DATE DUE

MAY 1 3 2004		

DEMCO NO. 38-298

A Japanese New Religion

Michigan Monograph Series in Japanese Studies

Number 1

Center for Japanese Studies
The University of Michigan

A JAPANESE NEW RELIGION

RISSHŌ KŌSEI-KAI IN A MOUNTAIN HAMLET

by

Stewart Guthrie

Ann Arbor

Center for Japanese Studies
The University of Michigan

1988

© 1988

by

Center for Japanese Studies
The University of Michigan
108 Lane Hall
Ann Arbor, MI 48109–1290

Cover design by Martha Cooper
Photographs by Stewart Guthrie

Index by AEIOU, Inc., Pleasantville, New York

Library of Congress Cataloging in Publication Data

Guthrie, Stewart Elliott, 1941-
    A Japanese new religion.

    (Michigan monograph series in Japanese studies; no. 1)
    Bibliography: p. 221.
    Includes index.
    1. Risshō Kōsei-kai—Social aspects. I. Title.
II. Series.
BQ8382.G88   1988   306'.6   86-33446
ISBN 0-939512-33-5

Printed in the United States of America

To Marty,
for her companionship and encouragement,
and to my parents

Contents

List of Figures

Preface

Humanistic descriptions and explanations of religion have engaged social scientists and others at least since the 19th century, when Sir E. B. Tylor made such an explanation central in his book *Primitive Culture*. To date, however, no common description or explanation has emerged, not even a common definition of "religion" within any one of the disciplines concerned. Many scholars have agreed on the non-Tylorian view that religion is a peculiar mode of thought and action distinct from ordinary thought and action, but this view has proved troublesome and has produced little further agreement.

Instead, the assumption that religious thought is peculiar has elicited correspondingly peculiar explanations. Depth and functionalist psychology and functionalist sociology and anthropology, for example, have held that religion is not what it seems (a plausible view of the world, and behavior appropriate to it), both to most believers and to many unbelievers. Rather, it is an unconscious (sometimes neurotic or hysterical) expression of emotions, a wish fulfillment, a covert code for proper social relationships, or some other transformed and disguised activity. The resulting difficulty of finding the "real" nature of religion by penetrating its camouflage and uncovering the hidden agenda behind its manifold forms has discouraged many scholars, who have concluded that "religion" covers phenomena too varied for any single explanation or definition.

For almost two decades now a renewed rationalism has held that religious and secular thought and action are not sharply different and that both are aspects, fundamentally similar in form and continuous in content, of the human endeavor to understand and cope with the world in general by unifying, simplifying, and regulating conceptions of it. This "rationalistic" or "intellectualist" view of religion shapes my description here of Japanese villagers who have joined a major religious movement, and of some who have not. My account describes religious meanings that the villagers find in their lives and suggests underlying models that unite religious and secular realms—or that, more accurately, do not divide them in the first place.

The renewal of rationalistic approaches to religion results in part from new awareness of the centrality of "meaning" to culture. During the time when many scholars thought religion too heterogeneous or well masked for comparative study, logical positivists similarly thought meaning too vague and unscientific and best left to prophets and poets. Since the decline of positivism, however, and influenced by recent philosophy and linguistics, anthropologists and others have found the need for meaning more and more central. Metaphysical or not, this need is both a human universal and a cultural variable. It is universal because humans must learn to interpret the world, and variable because we depend upon symbols to learn it and because learning with symbols makes possible alternate interpretations.

Problems of meaning vary with the culture framing them. In the industrial West and elsewhere, for example, science and technology have created new problems of meaning by more and more explicitly distinguishing the human from the nonhuman world. Science in fact is characterized by, among other features, its "strong aversion to anthropomorphism and anthropocentrism" (Barnes 1974:45). It has gradually purged anthropomorphism, and typical Western problems of meaning now inhabit a nonhuman and indifferent universe.

It is hard to relate ourselves to this universe that neither speaks nor listens, to which we are only the most distant and metaphoric kin, and much of which we see as accidental. Our estrangement is increased by the fact that not only the nonhuman world but also human societies often defy understanding, will, and purpose. This opacity and recalcitrance often have made anthropologists and others pessimistic about meaning in human life. Rodney Needham, for example, has remarked of the human situation, "We cannot make sense of it. If only it were at least a tale told by an idiot, we might arrive at some coherent meaning, but [it is not]" (1972:244).

Japan also has recently experienced new problems of meaning. At least once—when it was defeated in World War II, in which national deities had been said to promise victory—its loss of faith has been sharper than that of the West. In general, Japan's secularizing trend has been similar to that in the West, except that a postwar spate of new religious movements has, for many millions, countered this trend with a renewal and recombination of old beliefs. These "New Religions" (*shinkō shūkyō*) comprise several hundred groups, mostly of Buddhist or Shinto parentage, that grew rapidly or were founded shortly after the war. In the midst of defeat, occupation, and rapid social change they seem to have provided renewed meaning for their now roughly thirty million adherents, and they still continue to convey that meaning.

When I first visited Japan for about a month in 1964, I was attracted by what seemed a sense of purpose and cohesion, by Japanese esthetics, and by what little I knew of Buddhism. I resolved to spend more time there. A few years later, while I was in graduate school, these attractions and questions about religion and meaning led me to want to study some contemporary Japanese Buddhist group. The vigor of the New Religions made them especially interesting. Because its growing membership offered a large population and a choice of geographic areas for study, and because it was both amenable and as yet unstudied by Westerners, I eventually chose to look at Risshō Kōsei-kai, a Nichiren movement that is the second largest (it then had about three million members and now has about five) of all the new movements.

In the course of over a year in the mountain hamlet that was the main site of the study, I talked with members and others about why people had joined, and I discovered some problems they had faced and how the movement had solved them. Their responses seem to throw light on some old and general questions about religion, including ones of definition, connection to social relations, and features religion shares or does not share with other belief and behavior. One view that finds support here is that much religious thought and action, like much secular thought and action, can plausibly be called "rational" in at least a Weberian sense (i.e., as goal-oriented and as an allocation of means to ends). In this view, rationalism gives the most economical initial account of religion, taking adherents' statements at face value as beliefs about the world, not as mere metaphors for the social order or as otherwise sharply different from what they claim to be.

Rationalistic interpretations of religion have been scanted by many 20th-century anthropologists for whom religious accounts of the world have ceased to seem reasonable. Followers of Freud and of Malinowski have described religion as a fantasy "more akin to daydreaming and wish-fulfillment" (Malinowski 1979:43) when contrasting it with other thought and especially with science. Many followers of Durkheim have held it to be a way of representing, commenting on, and influencing the social order alone. In my view, distinctions of religion, science, and common sense as "modes of thought" have been overdrawn by most 20th-century scholars. I support the view that although they can be distinguished in several ways, it is important that they all attempt to represent, comment on, and influence the world in general, and to do so in an orderly, economical, and coherent way.

I owe many people thanks for their help. My major debt is to the people of the hamlet of Yamanaka (the name of which has been changed, as have those of persons and of nearby places) for their courtesy, generosity, and trust throughout my fourteen initial months and subsequent shorter visits. The Missionizing and Academic Research Divisions of Risshō Kōsei-kai provided useful information and an introduction to the Ueno Church, within whose territory most of the study took place. Professors Yanagawa Keiichi and Hori Ichiro of the University of Tokyo and Professor Morioka Kiyomi of the Tokyo University of Education made suggestions about the choice of a religious movement and about method and provided an introduction to Risshō Kōsei-kai. Professor Yanagawa gave me advice and encouragement on many occasions, and the Religious Studies Seminar under his direction at the University of Tokyo accepted me as a research student. The Yale Summer Language Institute and the Stanford Inter-University Center for Japanese Language Studies in Tokyo provided training in Japanese, supported by a grant from the Yale Anthropology Department and by a National Science Foundation Fellowship. The National Science Foundation also provided three more fellowships and a doctoral research grant, GS 3203. A Yale University Fellowship supported a year of writing, and a Short-term Fellowship from the Japan Foundation took me back to Japan in the summer of 1977. Fordham University assisted with some of the costs of publication. Friends from a hamlet neighboring the one studied have visited me several times in the United States, bringing this account up to date, in a number of ways, to 1981, and received me graciously when I returned to the hamlet again for a few days in the summer of 1984. My wife, Martha Cooper, accompanied me during the first and longest stay, giving support and encouragement. Among other contributions to the book, she designed its cover.

Drafts or portions of drafts have been read by, and improved by suggestions from, Barbara Bode, Keith Brown, John Campbell, John Child, Sarah Cooper, H. Byron Earhart, Walter Edwards, James W. Fernandez, Walter Guthrie, Sally Moore, Edward Norbeck, Harold Scheffler, Robert J. Smith, and Bruce E. Willoughby.

Personal names are given in the Japanese order, surname first.

Chapter 1
Problem, Theory, and Method

Introduction

I shall try to describe why some people in a Japanese hamlet have joined a major religious movement, what it has done for them, and especially how it helps them, as "established" (*kisei*) religion helps others, interpret and influence important events in their lives. In doing so I also address some general questions about religion as a kind of thought and action, including what connection it has to social relations and whether it is fundamentally different from secular, and especially scientific, thought and action.

My main setting is Yamanaka, a mountain farming hamlet on Honshu. As in the rest of Japan,[1] established religion in the hamlet has generally declined since World War II: attendance at Buddhist and Shinto festivals has decreased, a traditional dance at the Buddhist "All Souls' Festival" and a Shinto festival play have been abandoned, and a few people declare themselves skeptics or atheists and say that religion is "superstition."

While traditional religion in the hamlet has declined since the war, people say that scientific knowledge and technique, individualism, and a secular outlook have increased. New medical clinics have partially supplanted diviners and charms, and pesticides and mechanical noisemakers have partially supplanted Shinto in agriculture. Meteorology and physics had already displaced Raiden, Shinto god of thunder, before the war. Through television everyone has seen men landing on the moon, and even the oldest villagers now are skeptical of the moon deity. Other deities had been diminished by defeat in the war, in which the government had said they guaranteed victory, and television and travel have drawn people away from festivals. New agricultural machines continue to reduce the household interdependence that hamlet festivals celebrated.

1

Nonetheless, Buddhism and Shinto, though weakened, persist. Most households still contribute to temple and shrine. Every household over a generation old has a Buddhist altar, and almost every household has a Shinto god shelf; most households continue observances before them. Although beliefs vary from household to household and person to person, most still believe that ancestors and deities are somehow important for households and the hamlet.

While established religion in the hamlet has declined since the war, a new Nichiren Buddhist movement called Rishhō Kōsei-kai ("Society for Virtuous Human Relations"), second largest of the many New Religions,[2] arrived, grew quickly, and then subsided slightly. The first people in Yamanaka joined in 1953, and by the early 1960s people from almost a third of hamlet households had joined. By the mid-1960s some people began to drop out; membership now is stable. For some time, however, the movement flourished amid the general ebb of religion in the hamlet, and it is still growing, though more slowly, in the nation as a whole.

Trying to understand the local growth of the new movement as an instance of its national growth, I supposed that it might be a response to any or all of several kinds of local and national privation: the limited economic and social opportunities of the hamlet, its unequal distribution of resources, its formerly scanty medicine, its depopulation, and the shock of military defeat and occupation. Like many rural villages, Yamanaka, though better off than it used to be, has not shared equally in the national economic expansion. Its hierarchical social order is called "feudal" by young villagers. Until the mid-1970s its population was shrinking year by year. To a degree, people who joined the movement seem to have suffered more than others from these conditions and to have joined in order to ameliorate them.

Many scholars have similarly explained the rapid growth of religious movements throughout postwar Japan as a response to hardships, ranging from defeat in war to illness to the anomie of modern urban life.[3] Like these scholars, Risshō Kōsei-kai itself also credits such concrete causes of discontent for its success. Its publications mention physical illness in its early period, and strained family relations more recently, as chief factors in its growth. Its co-founder and president (Niwano 1978:95) writes that in its early period the "overwhelming majority of our new members were people who were seriously ill, who had mentally ill relatives, or who for economic or other reasons could not call on . . . doctors." Observers and leaders alike agree, then, that joining Kōsei-kai and other contemporary movements usually is a response to some special hardship.

Kōsei-kai's apparent relation to hardship is, moreover, an old one. The reforming monk Nichiren (1222–1282), founder of Nichiren-shū, from which Kōsei-kai and several other major movements (most notably Sōka Gakkai and Reiyū-kai) derive, survived Mongol invasions, natural disasters, and chronic social disturbances. A great earthquake in 1257 was followed by typhoon, famine, and plague, and the government was threatened internally by uprisings and externally by Mongols.[4] Nichiren and many contemporaries saw these troubles as the results of religious decay. In his "Treatise on the Establishment of the Orthodox Teaching and the Peace of the Nation" (Risshō Ankokuron), Nichiren quotes a visitor: "cosmic cataclysms [an eclipse and a comet], natural disasters, famines, and epidemics have filled the world. Oxen and horses collapse at the crossroads; skeletons fill the lanes. Already more than half the population has died." Nichiren lists popular religious responses to the disasters and says that none has been effective (Rodd 1980:58): "while we rack our minds and bodies, famine and plague grow more menacing. Everywhere we see beggars; our eyes cannot escape the sight of death. Bodies are piled as high as watchtowers, and lined up side by side like bridge planks." He notes that of disasters foretold in the sutras, only invasion had not yet occurred (this too came, in 1274 and 1281, from the Mongols), and he concludes that the country's salvation is to be found only in reciting the Lotus Sutra.

A link between distress and popular religious movements is familiar in millenial movements elsewhere in the world as well: in Europe in the 16th century, China and North America in the 19th, and Melanesia (and on a smaller scale Jonestown) in the 20th. Most observers of such movements (e.g., Wallace 1966 and Davis 1980) see a causal relation in which religious renewal is brought about, or at least touched off, by severe and widespread distress.

To explain such movements by privation, however, is simply to push the problem back a step (cf. Earhart 1980a and Hardacre 1984). Given that people join to solve certain problems, why should they choose religion as a means? Or if they choose religion, why a particular one? Many modern writers on religion, from Freud and Malinowski to Cohn (1970) and most observers of the New Religions, have treated it as particularly nonrational and often as an emotional panacea. As Hardacre (1984:31) writes, almost all scholars of the New Religions think that members "are seeking quick, emotionally satisfying solutions to problems whose complexity they do not correctly understand."

The difficulty for many anthropologists in viewing religion as rational behavior devoted to certain goals is that it does not seem to be the plausible account of reality, and the means to influence it, that believers think it is. Anthropologists see no evidence that the postulated gods, spirits, and demons exist, or that prayer brings rain. Religion then must be intellectually empty and adhered to, irrationally, for some other reason such as "emotional" security. Or, as many anthropologists (and theologians, including some non-Western religious thinkers such as Ogotemmeli in Griaule 1980) think, it must be allegorical, not literal, "representing," for example, social relations. Yet believers usually do not see their account as merely allegorical, nor are they necessarily irrational. They may well be as empirically and logically perceptive as others and lead reasonable lives even by secular standards. In such circumstances, one cannot agree with some psychologically inclined writers that religion is neurotic or mere wish fulfillment. What we need instead, for established religions and for new ones, is a general account of them as a plausible means of interpreting and dealing with the world.

In trying to define "religion" and to explain its near universality, most theorists since Durkheim have denied that it is "primitive science" (that explanation and control of phenomena are its primary goal), for any of several reasons. First, its major premise (if this is that spirit beings, or the supernatural, exist) is said (e.g., by Durkheim 1976) either to be apparently false or (Geertz 1966) to be so removed from experience that no one could derive it from observation and reason alone. If it is based neither on observation nor on reason, it may even be characteristically irrational. Among observers of the contemporary religious movements in Japan, for example, Murakami (1980:144) calls these movements "remarkably irrational," and Davis (1980:14) ascribes "religious delirium" and "collective illusions" to them. To cite Hardacre (1984:5) again, most scholars have treated them as "having only an expressive sort of significance."

A second argument (e.g., Malinowski 1925) for rejecting the primitive science view also assumes that religious premises are false and that if they were attempts to describe reality, they would be maladaptive. Since they often are not, they must actually do something else.

Third, it is said (Cohn 1970; Beattie 1970) that people do not want to know whether religious premises are true or not since they do not actively test them. Finally, it is said (Festinger, Riecken, and Schachter 1956) that unlike the case in science, negative evidence about religious premises is dismissed or rationalized so that when prophecy fails, mistaken premises still can be maintained. Davis (1980) has noted such rationalization in one of the New Religions, Mahikari, although he notes its empirical attitude as well.

Horton andl Finnegan (1973), Barnes (1973), and Barbour (1974), however, think that none of these assertions clearly distinguishes religious from scientific thought, and I agree. In my view, although religion and science differ in methodology and topical emphasis, they share a concern to explain and control experience systematically and economically, and do so by the same chief method, analogy.

Theory

Since the late 19th century when the natural sciences plainly were forcing religion into retreat along broad intellectual fronts, most comparisons have opposed these two as "modes of thought." The opposition typically is polar: science is logical and empirical and religion is not. Since human thought is taken to be usually, or at least ideally, logical and empirical, religion is to be explained as an anomaly.

Other oppositions have been suggested, but most contrast "religious" with "normal" thought. Fortes (1976:1–2), for example, asks whether ancestor worship should be regarded as religion or as an extension of domestic social relations, as though these were mutually exclusive. But Fortes's question and all oppositions of religion to other kinds of thought and action are unnecessary or overdrawn if the characteristics (such as rationality or its absence) they assert are in fact complementary, not mutually exclusive, throughout human thought. If heterogeneity exists elsewhere in thought and action, it should not surprise us in religion. A definition of religion proposed elsewhere (Guthrie 1980) and repeated briefly below, with a little epistemology, may obviate some apparent contradictions. This approach is in part the basis and in part the result of my interpretation of religion in Yamanaka.

A Definition of Religion

> There is a universal tendency among mankind to conceive of all beings like themselves and to transfer to every object those qualities with which they are familiarly acquainted, and of which they are intimately conscious. (Hume 1757, cited in Tylor 1924:477)

My definition of religion owes much to Robin Horton's definition, the "extension of the field of people's social relationships beyond the confines of purely human society" (1960:211). My version, following this view of religion as anthropomorphism,[5] is "the systematic application of

human-like models to non-human in addition to human phenomena"
(Guthrie 1980:181). This emphasizes the hypothetical and model-using
nature of *all* knowledge and an epistemology in which religious and other
models are similar. By stating that religion is a kind of model-use, it
addresses a question Horton answers slightly differently, namely, why
social relations should be extended to the nonhuman world at all. My
answer in brief is that like all models, religious ones try to interpret and
influence the world by drawing analogies among phenomena. Specifi-
cally, they explain nonhuman phenomena by analogy with human (for
Horton, "social") ones, for cognitive and instrumental purposes.

Several terms of this definition deserve comment. By a "model" I
mean any construct that allows us to understand phenomena by isolating
a set of them and identifying relations within the set. Models depend on
analogies (Black 1962; Hesse 1966) or, in Aristotle's definition, "four
terms such that the relation between the second and the first is similar
to that between the fourth and third" (Maranda 1971:192). Analogies
contain

> two kinds of connections between phenomena: similarity and
> contiguity, in other words metaphor and metonymy. . . . In
> the analogy formula A/B=C/D, two members in the same
> structural position (A and C) constitute a [metaphor, and] the
> members of one side of the equation mark are in a metonymic
> ["contiguous"] relation to each other (A and B). Thus, in an
> analogy, we have the interrelation of metaphor and contiguity
> in the same picture:

> ANALOGY

> METAPHOR

> $$[\text{CONTIGUITY}] \quad \frac{A}{B} = \frac{C}{D}$$

> In other words, contiguity is the relation of two terms,
> metaphor, the equation of two terms. (Maranda 1971: 193–
> 94)

The metaphorical identification of A and C in turn rests on an analogy of
subsets of A with subsets of C, as in $a^1/a^2=c^1/c^2$. For example, the

premise of the planetary model of the atom is solar system/large-scale matter=atom/small-scale matter. This contains the metaphor, solar system=atom, and the further analogy, sun/planets=nucleus/electrons, which may be further analyzed in the same way. Eventually, metaphoric discrepancies become too great, and the analogy is abandoned or supplemental analogies are made, as in the hybrid wave/particle model of light.

The same principles apply in such realms as social relations, religion, and magic. Among older people in the hamlet of Yamanaka and among most members of the religious movements, much thought both about society and about matters such as weather and traffic accidents, which most contemporary Westerners and Japanese alike see as nonsocial, is based on the analogy ancestors/descendents=parents/children. As we will see, ancestors "are" parents and descendents "are" children.

Again, Frazer's oft-maligned thesis that "magic is a spurious system of natural law" (1935:12) points out that magic too is based on the analogical principles of similarity and contiguity:

> If my analysis of the magician's logic is correct, its two great principles turn out to be merely two different misapplications of the association of ideas. Homeopathic magic is founded on the association of ideas by similarity; contagious magic is founded on the association of ideas by contiguity . . . in practice the two branches are often combined. . . . Both trains of thought are in fact extremely simple and elementary. (1935:12)

Frazer concludes that science and magic differ neither in logic nor purpose, but only in that scientific logic is explicit while magical logic is implicit. Therefore, magicians do not discover their mistakes; scientists do.

All generalizations about the real world, then, whether scientific, religious, or magical, are in the end of the uncertain but significant sort A/B=C/D, not the certain but trivial sort A/B=A/B, with which common sense and ordinary language (e.g., "pigs is pigs") confuse them. While Frazer's analysis of science and magic may not be sufficient, it is necessary. Similarity and contiguity, of which he offers so many examples from magic, appear everywhere in human thought, as they must if the world is not to seem infinitely complex, idiosyncratic, and chaotic.

The next term of my definition, "humanlike," describes a model constructed from experience with humans as distinct from experience with animals, plants, or inanimate objects. It hence has characteristically human features, chiefly language.

Last, "nonhuman phenomena" means nature as opposed both to man and to culture. Many phenomena, such as diseases, are in some ways nonhuman and in others human, but it is possible and useful to distinguish these. A disease is "natural" insofar as it is best explained by reference to some nonhuman agency such as germs, but cultural or human insofar as it may be explained by human relations, as in psychosomatic illness or biological warfare.

Some Aspects of a Human Epistemology

Some familiar yet noteworthy aspects of the human perceptual world shape this view of religion: (a) the world is, for humans, initially opaque; (b) to be understood it must be constructed; (c) what are constructed are hypotheses; and (d) these hypotheses tend to be messagelike.

The world as opaque. The world initially is opaque (Durkheim 1976) because for us the meanings of phenomena are not inherent as they are for, say, grasshoppers. When we first hear "dog," it does not evoke a dog, nor does our first smell of smoke mean fire. In fact, these mean nothing at all since connections among them are not genetically given but are acquired.

Science and religion both are procedures for making these connections. They may be distinguished in part as kinds of procedures and in part by the kind of connections they posit. Because of the initial opacity of phenomena, however, we can make this distinction only after we produce and recognize alternative connections. Since there is nothing in phenomena themselves as we encounter them to suggest what model is best, all kinds of models—mechanical, organic, anthropomorphic—are, *a priori*, equally worth testing.

The world as construction. Finding connections among phenomena amounts to making models and thus making phenomena intelligible. The observer (actively, as Kant noted) selects some phenomena as relevant (similar or contiguous) to each other, hypothesizes their relationship, and acts upon the hypothesis (Popper 1985a:368). Selection and hypothesis are necessary because phenomena are manifold and their relationships are not intrinsically apparent. As Durkheim put it, active interpretation is necessary because reality, as our senses show it, has the "grave inconvenience" of

> allowing of no interpretation. For to explain is to attach things to each other and to establish relations between them which make them appear as functions of each other. (1976:237)

The world as hypothesis. According to strict empiricists such as Berkeley (1939), all we can know for certain are sense impressions such as "red" or "hot," and we have no grounds for thinking that anything "corresponds" to them. This is equally true of impressions of pieces of chalk, electrons, and ancestors. Berkeley points out, however, that if things are not independent of individual observers then they must pop in and out of existence as we perceive and forget them. This is uneconomical because it requires endless creation and re-creation. Berkeley reestablished economy by suggesting that the world exists independently of human observers because it is continuously perceived by God (for whom Durkheim, it seems, substitutes society).

The common sense alternative to Berkeley is "realism" (e.g., Popper 1985b), the view that objects exist independently of perception. This view needs two strictures. First, we know the entities that it postulates only as *models*, which, however persuasive or commonsensical (as when Samuel Johnson kicked the rock to refute Berkeley), can never, as Popper has argued, be proved. As the evidence of phlogiston, ether, and Newtonian physics shows, models are perpetually subject to revision or abandonment. This is true even of everyday, seemingly self-evident models: whereas the sun once seemed to circle the earth, the reverse now seems true. Contrary to the usual view, then, there is no break between common sense and theory: both consist of models and both are hypothetical. Common sense is literally a consensus, of received hypotheses, while theory consists of hypotheses still explicit and self-conscious.

The second stricture about realism is a corollary: although we may (must, for social purposes) accept the existence of some external world, we can never know this world apart from some particular model of it. Lienhardt says of Dinka religion that

> the Powers may be understood as images corresponding to complex and various combinations of Dinka experience which

are contingent on their particular social and physical environment. For the Dinka they are the grounds of those
experiences. . . . With the imaging of the ground of suffering
in a particular Power, the Dinka can grasp its nature intellectually in a way which satisfies them. (1961:170)

Lienhardt implicitly approaches religion as a particular set of models.
The Dinka, like ourselves, are mostly naive realists who in daily life
suppose for intellectual satisfaction that their models are not mere
models but "grounds" of experience. Common sense, religion, and much
science normally suppose so too, but as Evans-Pritchard concludes in
Nuer religion (1956:322), "the significance of the objects, actions and
events lies not in themselves but in what they mean to those who
experience them." As Marwick (1973:68) notes, even within a single
society "the same landscape is seen differently by a farmer, a painter, a
geologist, a strategist, or an airman about to make an emergency
landing."

The dependence of perception on models and the dependence of
models on context are not news but are worth noting because of our
persistent (though chastized), careless, and frequently ethnocentric
dismissal of any models that differ from our own as irrational, uncritical,
emotionally motivated, or "symbolic." Anthropologists as diverse as
Malinowski (1925), Radcliffe-Brown (1922), Leach (1954), Wallace
(1966), and Beattie (1970) have thus ascribed functions and concerns to
religion that are different from what religious adherents take them to be.
Leach (1954, in Gellner 1970:40), for example, says that he makes

no attempt to find any logical coherence in the myths to
which I refer. Myths for me are simply one way of describing
certain types of human behavior . . . the various nats [spirits]
of Kachin religious ideology are, in the last analysis, nothing
more than ways of describing the formal relationships that
exist between real persons and real groups in ordinary Kachin
society.

As Gellner comments, Leach's exegesis has also "saved the Kachins
from being credited with meaning what they *appear* to be saying. Their

assertions are reinterpreted in the light of the author's disregard for the supernatural" (1970:41). To explain their society, Leach remakes the Kachin endeavor into his endeavor. But economical exegesis begins with the native view as it stands. Perhaps the Kachin are, as they think, trying to explain not just society but the world.

Structural-functionalists have assumed that if a society seems to use supernatural solutions for natural problems, the real problems must be others, of which the people are unaware. But this assumption magnifies our task unnecessarily. Occam's Razor tells us to assume only that the believers and practitioners are as reasonable as we and to try to take their statements, in context, at face value. If our world is in large part constructed, there will be many versions of it, and differences between even "literal" descriptions. Our beliefs, though based on the same external world, differ truly. Interpretation of the constructions of others as socially motivated, subconscious, or symbolic, although at some point necessary, should be deferred.

The world as message. To interpret experience humans, even more than other animals, must communicate—witness the general importance of language. Because of the vital role of language in cognition, a few suggestions are in order about it and a possible special relation to religion. First, whatever else language may be (e.g., emotional "expression"), it is an exchange of information and our primary means of understanding and controlling the world. Our capacity for it is built in: not merely an opportune exploitation of anatomy, physiology, and neurology by intelligence, but a biologically broadly based and deeply integrated system. We may conveniently distinguish it from other natural communications by such features as productivity, displacement, and arbitrariness, but neither its form nor its content can be narrowly specified. Its "arbitrariness" means that its information is not intrinsic but depends on interpretation by means of a learned system. To send and receive messages by such a system is a basic human orientation to the world, both by experience and by predisposition.

Although language typically uses speech, its media are unlimited since it depends on a code, not a medium. Any and all events therefore are potential messages and are scrutinized as such. There is no self-evident requirement that a sender or receiver of messages be human—or simian, divine, or of any other particular class—or communicate in any particular way. People therefore can believe in such message senders as ancestors and find messages in sickness, drought, or traffic accidents; no hidden symbolism or ulterior or unconscious motivations (unless our proclivity for language is itself one) are needed to account for this belief.

Religion and Language

> The ancestors said, "It would be dangerous to go today, so you mustn't go!" You can't hear the ancestors speak in words, so they gave him the message by keeping the car from going. If the car had gone, my husband might have had the accident. (Yamanaka resident and Risshō Kōsei-kai member)

Humans look for messages in, and send messages to, their environments—both human and nonhuman. There is no self-evident or genetic reason why we should limit this treatment to other people, and we do not. We are constituted by nature and nurture to send and receive messages, but this behavior is general, not targeted only on other humans. People find messages not only in road signs and semaphores, where no human is present but one is implied, but also in comets, earthquakes, entrails, and cracks in scapulae. In prevailing contemporary Western belief, the latter "signs" are neither linguistic nor even messages at all. In much of the world, however, people still use linguistic models to interpret and influence the (for us) nonhuman world as well as the human one. This is what we indicate first of all when we call a world view an attitude, or a practice "religious." When people in Yamanaka pray to ancestors, they are religious because "ancestors" and the phenomena in which they are discerned—crop failure and sickness, for example—are not, in the etic view, human and do not use language. Good or ill fortune interpreted by believers as communications from ancestors are in Western anthropological terms mere accidents.

On this view, religion, in employing message behavior, shares with magic an overestimation of organization in phenomena. What is called religion typically attributes a human level of organization to the nonhuman universe, in part or in whole. What is called magic, which typically uses signs rather than symbols, assumes subhuman organization in phenomena, which in the nonmagical view do not possess it. Religious and magical behavior both assume that certain phenomena have a systematic relationship with the message sender that enables them to send and receive messages, when in the nonreligious view they do not have such a relationship.

Phenomena as Orderly:
Religion, Magic, and Science in Consensus

Why do we overestimate organization? This is a general problem about thought with several possible answers. One is simply that we must assume that phenomena are integrated, not random, because we must have some regular framework within which to think and act. Given the necessity of such a framework, the most useful is the most general and encompassing. Aiming at generality, we sometimes overshoot.

Various writers have said that an assumption of integration among phenomena is characteristic, variously, of religion, science, and magic. Geertz (1966:13) offers as one definition of religion "what Salvador de Madariaga has called 'the relatively modest dogma that God is not mad.'" Simpson (1961:5) says of theoretical science that its whole aim is "the perceptual reduction of chaos . . . the most basic postulate of science is that nature itself is orderly . . . all theoretical science is ordering and . . . systematics is synonymous with theoretical science." Levi-Strauss says of magic that it may be that this

> gigantic variation on the theme of the principle of Causality . . . can be distinguished from science not so much by any ignorance or contempt of determination but by a more imperious and uncompromising demand for it. (1966:11)

He points out that Evans-Pritchard (1956:418) similarly remarks of Azande witchcraft that "as natural philosophy it reveals a theory of causation." Durkheim says of religion similarly that

> religious conceptions have as their object, before everything else, to express and explain, not that which is exceptional and abnormal in things, but, on the contrary, that which is normal and regular. (1976:28-29)

And a branch chief of Kōsei-kai expressed a basic Buddhist tenet when he told a gathering at which I was present, referring to karma or comprehensive causality, "There are no effects without causes" (the notion of regular causal interrelatedness is, indeed, fundamental to Kōsei-kai).

The assumption that phenomena are unified, integrated, and connected, then, is not peculiar to religion but is found in magic and in science as well. What varies is not the notion that they are orderly but only the rules of order. If magic and religion overestimate the integration of phenomena it is because they seek economy: driven by the human "compulsion to understand the world as a meaningful cosmos" (Weber 1963:117), they explain more phenomena by fewer principles than do secular alternatives. Azande witchcraft, for example, explains unfortunate events such as the lethal collapse of granaries, which for modern Westerners must remain meaningless accidents. To apply a humanlike model, witchcraft, is to make an established principle account for what would otherwise be anomalous (in another context, Thomas Kuhn calls such a process "normal science").

As noted, many 20th-century writers oppose such rationalism concerning religion, and they oppose it concerning magic as well. Beattie, for instance, refers to "Frazer's theory that underlying magic is a faith in 'the order and uniformity of nature'" as a "theory quite unsupported by ethnography" (1970:250). But Beattie does not mention any ethnography that refutes Frazer's theory, and I know of no literature that shows that magical thought assumes an unordered universe.

Another response to the question, why magic and religion are over-ambitious in their explanations, is to ask just how far they do overestimate the unity of phenomena or mistake their connections. The answer is not clear. They sometimes accomplish their aims, especially when they aim to cause or cure such conditions as human illness. As Horton (1970:137-40) among others has pointed out,

> modern medical men . . . are once more beginning to toy with the idea that disturbance in a person's social life can in fact contribute to a whole series of sickness . . . some of the connections traditional religious theory postulates are, by the standards of modern medical science, almost certainly real ones.

Similarly, Levi-Strauss (1966:11-12), noting the empirical value of much "magical" knowledge, says that it often anticipates science: "The nature of these anticipations is such that they may sometimes succeed. . . . In the history of scientific thought this 'anticipation-effect' has . . . occurred repeatedly." And Stephen Toulmin recently (1982:103) has written of science that "we cannot hope to decide in advance how far and in what respects the [natural world] can fruitfully be studied from alternative standpoints." Toulmin does not say that religion is such an alternative standpoint, but doing so would violate neither the logic nor the spirit of his argument.

Religion can usefully be distinguished from science, notably by its relative lack of self-criticism and by its anthropomorphism. However, it also has important similarities, and the two are as much contiguous as they are at extremes. As Barry Barnes (1973:183) has put it, "all belief systems, scientific or preliterate, 'true' or 'erroneous,' are most profitably compared and understood within a single framework." Toulmin (1982:111) says similarly of the alleged differences between the aims and methods of scientists and those of humanists that "critical judgment in the natural sciences . . . is not geometrical, and critical interpretation in the humanities is not whimsical. In both spheres, the proper aims [are] to be perceptive, illuminating, and reasonable." Again, Toulmin's dictum can be broadened to include religious thought as well. As Durkheim (1976:429) writes in a little-noted passage, the topics of both religious and scientific thought are the same ("nature, man, society"), and both attempt

> to connect things with each other, to establish internal rela-
> tions between them, to classify them and to systematize
> them. . . . It is true that [science] brings a spirit of criticism
> into all its doings, which religion ignores, [but perfection of
> method is] not enough to differentiate it from religion . . .
> both pursue the same end: scientific thought is only a more
> perfect form of religious thought.

Some Consequences

Let me note some consequences of this definition and approach, ending with my hypothesis for fieldwork.

Rationality. Since the definition is substantive, it imputes no particular function to religion other than understanding and control, which all models share. Hence, it is silent on such issues as the primacy of rationality vs. irrationality, latent vs. manifest functions, and individual vs. social goals. This silence eliminates some culture-bound and incidental properties from our Western notion of religion. Subconscious motives and obscure symbolism surely are present in religion, but they are present in other thought and action as well. The assumption that their religious form is peculiar prematurely abandons the attempt to find principles and processes common to all thought and action. It also discourages the search for coherent explicit meaning in religious acts, causing anthropologists to "spin notional complexities they then report as cultural facts through a failure to realize that much of what their informants are saying is, however strange it may sound to educated ears, meant literally" (Geertz 1975:22). To avoid issues such as rationality in *defining* religion is not to suggest that they are meaningless. But religion, as a kind of model, is a tool and is capable of being used in ways that may or may not be rational.

Unity in variety. My definition unifies such definitions of religion as Tylor's "belief in Spirit Beings" and Bellah's "set of symbolic forms and acts which relate man to the ultimate conditions of his existence" in that both attribute humanlike elements to the world. It unifies such religious adherents as Geertz's Javanese mystic staring into a candle flame, Evans-Pritchard's Zande discovering who bewitched him, and my Japanese villager curing her rheumatism or explaining her husband's balky car, who all are concerned with the meaning of events, who all search for it in a humanlike pattern, and who all wish to produce some desired result and suppose that the world understands and responds.

As Ooms (1976:73) notes, religion includes an "exceedingly disparate array of events." Religious goals include eternal life, escape from rebirth, victory in war, social harmony, communion with godhead, or prevention of toothache. My definition accommodates such diverse goals equally. "Religions" not only can have infinitely diverse goals but also can harbor equally speculative and pragmatic activities since religion like science may at one point be mainly model building and at another mainly model use.

Change in the model: Revision vs. revolution. Risshō Kōsei-kai arrived in Yamanaka when religion there, as elsewhere in Japan, was gradually yielding to secularism. Is this partial renaissance of religion a kind of irrationality, an aberrant regression to views already shown to be unsound, as many students of the New Religions and of millennial movements have decared? I think not.

Religious models like other models are subject to revision as well as to overthrow or "revolution." Revolution, as Kuhn says of science, occurs not so much when a current model is found flagrantly inadequate as when a new model is found more adequate. "Inadequacy" alone is insufficient reason to abandon an old model since all models appear inadequate at some time and since refining them is less disruptive than giving them up.

Both revision and revolution have occurred in world-views everywhere in recent centuries, often resulting in the supplanting of humanlike models with unhumanlike ones. This is perhaps the result of a new industrial milieu as well as of a scientific one. My elderly neighbor in Yamanaka, for example, said that people there treated thunder and lightning as manifestations of a Shinto deity (Raiden) until late in the 19th century "because they didn't know about electricity." When they acquired the idea and use of electricity, he said, they abandoned the deity.

But logic does not require that an inadequate humanlike model be replaced with a nonhuman one any more than it requires the reverse. These are not reciprocal alternatives such that the failure of one leads necessarily to the other. In millennial movements (Cross 1950; Worsley 1957; Cohn 1970) the failure of a humanlike model of the world often has caused not abandonment but only revision or replacement with another humanlike model. In Yamanaka, Sōtō Zen and Shinto have been supplanted not only by technology but also by Kōsei-kai, which has revived old models by revising and elaborating them.

Isomorphism in society and religion. Recognizing that models are analogical leads us to look for similarities and even identity between religious and nonreligious models and cautions us against making such dichotomies as "naturalistic" vs. "supernaturalistic" within non-Western cosmologies. In Yamanaka as elsewhere in Japan, for example, one model, the "parent-child relationship" (*oya-kō kankei*), is used both in religious and in secular contexts. Finding a single model crucial to both contexts is not new (Horton [1962] finds one in Kalabari culture) but still seems exceptional.

Many anthropologists, especially French and British ones, have noted the partial isomorphism of social relations and religious conceptions but dispute its cause. Most of them have been misled, in my view, by a partially Durkheimian interpretation of this isomorphism, namely, that religious statements are simply metaphors for, comments on, or attempts to make adjustments in human society. In my view (and often in Durkheim's), religious thinkers do comment on and attempt to influence society. They do not merely say what is or should be true of society, however, but say it of some larger world as well.

The question is, Why do they think it true? The answer seems to be that understanding is mainly the extension of old principles to new domains (Toulmin 1972) and that the first and most important principles people grasp are human ones, those of language and human social relations (Popper 1985c:433–34). In Yamanaka the primary religious model, the parent-child relationship, is central to important secular contexts as well. What makes it "religious" is its application to broader contexts than nonreligious views allow.

The working hypothesis. As Durkheim noted, religion connects superficially dissimilar events. In my view it especially connects dissimilar human and nonhuman events, using a humanlike model to integrate them in a single system. Presumably because of the unity it thus achieves, some scholars define religion with such inclusive, abstract, and heavily freighted phrases as "ultimate concern" (Tillich), "ultimate conditions" (Bellah), and "general order of existence" (Geertz).

When religions have concerns as broad and inclusive as these phrases suggest, as some do, conversion to them may mean that they meet correspondingly broad needs, unfulfilled by converts' previous models. In such a culturally homogeneous community as a Japanese hamlet, in which everyone has heard roughly the same ideas, one might expect people who join a new religious movement to have had experiences that peculiarly failed their expectations. If religious models interpret and influence experience generally, they will concern, among other things, such common wants as health, wealth, affection, and esteem.

I supposed, then, that people who joined might have been a kind of underclass in Yamanaka: poorer, sicker, and with fewer friends and relatives. I expected that they would be interested in the explanations and practical results of religious doctrine and practice, just as in secular explanations and effects. They would treat the movement and its doctrine with at least a partially rational and empirical attitude, and after joining they would have opinions about its economy and effectiveness as a means toward their ends.

Fieldwork:
Preparation, Movement and Community, and Methods

Preparation

I went to Japan for the second time in the late summer of 1969 to continue to study the language and do research for a dissertation. Ten months (daunting but fondly recalled) at the Stanford Inter-University Center for Japanese Studies in Tokyo, in addition to two summers and a half-time academic year of Japanese at Yale, gave me enough verbal fluency to interview and converse readily. My reading ability was adequate for wading through the most relevant primary documents, though for secondary and some primary materials on Kōsei-kai, other New Religions, and aspects of contemporary Japan I have relied heavily on English-language sources. As a research student in the Religious Studies Seminar at the University of Tokyo, I received invaluable advice, introduction, and encouragement from Professor Yanagawa Keiichi.

Choice of Movement

On suggestions from Yanagawa and from Professors Hori Ichiro of the University of Tokyo and Morioka Kiyomi of Tokyo University of

Education, and after visits to the headquarters of six major New Religions (Sōka Gakkai, Risshō Kōsei-kai, PL Kyōdan, Tenrikyō, Ōmoto, and Seichō no Ie), I decided on Kōsei-kai, which calls itself a "lay movement" of Nichiren Buddhism. Kōsei-kai's large size and continued growth (about 3,500,000 members in 1970 and 5,400,000 members in 1982, according to Kōsei-kai) promised enough recent members in some small town or village to make possible a study set in a single community. Further, Kōsei-kai willingly permits academic study by outsiders, unlike its doctrinal relative and militant rival Sōka Gakkai. Moreover, since it is less political than Sōka Gakkai, it has been much less studied. The main Western-language sources (for a complete list see Earhart 1983) are Thomsen (1963), Offner and Van Straelen (1963), Spae (1966), McFarland (1967), Watanabe (1968), Norbeck (1970), Weeks (1974), Dale (1975), and Morioka (1979). Of these, only Dale gives more than a short account, and none gives a community setting.

Risshō Kōsei-Kai, An Introduction

Risshō Kōsei-kai was founded in 1938 as an offshoot of Reiyūkai Kyōdan (Hardacre 1984), a lay Buddhist association whose doctrine is based on the Lotus Sutra. Reiyūkai, founded during the 1920s, grew rapidly in Tokyo during the 1930s amid growing fear of the war in China. It drew its members from the middle and lower middle classes, with promises of the practical benefits of pleasing the ancestors, largely by reciting the sutra and by self-cultivation (Morioka 1979; Hardacre 1984). Among its members were Niwano Nikkyō, a thirty-two-year-old shop-keeper and entrepreneur, and Naganuma Myōkō, a forty-seven-year-old woman who had been one of Niwano's customers, whom he converted to Reiyūkai. Niwano (1968, 1978) writes that he had become deeply committed to the Lotus Sutra, and when Reiyūkai's national leadership criticized the sutra, Niwano and Naganuma left the movement. They were followed by 30 of Niwano's more than 200 converts, and these became the core of a new movement, Risshō Kōsei-kai.

Niwano was born in 1906 in Niigata Prefecture, the second son in a farming household of evidently modest means. The household was Sōtō Zen Buddhist (the established Buddhism in Yamanaka, the hamlet described here, as well), and Niwano's grandfather was a semiprofessional healer. Niwano, according to his autobiography a bright and diligent student, was also interested in healing from childhood. During his youth he tried astrology, divination (*rokuyō, kyūsei,* and *shichishin*), "direction lore" (*hōi*), and asceticism (*shugendō*).

Later, in Tokyo, he joined Reiyūkai to cure his daughter's encephalitis. She recovered, and Niwano became an enthusiastic proselyte of the Lotus Sutra. He recalls (1968:87) his response to Reiyūkai's exposition of the sutra:

> the very fact I sought after became clear to me. I examined it from every point but could not find any defect . . . it is quite a perfect network vast and boundless to save all the people in the world to the last man.

As a base for proselytizing, Niwano started a milk shop, since customers for milk, regarded as medicinal, would be in poor health and thus potential converts.

Among his converts was Naganuma Myōkō, then forty-six. Myōkō (her first name, used affectionately and with the honorific *sensei* by members) was the sixth daughter of a poor farming household in Saitama Prefecture, dispossessed of its land soon after her birth. Her mother died when she was six, and she was raised first by an uncle and then by her older sister. As a young woman she went to work in Tokyo. She fell ill, however, and returned home. There she married, at twenty-five, but after ten years of her husband's "dissipation," during which her only child died, she left him and returned to Tokyo. She remarried and with her new husband started a small shop, selling ice in summer and roasted sweet potatoes in winter. But she had heart, stomach, and uterus problems and was barren.

When Myōkō converted to Reiyūkai, she had a "change of personality" (Risshō Kōsei-kai 1966:17) and her health improved. Like Niwano she became an enthusiastic proselytizer. Her personality change brought shamanic powers[6] (called by Kōsei-kai her "bodily reading," *shikidoku*, of the sutra), which remained important to Kōsei-kai until her death at sixty-eight, in 1957.

Although the movement now has shifted doctrinal emphasis to rationalistic exegesis (Hardacre 1984 notes a similar trend in Reiyūkai) of the sutra, in the early period both Myōkō and Niwano had frequent revelations, often with Niwano interpreting Myōkō's utterances. Niwano (1968:109) writes that

> Reiyūkai attached great importance to the practice of invoking a god to receive some revelation from him. I and Mrs. Myōkō had been systematically instructed in this and

relied also on such revelations after the foundation of Kōsei-kai. We were led around by the gods from morning till evening. The gods that revealed their wishes to us were mainly Fudō-myōō, Hachiman-daibosatsu, Dainichi-nyorai, Bishamonten, Shichimen-daimyōjin and Nichiren-daibosatsu.

Myōkō's visions and simple, comprehensible interpretations of sutra made her more popular than Niwano (Morioka 1979), and several officers planned to unseat Niwano with a splinter group under her, but she died before they acted. Since then Niwano has discouraged shamanism at the movement's national level, but some local leaders and group activities such as the "winter ascetic exercises" (*reikan shugyo*) still use occasional trance.

Since its founding, Kōsei-kai has grown steadily, despite setbacks from government suppression during the war, when Niwano and Myōkō were held by the police for several weeks, and from a prolonged attack on its doctrine and finances in 1956 by the newspaper *Yomiuri Shinbun*. After the war and the end of suppression, rapid growth began, which continued through the 1950s and early 1960s and, with only minor fluctuations and slight moderation, has continued to the present. According to Kōsei-kai publications it had 150 member households in five branch churches by 1940. By 1945 there were 1,300 households in ten churches, and by 1949, 22,500 in twenty-three churches. By 1953 there were 158,587 households; by 1956, 298,000; and by 1970 almost one million (Risshō Kōsei-kai 1970). At present the movement claims about 5.5 million individual members. These figures may be somewhat inflated, both by national headquarters and by local leaders, but Kōsei-kai clearly is second in size only to Sōka Gakkai among the new movements.

The movement is not only large but wealthy, as the architecture at its Tokyo headquarters attests. The main worship hall or "Great Sacred Hall" (*daiseido*) is a lavish, modernistic eight-story building of eclectic style that cost Y4 billion or about $11 million at its completion in 1964. In 1970 an even larger and more lavish hall, the "Hall of the Open Gate" (*fumonkan*), including an auditorium seating 5,000 people, was completed. It was followed in 1978 by a third building of equal size, the Horin-kaku Guest Hall, with more meeting rooms. Other facilities are a 330-bed general hospital, a kindergarten, middle and high schools, a nursing school, a sizeable library, a modern administration building, a youth training hall, an old people's home, a cemetery with 5,600 grave lots, and a publishing house (Risshō Kōsei-kai 1970 and 1980; see n. 46 for more description of the headquarters' buildings). In addition to these facilities at the headquarters, there is another large and modern "Hall of the Open Gate" in Osaka as the center for western Japan, and most of the regional "churches" (kyōkai) have substantial meeting halls.

National organization at the top level comprises Niwano (whose presidency is lifelong and hereditary), a board of directors, and a chief director. Under them are numerous departments including one for missionizing (this is first among departments, and its director works closely with the chief director and is responsible for religious affairs, for the Youth Director, and for administration of the regional churches), one for academic affairs, and others. Under the missionizing department Kōsei-kai is divided into thirty-three geographical areas or dioceses (kyōku), including one overseas, comprising 225 regional churches. These in turn are divided at several levels into smaller areas (chapter 5) and into divisions for men, women, and young people.

Members' activities include praying and making offerings before the altars at home, at local meeting places, regional churches, and occasionally at national headquarters; attending sermons and testimonies at regional churches; participating in group counseling; and missionizing, among others (chapter 5). Of these, group counseling, in which members present personal problems and get advice from a professional or semiprofessional leader, is most important.[7] Here the leader applies movement doctrine to personal problems, in the chief method of doctrinal teaching.

Kōsei-kai calls its doctrine "fundamental Buddhism" (kompon bukkyō). By interpreting and applying it, the movement aims to provide happiness to members and harmony to society. Exegesis is mainly of the Buddhist "Four Noble Truths," of which Kōsei-kai says its "other doctrines are the same principles considered from various angles" (Risshō Kōsei-kai 1966:44).

The first of the Four Noble Truths is the "Truth of Suffering" (kutai). Existence inevitably entails suffering, including the pains of birth, sickness, old age, and death. The first step toward happiness is to realize the inevitability of suffering, the reality of one's own present suffering, and the inadequacy of one's usual attempts to alleviate it. Most people conceal from themselves and others the extent of their unhappiness. A major obstacle to realizing the truth of suffering is self-delusion, such as nostalgic recollection of the past and hopeful expectation of the future. One must confront the present directly.

Second is the "Truth of Cause" (jittai), or comprehensive causality. All phenomena in the universe are causally connected. There are no events that are not both cause and effect of other events. Human suffering can be understood as the result of specific causes that result in complex "evil passions." Suffering is a state of mind, ultimately caused or cured by the sufferer's own actions. Each person is responsible for his own condition.

Third is the "Truth of Extinction" (*mettai*). Suffering may be eliminated by eliminating its causes and achieving quiescence. This requires recognizing the "Three Cardinal Signs" (*sanbōin*): "all things are impermanent," "nothing has an ego," and "nirvana is quiescence." Because all things are impermanent, suffering stems from attachment to people, possessions, and other conditions of life as though they were changeless. "Nothing has an ego" means that "nothing in the universe is an isolated existence, without any relation to other things. Things exist in connection with one another and are interdependent. . . . Is there even one who says, 'I live without any relation to the community?'" (Risshō Kōsei-kai 1966:53–54). "Nirvana is quiescence" means that happiness lies in mental peace and quietness, achieved by realizing the impermanence and interdependence of all things and thus freeing oneself of greed, aggression, and self-delusion. Mental quietude is both an end in itself and the source of social harmony: "Those who are troubled in their relations with others or unable to succeed in anything will . . . find, when going back to the cause, the fact that their own mind is not serene" (Risshō Kōsei-kai 1966:54).

Fourth is the "Truth of the Path" (*dōtai*), the course to quiescence: a set of moral principles, the "Eightfold Path," for thought and action. Its eight features, common to all Buddhism, are right view, right thinking, right speech, right action, right living, right endeavor, right memory, and right meditation. Each is elucidated in detail. Realizing the first three Truths is difficult, but one can do so by practicing the fourth.

Put abstractly as above, the Four Noble Truths embody the Buddhism most familiar to the West, a nontheistic, world-rejecting, psychological philosophy. In practice, however, Kōsei-kai, like most popular Buddhism in Japan, recognizes deities (principally incarnations of the Buddha) and ancestors and is explicitly world-accepting. It is optimistic and activist and urges members to pray, make offerings, and commit themselves to varied personal and social goals. Something of its tenor may be heard in its comments on the Lotus Sutra, held to be sermons by the Buddha to his disciples near the end of his life, and thus his summary statement. At its heart (Risshō Kōsei-kai 1980:6–7) are three concepts:

1. All sentient beings can attain Perfect Enlightenment—that is, buddhahood—and nothing less than this is the appropriate final goal of believers.

2. The Buddha is eternal, having existed from the infinite past and having appeared in many forms throughout the ages to guide and succor beings through the teaching of the Wonderful Law.

3. The noblest form of Buddhist practice is the way of the bodhisattva, one who devotes himself to attaining enlightenment not only for himself but for all sentient beings.

Kōsei-kai is concerned primarily with this world and claims to be grounded in ordinary daily experience. It promises present happiness through harmonious social relations, achieved largely by self-scrutiny and by prayers to ancestors[8]:

A happy family and good human relations with one's fellow workers are the indispensable terms of man's happiness. . . . Intimacy among the family members, health, and stable finances are the terms of a happy family. . . . At a believer's home, the symbol of the faith [a mandala] and the list giving the posthumous names of the deceased members of the family are on the family altar, the center of the family's faith. Thanksgiving to the ancestors by the whole family, the daily offering of water, flowers, tea and rice, the chanting of the sutra, and the practice of the Law brings happiness. (Risshō Kōsei-kai 1966:110)

Members are taught to practice the Law (hō, the Four Truths) in occasional sermons, but more often and more importantly in group counseling sessions or hōza (a term also used by the parent movement, Reiyūkai). Literally "law sittings," or discussions of the application of Buddhist principles to practical problems, they are regarded by Kōsei-kai and outside observers (e.g., Dale 1975) alike as the movement's most important activity and greatest attraction. Kōsei-kai calls them "circles of compassion" based on the Buddha's teaching methods:

less than twenty persons sit in a circle, and a leader gives answers to their questions on religious experiences and all other problems they meet in social life. The leader, on the basis of the Law of the Four Noble Truths, shows every person the way to properly understand the faith and the solution of his problem. (Risshō Kōsei-kai 1966:114)

The solutions most frequently recommended are cultivation of gratitude toward one's parents and devotions to ancestors. These closely related actions fulfill a central precept, that the child be grateful and respectful toward its parents. In Kōsei-kai's words,

> there is no difference between filial piety and ancestor worship. It is originally an act of expressing thanks, in which a grateful mind is extended from parents to grandparents, from grandparents to great-grandparents, and so on, infinitely to the most remote ancestors. (Risshō Kōsei-kai 1966:132)

Choice of Community

My formal introduction to Kōsei-kai, from Professor Hori, was to officers of its Academic Research Department. After helpful discussions of their own research, the officers introduced me to the Missionizing Department for help in finding a community for study.

My criteria for the community were that Kōsei-kai have grown there in recent years, that it be small enough to study by participant observation and informal interviews, and that it be within the Kanto region in central Honshu to preclude my having to learn dialect. At the same time I wanted it to be far enough from Tokyo to be rural and relatively traditional—more a personal and romantic than a methodological preference.

From our survey it seemed that the area around Ueno City (not its real name) in northern Gunma Prefecture, two hours by express train from Tokyo, was likely to have such a community. Ueno had a regional church established in the previous year, numerous old farming villages nearby, and a Kōsei-kai membership that had grown rapidly in the past decade. The Missionizing Department provided an introduction to the Ueno Church. After meeting the church chief, my wife and I spent several days driving about looking at villages and hamlets in the area.

The hamlet we chose, with the help of Kimura Hideo, a Kōsei-kai staff member delegated by the Ueno Church and himself a resident of the hamlet, was Yamanaka. Twenty-two kilometers into the mountains from Ueno City, it was the site of a Kōsei-kai "local meeting place" (hōza-jō) in Hideo's (villagers go by their given names) home. It claimed over 200 members from some twenty surrounding hamlets. It also had a house for us. This had been a schoolhouse before the turn of the century and then the home of the hamlet's first electrician. It was owned by the hamlet communal property association and had just been vacated by its tenants of forty years.

Hideo explained my study to the communal property association and asked whether we could rent the house. The association met for discussion and several days later agreed to rent it for Y12,000, or about $36.00, for the entire year. Their agreement, especially for this modest sum, appeared to represent the tacit consent of the hamlet people, at least of that majority who were association members, to the study. One of them later told me that it had represented such a consensus, though not one without apprehension. Somehow it occurred to me only later that we had slipped into town with the very barest formalities—and although it never produced any apparent difficulties, had bypassed the headman altogether.

Methods

We moved in on a bright November morning in 1970, with the help of Hideo and his whole household (among other things, his son and the son of a related household had driven a small truck with our belongings from Tokyo the night before). Hideo vigorously dusted out the house from rafters to floorboards with a long, fresh bamboo duster, in what I mistook, partly because of his pure white headband, for a purification ritual.

When we had settled in for a day or so, I began informal visits to hamlet households, particularly to our immediate neighbors, to hamlet and village leaders, and to households belonging to Kōsei-kai. Hideo became my chief Kōsei-kai informant. He introduced me to a number of Yamanaka households, to the mayor and administrative staff of the village (*mura*) of which Yamanaka is part, and to the Buddhist priest, in several walks through the village. For several months my research remained informal and exploratory, consisting of conversations and taking part in hamlet festivals, household memorial services, and "bad luck year" (*yakudoshi*) parties. I went regularly to the services, five a month, at the Kōsei-kai meeting place and occasionally to counseling meetings at the Ueno Church and throughout its area.

It soon seemed that there were fewer active Kōsei-kai members in the hamlet and in nearby hamlets than I had thought. In fact, scarcely half the 200 members listed for the meeting place seemed to be coming. In Yamanaka only 11 people said they were members, and only 6 regularly came to meetings. The most recent convert in Yamanaka had joined eleven years before. Since most members had joined between fifteen and twenty years before, the circumstances of their joining appeared potentially difficult to establish. Records of household health and landholdings kept by the village, for instance, were available only for the last five years, and Kōsei-kai's records appeared sketchy.

This relative scarcity of members was disappointing, and I considered options of finding another hamlet with more and newer members, changing my scope to a larger subdivision of the Ueno Church, or staying in the same hamlet but drawing on neighboring ones for more material when necessary. I decided to stay put. By the time I was fairly sure of the number of members (no records were available at first), I had been in Yamanaka several months and had found it congenial, helpful, and hospitable. Another hamlet might turn out also to have fewer members than it seemed, or to present some other problem. Expanding the area of the study to include more Kōsei-kai members would have meant abandoning a natural community, the hamlet, for some more arbitrary unit. Since most people in Yamanaka expressed loyalty to it, and since Kōsei-kai members' relations with it were of interest, it seemed best to keep the hamlet as the primary unit. Still, I spent considerable time with both members and nonmembers in nearby hamlets, and some time at the Ueno Church and at the headquarters in Tokyo.

My first formal survey was made with copies of the national census form (from a ward office in Tokyo), together with a written statement of my purposes, which the hamlet headman passed out for me to every household. This census provided the name, relation to householder, date and place of birth, sex, level of education, occupation, place of occupation or school and means of transportation to it, and number of children born, for each member of every household. It also specified the relationship of inhabitants to domicile (owned or rented), number and size of rooms, and principal source of household income. All fifty-two households responded, with the exception of one consisting of a single, mentally incompetent woman, for whom a relative in another household supplied most of the information.

The second and more important instrument was a thirty-page, 182-item questionnaire developed over my first year in Yamanaka and administered in the last two months. I wrote this in English and translated it into Japanese, and a young Yamanaka poet and friend checked, discussed, and corrected it for me. It covered kinship, marriage, neighborhood relations, religion (at fourteen pages, religion was almost half the questionnaire), education, news media, economic activities, health, politics, recreation, and travel, in that order.

I used the questionnaire as a guide in semiformal interviews, either in the home of the person being interviewed (usually the head of the

Author and informants in a Yamanaka household.

household) or in mine. This took an average of about three hours, often in two or three sessions. I wrote the answers out as fully as possible without interrupting the flow of talk, writing in a mix of romanized Japanese and English in booklets with spaces pre-numbered by question, and recorded the interview on tape as well. I used the whole questionnaire for only half of the fifty-two households, but this was a complete cross-section and included every past or present Kōsei-kai member. I asked members an additional six pages and also used the questionnaire for three Kōsei-kai households outside the hamlet and for the younger priest of the Buddhist temple. After each interview I gave the respondent (usually weary but almost always still courteous) a few gifts, including a moderately priced Parker (a name well known in Japan) pen and a few other mementos, and on a few occasions a bottle of Johnny Walker Scotch, at that time heavily tariffed and rather coveted, but of which a foreigner entering Japan could bring in three bottles duty-free.

Various documents were kindly supplied by Kawa Mura (the administrative village); by Kōsei-kai's local meeting place, Ueno Church, and national headquarters; and by the Sōtō Zen temple, the Yamanaka Shrine Parishioners' Delegation, and several hamlet common-interest groups. Village records included agricultural surveys, a health survey and a record of household visits to a doctor, household property taxes, maps and aerial photographs, and a public information pamphlet with surveys of village matters from climate to consumer goods. My wife and I took several thousand 35-mm color slides and black and white photographs and about 1,500 feet of super 8-mm movie film. Copies of the photos and film screenings were given in exchange for the material.

Our relations with people in Yamanaka were friendly and informal. We received great hospitality and aid, thanks in part to Japanese courtesy and forbearance toward guests, toward Westerners in Japan, and toward students, and in part to village curiosity about Western life (people commented on our consumption of milk and on my drinking beer at lunch). As neighbors we were regularly given fresh vegetables, prepared foods, and souvenirs, and as Yamanaka residents we were recruited to run a 1,500-m race and a balloon-squashing race for the hamlet in the annual village field day. We conducted several months of English lessons for Yamanaka children, an hour each Sunday, an event popular with hamlet parents.

The original study lasted fourteen months, from November 1970 to January 1972. The "ethnographic present" used, including prices (which have more than doubled), is primarily from that time, though partially updated by correspondence, by several subsequent briefer visits, and by visits to the U.S. by friends from a neighboring hamlet. My wife and I returned for a few weeks in 1973 in the course of making educational filmstrips. In the summer of 1977 a Japan Foundation fellowship returned me for a month to gauge changes and fill gaps in the study. In the summer of 1984 I visited Yamanaka for a little over a day and spent another day in Tokyo with friends from the nearby hamlet.

Chapter 2
The Hamlet

Nihon jū kome no meshi
Yamanaka bakari wa
Soba no yakimochi

Throughout Japan the food is rice;
in Yamanaka alone it's
baked buckwheat cakes.
(traditional Yamanaka poem)

Introduction

Yamanaka is a farming hamlet of fifty-two households, with 220
people in 1972 and somewhat fewer in 1984. It lies along the slope of a
low mountain on the northern border of the Kanto Plain near the center
of Honshu. Throughout the plain, rivers, roads, and railroads descend
from the semicircle of mountains and hills to the north and west and
converge on Tokyo to the east. Yamanaka is an hour by car into the
mountains above the northern rim of the plain and four hours from
Tokyo, or a little over three hours by express train and bus (a super-
highway and a bullet train line to Niigata, under construction, will soon
cut these times considerably). To reach the hamlet from Tokyo, a
traveler crosses the width of the plain, winds up through foothills to
Ueno City, and crosses a pass by road.

The Kanto region as a whole is prosperous. It is the chief rice
supplier to Tokyo and satellite towns, and its mountainous fringe is a
major silk producer. Most important, its factories, mainly in the coastal
cities of Tokyo, Yokohama, and Kawasaki, produce about a quarter of
Japan's industrial output. But hemmed in by mountains and apart from
the main flow of Kanto commerce and industry, Yamanaka is marginal

Yamanaka from a mountaintop to the west, February 1971. Its rice paddies are mostly east of the river, and its dry fields and mulberry orchards are on the west.

to the region. New economic opportunities are few, and as in most rural areas, young people left for the cities steadily between the end of the war and the mid-seventies. Some traditional hamlet organizations, such as the young men's association, have been dissolved for lack of participants. On the other hand, some people are pleased that Yamanaka's isolation has helped preserve its intimacy, cooperation, and household tradition.

Environment

The Kanto region is an uplifted plain that has been tilted, eroded and dissected, and largely flattened by riverine deposits. The northern circumference in which Yamanaka lies is dominated by low but rugged mountains. The hamlet lies at an altitude of 660 m on a narrow, tilted plateau near the bottom of the eastern slope of a low mountain ridge. At the east edge of the plateau a steep wooded embankment drops 30 m to a swift, shallow river. At the west is the steep upper flank of the mountain, and at the north and south the plateau is pinched off by the convergence of river and mountain. A narrow valley floor east of the river, a few hundred meters wide, is the most extensive rice field.

The climate is temperate and monsoonal. In winter, cold continental air flows east and south across the Japan Sea, bringing freezing temperatures (a mean of 2° C in February, for instance) and moderate snowfall to Yamanaka. In summer the wind goes back across Japan from the Pacific to the continent, bringing heavy rains in spring and fall, with occasional typhoons. Total precipitation in Yamanaka is moderately heavy, about 1,000 mm, and irrigation water from the river is ample. Summers are warm and humid but not hot, with a mean of 23° C in August. The hamlet is protected by mountains from the highest winds of winter storms and late summer typhoons. It is also relatively stable geologically, so local damage was minor in, for example, the great Kanto earthquake of 1923.

The natural vegetation is a mixed forest of oak, maple, spruce, fir, and larch, but conifers for lumber and pulp now cover 80 percent of the hamlet's land and are second only to silk as a source of income. Until the postwar period, hardwood was also used locally for cooking and heating, directly or as charcoal, but it has been largely supplanted by bottled gas for cooking and by bricks of powdered coal and "electric hearths" for heating. The growing season of 200 days permits multiple cropping, but not double cropping of rice as in southern Japan. Climate and soil are suited, however, to cash crops, including silk, and subsistence crops, including rice, rye, wheat, vegetables, and apples. Deer, bear, grouse, and pheasant are taken by a semiprofessional hamlet hunter and occasional visiting sportsmen, and small trout and a few other fishes in the river provide sport for boys, and sometimes girls, with spears.

Economic Resources

The mountains restrict Yamanaka's economic potential. Its chief occupation has always been farming, but rice is limited by steep slopes and narrow valleys that make paddy construction difficult. Until the postwar period, rice was a holiday luxury imported from the Kanto Plain. Subsistence crops were plainer grains—wheat, buckwheat, and barley—not requiring paddy, and sweet potatoes. Now enough paddy has been built for rice for domestic use, but not for significant income. Silk has provided the main income for most Yamanaka households since the end of the 19th century, when it was a major national export, and still provides 70 percent of the cash income of farming households. Timber is next most important, followed by vegetables and, since the war, apples.

Although farming is the major occupation, only about half (969 of 1,758) the households in Kawa Mura, the administrative village of which Yamanaka is part, are classified by the national census as farm households. About 10 percent (191) farm full time. Most are "part-time" farming households with one or more members in nonagricultural work, from clerking at the village office, to auto repair, to hotel service at a local hot-spring spa. In Yamanaka one part-time farmer is the Shinto priest for all hamlets in Kawa Mura and the adjoining village as well.

Many people say that they would like to farm full time but that land is scarce. The mean area cultivated is 127 ares (3.1 acres) per household, more than the average in Japan, but only about 5 percent (one-tenth the ratio in the nation as a whole) is paddy, the most productive land. In the village as a whole, 83.6 percent is forested mountain, 5.6 percent is unirrigated farmland, 2.6 percent is meadow, 0.3 percent is building sites, and only 0.2 percent is paddy. Labor, fertilizer, and insecticides are already used liberally. Expanding paddy or even dry fields would mean terracing steep slopes, unjustified by current or prospective crop prices. Slight consolidation of small holdings, and mechanization (in 1972 over two-thirds of farm households had tractors—twice the rate six years before—and several had mechanical rice reapers, and by 1984 mechanized transplanting was general) are occurring, but neither is likely to have a major economic impact.

Prospects for other jobs are also limited. The closest railroad runs through Ueno City, so any prospective enterprises face expensive transportation. The two small factories in the village, making shoes and watch bands (the latter in Yamanaka), depend on unskilled farm women at (in 1972) ¥1,000, about $3.00 a day. Both were built in the late 1960s. They may eventually be followed by other light industries, but none had arrived by 1984.

Tourism and related service occupations are growing slightly. Kawa Mura has brilliant fall foliage, an extinct volcano, a waterfall, and a hot spring with twenty small hotels. It is also traversed by a national highway, completed in 1970, which leads to a "quasi-national" park and a perennial tourist attraction, the famous shrine complex at Nikko. Now cars and tour buses from Tokyo travel the highway throughout summer and fall, and many pause at the spa or waterfall. The highway passes through one end of Yamanaka and half-circles the rest, and by 1973 four Yamanaka households had built permanent roadside stalls with apples, corn, and a folk medicine: an adder (*mamushi*) pickled in white liquor for its aphrodisiacal and other virtues. In 1979 a new building was put up at the north end of the hamlet to house a hamlet meeting place and the neighboring hamlet's chamber of commerce. In 1980 a sushi shop, a used car dealership, and a coffee shop were built, all by people from outside the hamlet and all at the northern end, and a medical clinic was moved there from the neighboring hamlet. In 1983, a pinball (*pachinko*) parlor and a guesthouse were built (the latter by the young Yamanaka poet), and in 1983 a noodle shop.

Agriculture

Farmers here, as elsewhere in Japan, have a busy and varied summer and a slack winter. Within the growing season are shorter cycles: three generations of silkworms in spring, summer, and early fall, and small amounts of soy beans, wheat, buckwheat, sweet potatoes, Chinese cabbage, giant radish, and cucumbers. Many households grow pears, Japanese plums, and persimmons for their own use, and several have small commercial apple orchards.

Four cold and often snowy months, December through March, are relatively idle. Four households do piece-work button making, quilting, assembling a seaweed condiment, or assembling watchbands for the little factory. For all but the watchbands, company drivers bring materials and take away finished products. Men from four or five farm households leave in winter for factory work or day labor in cities of the Kanto Plain.

Rice cultivation begins and ends the main growing season. In 1972, seedbeds near each farmhouse were plowed in late April with small diesel hand tractors, flooded, and harrowed. Seed rice was broadcast by hand and covered by a thin layer of soil, a layer of straw, and a translucent plastic sheet as a temporary hothouse for germination. At the end of the month, the spring festival at the hamlet tutelary shrine signaled the official beginning of the agricultural year (chapter 4). A month after being sown the rice seedlings were transplanted to the main fields. Several households (usually neighbors but sometimes kin) cooperated, making a single line of workers across each field to transplant evenly and quickly. All fields were transplanted in about a week, and each household finished with a celebratory feast for helpers. By 1984, transplanting had been largely mechanized and cooperation and feasting reduced.

After transplanting, the rice is protected against birds and rice borers, and weeded. The hamlet deity is invoked against pests at three festivals during the season, but mechanical and chemical means now supplement the festivals. Birds are frightened with scarecrows, plastic ribbons stretched across the fields, and noise makers periodically exploding a charge of acetylene gas; pesticides are used on insects. Early in November the rice harvest brings another spate of work. The rice is cut, bundled, and hung on racks to dry. In 1972 most people still used the old rice sickle, but a few were experimenting with small hand- or motor-driven machines that cut and bundle in one motion, and by 1984 almost all had motorized harvesters. The dried rice is threshed, polished (with electric or diesel machines, some rented and some owned), and stored at each household. The season concludes with the third festival, for the harvest, at the tutelary shrine.

Between rice planting and harvesting, farm households are busy with other subsistence and cash crops, most importantly three batches of silk. Households buy week-old caterpillars from the agricultural cooperative, which incubates them in a humidity- and temperature-controlled hatchery in a neighboring hamlet. Householders install the caterpillars in their second-story lofts and feed them mulberry leaves for three weeks, after which they stop eating and spin cocoons. After each batch spins, the cooperative weighs each household's lot, sifts it for dead caterpillars, and sells the cocoons of the whole village as a lot to raw silk mills in southern Gunma.

As there are for rice, there are Shinto practices for sericulture, such as a New Year's display of small branches with "cocoons" of glutinous rice cake, near the god shelf. But although this was still made in villages a few kilometers up the valley in 1972, it was no longer made in Yamanaka. According to several people, it had been supplanted by new

Transplanting tobacco seedlings, typical of the region's labor-intensive agriculture.

techniques and devices from the agricultural cooperative, and most importantly by the hygienic modern hatchery.

Education

Residents say that Yamanaka is hampered by "country education." Most children finish school within the village, but some parents think local education is inadequate for modern life (education is highly valued, here as elsewhere) and send their children outside for high school. Although few children from Yamanaka—perhaps none—go to the better universities, several do go to the high school in Ueno City or farther, and thence to a less well known university. Thus, a move from country to city may begin at the end of the ninth grade. Only a few students who make it return, since there are few jobs commensurate with a university education. Moreover, students who have tasted the anonymity and freedom of Tokyo may find it hard to return for other reasons. Many find the intimacy of hamlet life oppressive, and relations between households "feudal." "You can call it 'intimate,'" the young poet said, "or you can call it 'meddling.'"

Of the older generation, nearly all are literate but few have more than a grade-school education, particularly among those who reached high-school age in the prewar or war years. Several active members of Kōsei-kai say that the movement is a means to educational improvement otherwise unobtainable.

Depopulation

The population of Kawa Mura, including Yamanaka, has been declining for several decades. Between 1965 and 1970, for example, it dropped by over 12 percent, though by 1984 the decline had slowed. Depopulation (as in other rural areas; cf. Smith 1978 and Dore 1978) has reduced the effectiveness of hamlet services and the self-sufficiency and diversity of hamlet life. The fire-fighting association and other community labor forces lack able-bodied young men, so older men must serve longer. The All Souls' Festival (*obon*) dance is no longer held in the hamlet, and people who want to dance must go to the larger neighboring hamlet. The shrine festival's play (*kagura*) lost sufficient performers in the mid-fifties and was abandoned, and the young men's association (*seinenkai*) was dissolved in 1970.

The most serious consequence, however, is the extinction of household lines. The household is a fundamental unit whose perpetuation is a primary concern for all members, but from the end of the war through the early 1970s, households died out as young people left. In 1950 there were sixty households in Yamanaka. In 1955 there were fifty-seven; in 1970, fifty-six; and in 1972, fifty-two. Of these fifty-two, moreover, five had only one member and no prospect of reproduction.

Progress and Self-sufficiency

Despite Yamanaka's limitations, older people prefer present to past and hamlet to city. They eat rice and other formerly expensive foods regularly and live in adequately heated and markedly bigger houses than do city people. Two medical clinics, one in the larger neighboring hamlet and one moved from there to Yamanaka in 1980, provide modern medicine at reasonable cost, and the major health problem now is high blood pressure. Roads are paved right into household courtyards. There is half-hourly bus service along the highway, and in 1972 there was already a car or light truck for every ten persons and a motorbike for every seven. By then almost every household had a local telephone, and one in six had long distance; by 1978 all had long distance. There was a television set for every 1.3 households; only three (ours was one) had none. People also have time and money for travel, almost nonexistent until the 1960s, and what they see makes older people happy to be home again. As a man who had lived briefly in a southern Gunma city said, "Relations there are too cool—you don't even know your own neighbor!"

Yamanaka is reasonably representative of Kawa Mura hamlets, and Kawa of contemporary rural villages. At fifty-two households, its size is about average, as are household size (4.3 people), landholdings, education, occupations, and depopulation. But it has a distinct sense (which Brown 1979 points out is common in Japanese villages) of its own identity, somewhat ascetic and reflected in the traditional poem about buckwheat cakes.

In the past this feeling was reinforced by relative self-sufficiency, and even now farming households grow most of their food, buying mainly salt, sugar, tea crackers, sake and beer, and occasionally fish, fruit, canned goods, and ice cream. Most of these come to Yamanaka twice a week in a small market truck. Only one household in three is employed mainly outside the hamlet, and even these raise some of their own food. A few professional services come from within the hamlet as well. Besides its thirty-four farming households, Yamanaka has a carpenter, a tatami maker, a Shinto priest, an aged "mountain ascetic" or diviner (*yamabushi*), a masseur, an owner-operator of a gas station and appliance store, a beauty parlor, a hunter, a furniture maker, a policeman, a government forester, and a shop with tobacco, confections, light bulbs, salt, soap, and cigarettes. Most recently it has acquired the clinic and the coffee, sushi, and a few other shops, although the latter are on the highway, mostly oriented to tourists, and mostly owned by outsiders.

Ready-made clothing, motor vehicles, farm equipment and supplies, building materials, primary and secondary education and other government functions, and a number of other goods and services are supplied by the neighboring hamlet (one of 300 households, numerous shops, two schools, and the village office) or by Ueno City or, occasionally, Tokyo. Otherwise, most needs are met by each household or by hamlet cooperative organizations, so that although the hamlet is more dependent on the outside than before, it still has an air of self-reliance.

Social Organization

The principal units of social organization in Yamanaka are residential households, neighborhood associations, and the hamlet as a whole. These three, each corporate to a degree, are crosscut by such common-interest groups as the fire-fighting association, women's association, and agricultural cooperative.

Residential Groups

The household. The household (*ie*) is the basic unit of social organization in rural Japan (Embree 1939; Nakane 1970; Hsu 1975; Dore 1978; Smith 1978) and so central to social thought that it has at times been the ostensible model for the state (Morioka 1977). Households in Yamanaka are similar to those in other rural areas.[9]

Under the postwar constitution the individual adult has replaced the household as the basic legal unit, and inheritance legally is equally divided among all children. But in popular thought and practice (Takeda 1976), the rural household still is corporate in most local rights and obligations. Succession to the household and its landholdings in

Yamanaka normally is by male primogeniture. Other children are compensated to some extent, frequently by further education. Occasionally an eldest son chooses education and career, and succession is to a younger brother. If there is no son or if none wishes to succeed to the household (or, as was frequent among the wartime generation, none survives), a daughter usually marries an "adoptive husband" (*mukoyoshi*) who takes the family name and succeeds as head of the household (Smith 1974). Since such adopted husbands are chosen from a number of candidates, they are expected to be more talented and ambitious than average. At least two adopted heirs in Yamanaka currently live up to this expectation. One, the able and affable head of the wealthiest household in the hamlet, is already village mayor in his mid-forties—considered a young age in Japan. The other is a local Kōsei-kai leader (Kimura Hideo), politically less advanced but probably no less ambitious.

If a couple has no children, they may adopt a young adult. He or she marries and succeeds to the household as would a natural child. If the person adopted is female, both she and her future husband are adopted. There is now one such adopted couple in Yamanaka, the proprietors of the little general store. The husband is also principal of the middle school in the next village. Their adoptive father also was an adopted son, from another village. He did not succeed to the household that adopted him, however, but instead founded his own household. He had no children, and in his middle years adopted the woman and her subsequent husband. Since this couple has two adult daughters but no son, the third generation also will be adopted.

Biological descent, the usual mode of succession, thus is not the only one. Nor are "ancestors" limited to genealogical ascendants since anyone who dies in the household, whether child or adult, kin or nonkin, becomes an ancestor (Smith 1974; Takeda 1976:120). The aim of succession is to perpetuate the household, defined more by coresidence and economic cooperation than by biology. The relation central to the household is the social one of "parent and child" (*oya-kō*), whether adoptive or biological.

A wealthy household may establish a "branch household" headed by a younger sibling and thus become a "main household" owed loyalty by its branch. A branch was established several years ago by a household whose highway gas station and appliance shop bring it the highest income in the hamlet. The head of the household and founder of the gas station (a member of Kōsei-kai, to which he attributes his success), besides establishing his younger brother and a bride as a branch, employs his brother in the station.

Household corporateness may be seen also in minor daily exchanges: in gift giving, household representation at common functions, linguistic usage, and ideas about karmic retribution. Holiday souvenirs, for example, are exchanged not between individuals but between households. For common-interest meetings, neighborhood association work, or Shinto festivals, households send any competent adult. Corporateness is also reflected in the frequent use of "my household" (*uchi*) for "I" or "me," and "your household" (*otaku*) for "you." Karmic retribution (*go*) in the form of sickness or other mishap may be suffered by any member of a household for the misdeed of any other member, past or present, and results of good deeds are similarly transmitted. A household's social relations as well as its material wealth thus are shared within and between generations, and between living and dead.

Within households, relations are both hierarchical and, so far as I could see, intimate. They center on the relationship of parent and child, which provides the model not only for ancestor-descendant relations but, beyond the household, for employer-employee and many other nondomestic relations as well (Nakane 1970). Morioka (1977) has noted that 20th-century ideologists have extensively invoked it, for example, to describe the relation between emperor and subjects. A seventh-grade textbook of 1911 says that "our country based on the family system forms one large household with the Emperor as its head" (Morioka 1977:187). A 1915 imperial rescript from Emperor Taisho says that the "personal feeling between you and us is the same as that between father and sons," and a 1928 rescript from the present emperor says that "the Imperial Ancestors who built up the country treated the people like their children and made the whole country the same as a household" (Morioka 1977:187–88).

The centrality of this relationship is in part a legacy of the Confucianism brought from China early in Japanese history, but it has a distinctly Japanese cast. Tomikura (1972:111) notes that in China the parent-child relationship was considered "completely different from all other relationships and utterly binding on those involved." In Japan, on the other hand, it was regarded as a basic model on which to pattern other social relationships, a prototype of social organization.

This relationship is, then, a dominant metaphor (a popular dish, rice topped with chicken and egg, is "parent-child broiled rice") with several dimensions. Most salient is "superiority-inferiority," which Nakane (1970) thinks central to Japanese society generally. The parent is superior to the child as the source of the child's very existence, and in taking this responsibility the parent is morally as well as practically superior. A closely related dimension, seniority, is in principle the major component of superiority among household members, village households, company employees, and most other groups. Parents are senior to children, and ancestors to descendants. But seniority does not require a genetic relation. "Ancestor," *senzo*, literally means "born before," and most people in Yamanaka define *senzo* as "those who came before oneself in the household."

The importance of seniority in household relations may be decreasing elsewhere in Japan. As in the West, equality and fraternity between urban parents and children seem to be increasing, often signaled by the loan words "mama" and "papa" (Smith 1974). But in Yamanaka the household hierarchy still is strong (the Kōsei-kai staff member and his son, who said several times that they are "more like friends or brothers than father and son," are an exception).

Superiority and seniority establish the framework for a third relation: *on*, the indebtedness of an inferior to a superior. *On* (Benedict 1946) is a debt intrinsically beyond repayment, but which the debtor nevertheless must repay as much as possible, by gratitude (*kansha*) at the least. *On*, as much as seniority, characterizes the relation of child to parent, from whom he has received existence. The unrepayable *on* of children to parents transcends death and is owed by all descendants to all household ancestors. The gratitude associated with it is sometimes said to separate humans from animals and is the feeling most people in Yamanaka report, if asked, toward ancestors. It is prerequisite to a virtuous life and expressed in all ethical behavior. Grateful children repay parents, first by being good, as adults as well as in childhood. Lack of filial gratitude is considered a prime source of social discord; fostering it is a central aim of Kōsei-kai.

The parent-child relation includes the continuing responsibility of parents to nurture children, evidently so pleasant and self-evident as to require little encouragement. It is relatively seldom cited. When it is, it is usually as an obligation not to the children but to the parents' parents, as part of the obligation to perpetuate the household (villagers occasionally asked why my wife and I had no children, when we would, and how our parents felt about their lack).

The household also is central, as elsewhere in Japan, to religion. Plath has said (1964:307) that the "family of god is the family," and Ooms (1976:71) that the household is a "spiritual community and ancestor worship is its religion." Yanagawa and Abe speak of the "intrinsic religiosity of the household" (1978:15) and say that the "counterpart in Japan of the 'church' in Western societies . . . has always been and will remain" the household. The core of these religious conceptions is, again, the parent-child relationship.

Kumi: Neighborhood associations. The residential unit a step up from the household is the *kumi* ("neighborhood association"), neighboring households that provide services for each other and for the hamlet. Services range from circulating a weekly message board from the village office, to hamlet road cleaning, to preparing weddings and funerals at member households. The *kumi* is also a level of organization for most common-interest groups.

Yamanaka comprises six *kumi* that include every hamlet household and range in size from three households, half a kilometer north of the main settlement, to twelve. Each *kumi* is headed for a year at a time by one household, a rotating task.

The *kumi* regularly circulates village message boards and collects village and prefectural taxes. Two mornings each year, in spring and fall, *kumi* of the entire village recruit a member from each household to spend several hours cleaning roads and gutters. Each *kumi* works by itself. On finishing, each retires to the house of the *kumi* head for a few minutes of tea, crackers, and conversation.

Less regular but just as important as these scheduled functions are unscheduled ones: weddings, funerals and memorial services, emergencies, and general neighborly cooperation. At weddings and funerals the principal guests are relatives and friends from the hamlet and beyond. *Kumi* members make the preparations, joining other guests afterward. In emergencies people turn first to fellow *kumi* members, usually the closest help. Members exchange frequent gifts of food, and of souvenirs after even minor travels. On New Year's Day each household should briefly visit every other household, although in fact few do. In all, the *kumi* is an encompassing net of relationships with people who share much of the round of daily life and almost all major transitions. These relationships are expected to be, and generally are, egalitarian and close. People commonly say that *kumi* members are more intimate than nonhousehold kin and are "like one's family."

Relations within a *kumi* are not always equal and amicable, however. Animosities, infirmities, jobs outside the hamlet, and economic handicaps preclude full participation by some households. Ten households among the fifty-two never serve as *kumi* head, and two or three do not even get the circular message. Four households that do not serve as head are small, work outside the hamlet, are almost never home, and have little contact with other households. Two others, those of a national forestry officer and a policeman, undergo frequent regional transfers. They get the circular message but do not serve as head and have little to do with the community. Two more consist only of a single, elderly woman each, one of whom is virtually incompetent and the only person in Yamanaka receiving prefectural welfare. Another is a single, blind, and aged masseur. The tenth consists of a middle-aged day laborer, eccentric and distrusted by other households, and his wife.

The head of one of these households, the retired village superintendent of education, is widely respected and still influential. His wife's
chronic illness, his own age, and his present work (a history of the
village) prevent them from acting as *kumi* head. With this exception,
households that never act as head are marginal to their neighborhoods
and the hamlet. None belongs to such common-interest groups as the
women's association and fire-fighting association. One is a virtual
pariah.[10] None has a voice in hamlet decisions, nor is any a member of
Kōsei-kai.

Some animosities also exist within *kumi*. One household, as noted,
is distrusted for the householder's eccentricity and for his indigence and
refusal to provide money and labor for festivals and work projects.
Another (a leading Kōsei-kai household) is criticized for not providing a
fire fighter despite having two able-bodied men. One branch household
is on notoriously bad terms with its wealthier main household and
closest neighbor, and one woman, a lone householder, said that
"jealousy" made a neighbor pour motor oil on one of her rice paddies one
night, a serious act of vandalism. Members of Kōsei-kai generally are
regarded skeptically.

Nevertheless, relations within *kumi* usually are friendly and even
familistic, as they are supposed to be, with easy informality and
intimacy. Despite growing independence offered by mobs, services, and
entertainment outside the hamlet and despite occasional antagonism,
kumi familism is still important.

Hamlet. Yamanaka as a whole has clear geographic boundaries,
administrative and service functions, and a corporate identity. It is a
primary unit of organization for common-interest groups. It is a set of
intimate, continuous household and individual relationships, with links
of kinship, daily encounters in the fields and on the road, and cooperation in fire fighting, maintaining roads, regulating water for irrigation
and domestic use, and other activities.

Its identity seems not only geographic and social but also
biological, with an organic unity of people and natural locale. The
hamlet was founded, according to incomplete local records, some 600
years ago by a few warriors fleeing north with their families from a military defeat in Edo (now Tokyo). Tradition says that their tracks were
hidden from pursuers by a strangely early November snowfall as they
reached this area, allowing them to stop. Every year since then, it is
said, snow has fallen on the same date.

Another sign of the unity of hamlet and locale is a lofty, massive
pine tree (a Japanese symbol of longevity) at the southeastern edge of
the hamlet's plateau. Called the "single pine" (*ippon matsu*), it is said to

have been planted when the hamlet was founded. It is emblematic not only in its origin and age but also in its prospects (it will live as long as the hamlet does), individuality, and powers of self-protection. The tree is said to produce hallucinations in anyone who climbs it with malicious intent. Some sixty years ago a villager climbed it to cut off branches interfering with his adjacent fields. Beginning to cut, he found himself and the tree surrounded by a sea. Frightened and confused, he quit and began to descend, and the sea disappeared.[11] The tree is also said to be protected by an unusual number of adders in its vicinity. It is further protected by hamlet residents. In 1971, for example, the Yamanaka old people's association used their annual outing to clear the underbrush beneath it and to put up a fence protecting its roots from visitors and a signpost with a brief history of the tree and its association with the hamlet.

Politically, Yamanaka was originally a village (*mura*), a legal and self-governing entity. Later it was consolidated with neighboring villages into a larger one, and later still postwar consolidation made it and its neighbors a still larger village, Kawa Mura. Now it is a hamlet (*buraku*) within village administration, but residents often still refer to it as a village, especially when speaking of its Shinto festivals. Another sign of its continuing sense of independence is that although the twenty-two seats on the village council are an ostensibly open pool for the entire village, Yamanaka, like other hamlets, seats its own candidates.

In each hamlet information needed or produced by village administrators is collected or disseminated, taxes are collected, and decisions of the council and mayor are implemented by the hamlet headman (*ku-chō*) and, in turn, by *kumi*. The headman is elected for one year by a simple majority of secret ballots. The post is open to any of the fifty-two households, but the twenty-three terms from 1948 to 1971 were served by only fourteen households, one of which served four times. This concentration, however, is said to be not monopolization by ambitious households but *noblesse oblige* since the post has neither power nor other tangible reward. It is, rather, a duty for households with labor to spare and enough knowledge of hamlet affairs to make recommendations to the village council. There is informal consensus before elections about which households can serve adequately and whose turn is next. Thus, although no candidates are announced, only two or three names turn up on ballots.

The hamlet is conceived not only as a natural, social, and quasi-political unit but as a moral one as well. Its ethical standards are supposed to be high. "All the people of Yamanaka are good people," several residents said, implying that they are better than in other

The Single Pine, emblem of the hamlet, with Nami and Obaa harvesting rice in the foreground.

hamlets. This opinion was offered several times at hamlet shrine festivals, where conversation tends toward hamlet affairs. Such loyalty is generalized. People admit that Yamanaka has slightly less cultivable land than other hamlets, but several, including the retired superintendent of education, assert that it has correspondingly more professional and other educated people and is therefore more intellectual (*chishikiteki*).

Common-interest Associations

The three levels of residential unit—household, *kumi*, and hamlet—are cut across by common-interest groups. Membership in most of these is restricted by age or sex but, apart from one group, is in principle open to all households. Beyond their special services, most of them also provide channels of communication and ties of hamlet loyalty across household and *kumi* lines, and membership is a measure of household participation in Yamanaka affairs.

The fire-fighting association. The most specialized and vital group is the fire-fighting association. Every household with an able-bodied man between seventeen and thirty-five is expected to serve in regular drills and several other functions as well as at fires. But employment outside the hamlet and a lack of young people keep over half the households from contributing anyone, and in 1972 there were only twenty-two members from the fifty-two households (though this rate is almost twice the Kawa Mura average). The village government supplies hamlet divisions with equipment (uniform jackets, helmets, hand tools, portable engine-driven pumps, two-way radios, and water tanks) and Y2,000 (about $6.00 in 1972) per member each year, but each hamlet does its own recruitment, maintenance, bookkeeping, and drill scheduling.

The association contributes not only to public safety but also to communal sentiment. The village averages two or three fires a year, which usually call divisions from all hamlets. There are four practice sessions a year, including a village-wide competition to determine the fastest association. During the week before the New Year, a night-long fire watch is kept by the men of each *kumi* in turn. A few firemen also keep watch at the All Souls' Festival dance and at a bonfire festival after the New Year, when Shinto and Buddhist holiday decorations are burned. Drills—especially competitive ones—require concentration and cooperation, and fires strengthen bonds by rewarding intense coordinated effort in crises. After a fire the men retire to a small communal hall beside the equipment shed for an hour or more of sake and snacks, and once a year the Yamanaka division pools its year's pay for a party at the hot-spring spa.

The women's association. The women's association, descended from a national women's auxiliary of the prewar and war years, is organized at the village level but (unlike the fire-fighting association) is independent of village government. Most activities are at the hamlet level.

Yamanaka's thirty-one members divide their activities about equally between recreation and hamlet service. They hold folk-dance practice for the annual village field day, day excursions, an annual cooking class with a nutritionist, an annual dinner for the old people's association, and an annual chemical sterilization of every household's toilet. At spring and autumn equinoxes they visit the graves of men killed in war or fire fighting with flowers, incense, and crackers. When a forest fire in the Yamanaka communal forest kept the fire-fighting associations of six hamlets busy for nearly a day, the Yamanaka women's association prepared food and drink and drove them up the mountain in pick-up trucks. Once a year, at the village field day, members yield their hamlet identity by dancing together in light cotton kimonos of a single pattern for the whole village. Membership thus links households across *kumi* and occasionally hamlet lines.

Communal property association. The communal property association was formed in 1922 to buy adjacent national forest land. Thirty-six households joined, of which four or five later left the hamlet. Two of these still keep their shares, but no other households have been admitted.

A director and one officer in each *kumi* are elected each year to sell timber and keep records. Transactions over Y10,000 require convening the entire association. Members assemble nine or ten days a year to clear brush, plant seedlings, and maintain mountain roads and boundary markers. Work days end with several bottles of sake, crackers, and good cheer in the little communal hall near the center of the hamlet.

Member households are, by and large, the oldest and wealthiest in the hamlet. With its long-term common interest in land and its communal labor, this group, like the fire-fighting and women's associations, comprises the households that have most at stake in the hamlet and are most fully a part of it.

The agricultural cooperative. The agricultural cooperative is important mainly to households that also belong to the first three groups. Unlike these groups, however, the co-op has almost entirely commercial, not communal, concerns and is organized not at the hamlet but at the village level.

Like the women's association, the co-op grew out of a government program of the prewar and war years, but now it is independent. It serves its 776 members in Kawa Mura by marketing nearly all crops and providing seed, fertilizer, insecticides, expert advice, and saving and loan services. It has a two-story, ferro-concrete office in Yamanaka (moved there from the neighboring hamlet in 1977), a modern silkworm hatchery, a warehouse, a small retail store (the latter two also in Yamanaka), and several trucks.

A board of twenty directors decides pricing and related matters. Like being on the village council, being co-op director gives one moderate power and prestige. Two Yamanaka householders (one of them the wealthiest and most influential in the hamlet) are currently directors. The most active member of Kōsei-kai in Yamanaka, Hideo, was a director before giving all his time to religion, and giving up this post is one of a number of ways in which he has shifted his concerns from the hamlet to Kōsei-kai.

Shrine parishioners' delegation. The shrine delegation (chapter 4), like the agricultural cooperative, promotes hamlet agriculture and general welfare. Unlike the co-op, it does this for the hamlet as a whole, not for individual households, and by different means. Its members, one from each of the six *kumi*, maintain the hamlet shrine and collect contributions for three annual festivals. Since festivals are held to secure good crops for the whole hamlet and to remind people of their mutual obligations, each household is expected to send someone.

The Buddhist temple. The other "established" (*kisei*) religious institution for Yamanaka, the Sōtō Zen temple (chapter 3), is in a sense more like the agricultural cooperative than the shrine delegation in that it serves individual households rather than the hamlet. The temple, to which almost every household belongs, lies in the next hamlet, and unlike the shrine it has parishioners from all hamlets. Its representatives in each hamlet take collections from all households but record them in the names of households, not the hamlet. Similarly, visits to the temple (or by the priest to Yamanaka) are not on behalf of the hamlet but of particular households. Also like the co-op, the temple has a board of directors from leading households.

The children's association. The *kodomokai* ("children's association," although it includes no girls) is an informal, self-governing group of middle-school boys. It prepares two minor festivals (chapter 4) and holds a New Year's fire watch preceding that of the adult firemen. These activities are planned in the little hamlet meetinghouse, where soft drinks and crackers are consumed and the division of labor decided. The preparations and the festivals themselves are said to be "amusement" (*goraku*) for the boys and a "chance for children from the far ends of the hamlet to get acquainted."

Communal property owners' association work party poses en route home from planting timber seedlings.

Old people's association. Most people over sixty-five belong to the "old people's association," founded in Yamanaka in 1963 for recreation and, according to the retired superintendent of education, to return respect to the aged. It meets only a few times a year, for a dinner held by the women's association, a work day clearing brush around the venerable pine tree, or a visit to the nearby hot-spring spa.

PTA. The "PTA" (written in Roman letters) is a postwar import from the United States for "democratizing" the school system. Membership is automatic for parents of schoolchildren. Members attend matriculation and graduation exercises, help school faculties organize an annual sports day, and distribute school announcements.

Household Status: Stratification and Mobility

While the residential units and common-interest associations constitute the hamlet's formal organization, differences on another dimension, household "status" (*chii*), are also informally but generally recognized. One mark of status is election to the village council, agricultural co-op board, hamlet headship, or chairmanship of common-interest associations. Another mark, in Yamanaka as elsewhere, is seating order at meetings. The person of highest status sits farthest from the entrance to the room, facing it. The order varies slightly from group to group and from meeting to meeting, so each occasion requires decisions and polite mutual offers and refusals of "superior" (*kami no*) places. Still, similar patterns appear regardless of occasion, and most people seem comfortable with them; Dore's (1978:57) reference to the "part-hierarchial, part-egalitarian solidarity of the traditional self-governing village" is apt. Only a few younger or more restless people appear to chafe.

The components of status are said (by at least a few people, including the young poet whose college sociology had included exercises in status ranking) to include, in order of importance, wealth (mainly land holdings), seniority in the hamlet (in generations since establishment of the household), education or "culture" (*kyōyō*), and the trust (*shinyō*) and affection inspired by current household members, particularly by the head. Each of these varies widely. The wealthiest household (called the "rock-cliff millionaire" for a stone retaining wall in front of the house) was assessed by the village tax office at Y2,500,000 in 1972, five times the Yamanaka mean. At the other extreme, eight households own no real property at all—none of these is a farming household. Two (the policeman and forestry officer) are subject to frequent transfer. Three more, including one of the most active members of Kōsei-kai, have adequate nonagricultural work, while another three are impoverished. Only one of these eight has any regular role in hamlet affairs.

Households vary similarly in seniority, education, and (it is said) in trust. The two oldest households claim fifteen generations, from the founding of the hamlet. Three or four others are almost as old, and after them is a continuous gradient to four households now in their first generation.

Regarding education, the heads of two households (the retired superintendent of education and a high-school teacher) are university graduates, and several young villagers are now at universities. The majority of adults have only a primary-school education, however, and four older people (all women and none heads of households) are illiterate.

The level of "trust" enjoyed by households, cited most frequently after wealth as needed for election to office, is difficult to gauge. But this also ranges widely and apparently consensually, from the unanimous mistrust of the small household of the eccentric day laborer to the generally high regard for the household of the gregarious rock-cliff millionaire.

Opportunities for households to change any of these circumstances are limited. Chances to make money are circumscribed by the stability of local agriculture and the local economy generally. Monetary ambition usually leads away from the hamlet. For house heads or presumptive heirs, however, moving conflicts with duty to the household. Seniority is even less subject to control than is wealth. A household may in a sense achieve seniority by establishing branch households, but this takes wealth. Educational opportunity also is limited. Ambitious students must leave home even for a good high school, and for a university education they must go to Tokyo. This too takes money. Moreover, people who leave for education usually do not come back. For the generation of high-school-age individuals before and during the war (most numerous in Kōsei-kai), higher education was simply unavailable. Trust, while influenced by the varying personalities of successive generations, is no easier to achieve than wealth, seniority, or education, and a notion that households run true to type is occasionally expressed, as when the eccentric day laborer told me that all households with the surname Kimura tend to go mad. Trustworthiness or untrustworthiness, like wealth, seems to carry over from generation to generation.[12]

Mothers' kimonos reflect the importance of the school induction ceremonies, Kawa Village primary school.

Risshō Kōsei-kai

In the early 1950s a new opportunity appeared, at least for a while and to some people, to circumvent the blocks to mobility and to enable people to achieve wealth, education, the confidence of others, and even a new kind of seniority. This opportunity was the new movement, Risshō Kōsei-kai, which offered, among other things, rudiments of an alternative social system. Within this system seniority was not by generation in the hamlet but by time of joining the movement and by converting others. By persuading other households to join, a household could become a "parent" without waiting a generation to establish "child" or branch households. Just as important, enthusiasts claimed that adherence to the movement's principles would bring not only social but material benefits, principally health, and solution to all other personal problems as well.

Summary and Implications

Yamanaka, compared to Japan as whole, is, like other mountain hamlets, a small, stable, and closed society. Its economy, mainly agriculture though with a growing service sector and a little light industry, has been comparatively stable since the mid-1950s; it has improved greatly since the war but has not kept pace with other areas, particularly cities, which continue to draw young people away.

Yamanaka includes three residential levels of organization: the household, neighborhood association, and village, crosscut by common-interest groups. There is competition and even conflict between households, but most are tied amicably by common interests, kinship, and intimate association from birth to death.

The hamlet ethic of amity and intimacy includes egalitarianism, at least within neighborhood associations, but there are wide and stable differences in household status. This stability, and inherited obligations between main and branch households, help maintain a closed, inflexible social order some people call "feudal." When Kōsei-kai came, it appeared to some people to be a chance to improve their lot in several ways.

Chapter 3
Established Buddhism in Yamanaka

Introduction

Organized religion in Yamanaka, apart from Kōsei-kai, consists of Sōtō Zen Buddhism and Shinto. (Confucianism and Taoism have left traces in these and in folk belief but have no organization.) Generally, Buddhism is the religion of the household and Shinto that of the community, but the distinction between them often is unclear, here as elsewhere. Both seem to be of generally declining importance to villagers.[13]

Religious belief and practice in Yamanaka vary between households and between individuals. Some are more pious or skeptical than others. Most but not all say that Shinto and Buddhism are separate entities, but people have trouble assigning some elements (e.g., the good-luck *daruma* dolls, which in fact represent Bodhidharma, who brought Zen to China) to one or the other. A few hold that the deities of the two are the same. Most people, including the Shinto priest and a few who say that both Shinto and Buddhism are "superstitions" (*meishin*), still say that Shinto is not a "religion" (*shūkyō*, a word with sectarian connotations) since it is something that all Japanese share.

This heterogeneity may stem in part from changing relations among religion, education, and national policy. After a long history of syncretism between Buddhism and Shinto, the two were separated by government decree in the late 19th century as the first step in using Shinto, the indigenous religion, to foster nationalism. Shinto became a legal part of the national polity (*kokutai*) and therefore no longer a "religion." As Earhart (personal communication) has said, "the state, especially from the 1890 Edict on Education, and more rigidly from the twenties and thirties of this century, was involved in a nationwide thought-control system." People in school in Yamanaka and elsewhere before and during World War II were taught that the emperor was a "deity" (*kami*) descended directly from the Sun Goddess and that Japan was the "country of the gods" (*shinkoku*). Religious groups of suspect loyalty, including Kōsei-kai, were suppressed, their leaders jailed, and their headquarters damaged. When the postwar American constitution separated church and state, it ended half a century of government control of religion. Many sects and movements grew rapidly, and many more were founded.

At the same time, people seem to have come to express—and accept—divergent opinion more freely. In Yamanaka the arrival of Kōsei-kai appears to have been only one instance of increasing diversity since the war. The diversity displeases some people, however. My closest neighbor, a man of seventy-three, said that freedom of speech and "freedom of behavior" (*kōdō no jyū*) are concepts imported by MacArthur and have gone too far. "It's hard to decide about building a road or selling communal timber now because too many people object to community opinion. If some agreement is reached with half, the other half object. *That's* the result of MacArthur's 'democracy.'" Moreover, according to the retired superintendent of education, in the younger generation respect for parents, teachers, and *kami* has declined since the removal of Shinto from school curricula.

Nor is there unanimity about an authority on religion. Although virtually everyone, including Kōsei-kai members, belongs to the same shrine and temple, some refer questions about religion to the retired superintendent, some to the Shinto priest, a few to the Buddhist priest, and a few to the local leader of Kōsei-kai. Despite the fact that Yamanaka is a small, old, stable, and closely knit community, in which consensus and harmony are said to be important, scrutiny shows its religion, like other aspects of its culture, to be somewhat heterogeneous.

The Temple

Sōtō Zen, the "established" Buddhism in Yamanaka as in much of rural Japan, may be described at two levels: the temple and the individual household. These two meet only at funerals, memorial services, collections by officers in the hamlet, and several annual services at the temple. The temple, Eizōji, is located in the adjoining hamlet, and its parish includes twelve of the twenty hamlets of Kawa Mura, or 672 households.

Organization and Recruitment

The "main temple" (*honzan*) and source of authority of Sōtō Zen is Eiheiji, established by Dōgen in 1243 in what is now Fukui Prefecture. It is ostensibly the goal of every member to make at least one pilgrimage, but it is a rather distant reality for most people in Yamanaka. Few have visited it, even though religious pilgrimages have long been popular in Japan as occasions for travel. Only a minority in Yamanaka could even name the main temple or their school of Zen, or identify "sitting meditation" (*zazen*), central to training at Eiheiji and not uncommon among educated city dwellers.[14]

Priests are accredited by the main temple, preferably but not necessarily after a year's training there. After this the priest's contact with the main temple is limited to occasional pilgrimages with parishioners, receiving periodic administrative directives, and sending a yearly remittance of about 15 percent (¥200,000, or $660, for Eizōji in 1972) of his temple's income. Doctrinal exposition (which in any case appears to concern the local priest very little) is largely left to local discretion.

The priest's position is hereditary. He is the chief administrator of the temple as well as chief celebrant, but he shares administration with a board of four lifetime trustees (*yakuin*) from prominent households who serve without pay as advisers, fact-finders, and treasurers. They set fees for funerals, arrange for building repairs, collect donations at New Year's and other festivals, and manage the treasury. Below them are six delegates (*sōdai*) chosen from prominent households by the trustees. At the lowest level are representatives (*sewanin*), one in each of the twelve parish hamlets, through whom delegates address members at large. The present priest, with his wife, son, and new daughter-in-law, lives in comfortable quarters attached to the temple. He is aided by his twenty-five-year-old son, graduate of a Tokyo Buddhist university and of a year at Eiheiji.

Facilities

The temple is physically imposing. It is about 500 years old and one of the largest buildings in the village, and its high peaked roof, a dull but visible red, can be seen from most points. According to "direction lore" it occupies one of the best sites in the village, facing down into the village from a steep southern slope. The interior is quiet, spacious, and uncluttered. A seated, larger-than-life gilt statue of the Buddha

(Śākyamuni, patron of the temple), flanked by two Bodhisattvas and two fierce Deva kings, faces south into the main hall from a gloomy alcove. A smaller room to the Buddha's left contains a smaller statue of Kannon, goddess of mercy, rescued at some point from an abandoned temple on an island in the nearby river. Another room to the Buddha's right contains tablets for the war dead of the parish. Water, incense, and fruit sit in dishes before the statues. Attached buildings include the priests' quarters, a festival hall, reception rooms, and a grain storehouse.

Activities

Parishioners' activities at the temple are scant and, according to the priest, decreasing. Mornings and evenings at six o'clock the priest chants a solitary prayer to the ancestors and to the Buddha on behalf of the parishioners. The only role for parishioners at the temple is attending an annual series of nine services (*gishiki*).[15] Once popular, these now draw small audiences. The best attended, the April reading of the Sutra of the Great Wisdom (*Daihannya-kyō*), features a vegetarian luncheon prepared by parish women, extra priests from other temples in the area, and a showy "reading" in which the priests spin portions of the text from hand to hand. Even this, however, draws only about 400 of the roughly 2,000 parishioners, and fewer than 100 stay for the whole service, numbers down from those of prewar times by about half. The service for "All Souls' Festival," the most important Buddhist holiday, brings still fewer. Other services bring almost no one but the officers and a few elderly parishioners.

Doctrine

The temple transmits little doctrine to parishioners, even at services. People who do attend say services are "amusement," and the priest concurs. People show little interest in their meaning and, if asked, usually lump the nine services as "services for the ancestors" (*senzo kuyō*). This description contrasts with that given by the priest, who designated only four ("All Souls' Festival," the Spring and Autumn Equinoxes, and the April fifth "Mass for the Dead") as ancestral services. Three more are for the Buddha (one each for his birth, enlightenment, and death), and one is for Dōgen, founder of Sōtō Zen.

The divergence of opinion between priest and laity reflects the absence of sermons and other instruction and differences between the training, experience, and interests of priestly and other households. Some Sōtō priests do give lectures (*sekkyo*) and occasionally one of these visits Eizōji, but only eight people in Yamanaka had ever heard one (a situation typical of established Buddhism elsewhere in Japan as well).[16]

There is some feeling, at least among the priests, that Buddhist clergy *should* provide guidance. Asked whether Shinto is a "religion" or not, the younger priest of Eizōji said,

> Yes, that's religion too . . . because there are people who believe in *kami-sama*. But *kami-sama* don't give guidance, you know. For instance, there's Kimura Taro, the Shinto priest . . . has he ever said, "Your household should do such-and-such?" No. But a Buddhist priest does do that.

This priest considers religion a source not only of morality, but also of general philosophical truth. Asked for a definition of "religion," he said, after a pause,

> Religion is what teaches truth (*shinri*), is what I think . . . the philosophical term, "truth" . . . "honest reason" (*makoto no kotowari*), you know, "true logic" (*makoto no rikutsu*), should I say . . . "true teaching" (*makoto no oshie*). For example, that people die is the truth, you know . . . that's the philosophical meaning of "truth." . . . That's why it will never die out. If it were a lie, it definitely would be found out. But it doesn't perish because it's the actual case (*shinjitsu*). Yes, it means "what is real." If man is born, then he dies; that's no lie, that's the truth. That people don't want to die, that's also "truth."[17]

The "truth" of Sōtō Zen is taught to priests at the main temple of Eiheiji, as recounted by the younger priest, largely intuitively, not as formal doctrine. There is no set of riddles to induce enlightenment, as in Rinzai Zen, and indeed no canon at all. There are only minutely detailed, austere regulations for training and prayers for funerals and other parish functions. The younger priest said,

We don't get formal training in doctrine . . . just after tea, or after reading a book. It's not like school. At school, they say, "Learn!" to the students, "This is the way it is!" But not at the temple. If they did, there would be no progress. The human world is always changing, and it can't be set out in doctrine.

The goal of Sōtō monastic life (though not of the hamlet laity), the priest noted, is "enlightenment" (*satori*). But enlightenment cannot be taught. One understands only through experience, in Sōtō Zen, by "one's own efforts" (*jiriki*). Nothing specific can be done to induce it, not even using riddles. At Eiheiji one either sits formally or works, thinking of nothing except, if one is a novice, the pain in his legs. The procedure is simple, the priest said:

One gets up at three o'clock in the morning, washes his face, and does *zazen* (sitting meditation) for an hour. Then there are the morning memorial service, morning duties, and breakfast. Then work cleaning the garden, cleaning glass, and so on; then noon duties. Then lunch and then afternoon, the same as the morning: work, evening duties, supper, *zazen* for two hours, and then sleep at nine o'clock. That's the outline . . . it's determined down to the last detail, which you couldn't understand without doing it, with a special vocabulary. It's all *zazen*: sitting *zazen* and moving *zazen* . . . "action" *zazen* . . . it's whatever you're doing if you do it with complete concentration, without being distracted. *You* don't think of your wife while writing this, and I don't think of going home for supper.

Training at Eiheiji teaches austerity, gratitude, and the frailty of life, "more evanescent than the dew," as the young priest quoted an aphorism. Gratitude includes "gratitude for things" (*mono no arigatasa*), especially food:

"Gratitude for things" . . . for instance, your tape recorder and your pen, essential to your work. . . . At Eiheiji there are no things. The life is that of 700 years ago, of the days of sword fighting . . . there are things but their use isn't permitted . . . and the food year-round is a few grains of rice in lots of water—rice gruel—and two slices of pickled radish, and at the left of your bowl, a little pile of salt. That's all morning, noon, and night. You don't want to eat very much . . . and you realize just how hungry you can get, and what food is worth . . . just as when you run out of money, you know for the first time the value of money: "Ah! I wish I had just a dollar!"

Here he stopped to make a bowl of gruel to show its tastelessness.

His year at Eiheiji had made a profound impression. One experience was particularly poignant. While doing *zazen*, he suddenly thought that "everything was alive . . . the earth, dirt, trees, the mountain . . . things you don't normally think are alive." Asked to describe it, he told of his first period at Eiheiji. It was miserable. One did nothing but sit in *zazen* outside the temple proper, continuously from getting up until bedtime, for a week or a month or however long was necessary. "Then an old monk decides you're ready, by looking at you . . . until then, you're not let into Eiheiji itself. Then there's a time of staring at the wall with your legs hurting like mad, wanting to quit but not giving in." Suddenly he had felt the passage of time and the changing of the season—it was spring—and thought, "Ah! The earth is alive!" He felt the wind become warmer and thought, "Ah! *It* was alive! and the trees too, and the rocks."

Since then, he had told only the master of the Ueno City Sōtō Zen temple of his experience, when the master had asked what had been best in his year at Eiheiji. Now he could capture the feeling only fleetingly and never with that intensity—perhaps briefly up on the mountain, sitting in the grass and looking up at the sky.

But most of the young priest's year at the main temple remains private. He seems to communicate neither austerity nor "gratitude for things" nor the vision of the world as living to parishioners, from whose experience they are far removed; nor do his television, stereo, car, and wife suggest the poverty or meditation of the main temple. He does feel that he should provide some moral leadership and doctrinal instruction. He says that he can exert influence at the service of the Sutra of the Great Wisdom and at funeral and memorial services, but his description is ambiguous:

One can't say, immediately or in the short run, but there's surely an influence; one can feel the reaction . . . they ask questions like, "Where is the principal image?" or "What does Yakushi-sama do?" Or they ask the meaning of the service.

Moreover, most people in the hamlet say that they never talk with either priest. In sum, despite the younger priest's qualms, the temple offers little active guidance to parishioners. If Sōtō Zen in the village continues to interpret the world to its adherents, the role of the temple apparently is small.

Eizōji's source of income, like its limited teachings, is typical of "established" Japanese Buddhism (Norbeck 1970; Tamaru 1972; Smith 1978:155–56; Shibata 1983), which, it is often said, is now no more than a "funeral religion" invoked at death and on memorial dates. In Japan as a whole, Shibata (1983:47) writes, "more than 90% of the active temples today are [ones] whose primary purpose is to perform the funeral rites and to pray for the deceased." Describing the conditions under which Reiyūkai was founded, Hardacre (1984:14–15) writes similarly that "because the Buddhist clergy was content to draw an income from the performances of ancestral and funeral rites, they took no initiative in aiding their parishioners' desire to lead ethical lives." In Yamanaka, funerals and memorial services are almost the only contact people have with temple or priest. Their importance is reflected in Eizōji's budget: in 1972, for example, these services brought in 74 percent of the temple's income (¥1,000,000 of ¥1,350,000), while another 15 percent came from contributions for the series of annual services, and 11 percent from special levies for building maintenance.

Households

Just as every Yamanaka household older than a generation belongs to the temple and has a Buddhist altar containing memorial tablets for everyone who has died in the house, so most adult householders among them say, if asked, that they "believe in" (shinjiru) Buddhism. Even people who say they are "unbelievers" (mushinjin) perform its ceremonies occasionally. Most householders pray and put cooked rice and water or tea in the altar daily, and almost every household observes the major holidays. What this means to them, however, is somewhat different from what it means to the priest.[18]

Recruitment

Only households older than one generation belong to the temple, have altars and offerings, and "believe in Buddhism," because all these are aspects of a household's relation to its dead.[19] Most people, in fact, say that "Buddhism" means "praying to the dead" (*hotokesama o ogamu*) or "praying to ancestors" (*senzo-sama o ogamu*). Until someone in a new household has died, "Buddhism" is simply irrelevant. As a high-school teacher (a graduate of a Buddhist university, with a "philosophical interest" in Buddhism) put it, "Our household is new, so we don't have any memorial tablets; so we don't have any religion."

"Ancestors" and "Spirits of the Dead": Senzo and Hotoke

Two words are most often used in Yamanaka for the recipients of Buddhist prayers and offerings: *hotoke*, literally "buddhas" but often glossed "spirits of the dead," and *senzo*, "ancestors." As used by most people in Yamanaka,[20] the two terms may be rendered "people who have died" and "the dead of one's household." Asked to compare them, most people say initially that they are the same. Pressed for a distinction, most say that *hotoke* are simply "people who have died" (*naku natta hito* or, less delicately, *shinda hito*), while *senzo* are either "people who came before oneself [in a household]" (*jibun no mae no hito*) or "the earliest people of the household" (*sono uchi no ichiban furui hito*). Both are the dead, in somewhat different capacities.

Taken literally as "buddhas," *hotoke* implies assimilation to the Buddha and hence purity, serenity, and detachment from this world. The temple priest and the local Kōsei-kai leader have theological precedent when they say that not all dead are *hotoke*, since to "become a buddha" (*jobutsu suru*) requires specific transformation (Smith 1974), in part by prayer and other services by survivors. But in lay usage in Yamanaka as elsewhere (Takeda 1976), all dead are *hotoke*. These *hotoke* may or may not be serene; they retain individuality and remain involved with their households. The term *hotoke* is respectful (it is almost always used with the honorific *sama*) and implies seniority, elevation, and moral refinement. (Ooms [1976:71] remarks that "becoming an ancestor [is] a ritual socialization . . . of the soul.") Although *hotoke* retain idiosyncracies for a while, they tend to leave moral failings behind. Offerings of food and drink, for example, are vegetarian and usually nonalcoholic. If ill-treated, however, they may be vengeful.

Senzo, literally "born before" and usually rendered "ancestors," are the dead as household progenitors and senior members. Being an ancestor is not necessarily biological[21] since "ancestors" include all who died in the household, whether they have left children or not. Depending on context, "ancestors" may be either the household dead collectively or only the founding generation. *Hotoke*, as noted, normally include all

ancestors, even though the Sōtō Zen priest and Kōsei-kai leaders say
that becoming *hotoke* is not automatic at death. In addition, a few
people in the hamlet say that *hotoke* are the same as Shinto *kami*, again
an idea with precedent (Matsunaga 1969; Gōrai 1984). This syncretistic
view was attacked by the Meiji government (1868–1912), which to foster
nationalism disentangled Shinto shrines from Buddhist temples (Ueda
1972).[22] The syncretism now seems to be rejected by many people in
Yamanaka,[23] who say that some dead may become *kami* as well as
hotoke, but that to do so they must have been, while alive, of outstanding
service to their community.

Variations in usage reflect, among other things, several taxonomic
levels. Lay usage in Yamanaka can be seen in figure 1.

At the most general level opinion differs about whether *hotoke* and
kami are the same or different. The view that they are different now
prevails.[24] But although household Buddhist altars and Shinto god
shelves usually are kept separate, and although *hotoke* and *kami* receive
different offerings, the distinction does not interest most people. It is
generally assumed but neither elaborated nor vigorously defended if
questioned.

At the next level down, *hotoke* are the dead generally, while those
such as the war dead, who had rendered outstanding service to
community or nation, are *kami* as well. As with *hotoke*, virtually none
are *kami* before death; the official place of the emperor from the Meiji
Restoration until the end of the World War II, and sporadically
throughout Japanese history, as a "living *kami*" (*arahitogami*) is an
exception. The younger priest at Eizōji found anomaly in it:

> If he [a past emperor] was a *kami*, and shouldn't die . . . well,
> he died anyway. So he is a *kami* who died. But according to
> the books, a *kami* is supposed to be able to give life to things,
> and a *kami* created Japan. A person [*hito*] of the kind who
> made Japan—why should he die? . . . It's points like that at
> which *kami* don't stand to reason . . . they don't make sense.

At the next level are two kinds of *hotoke*: the dead of one's own
household, or ancestors, and the dead of others. The dead of other
households usually are unimportant, so the further distinction between
those with "homes" (*en*, literally "connections") of their own (*yuen-
botoke*) and those without homes or "wandering spirits" (*muenbotoke*) is
of little interest. As elsewhere in Japan (Smith 1974, 1978; Ooms 1976),
however, "wandering spirits"—i.e., people who have died unjustly or

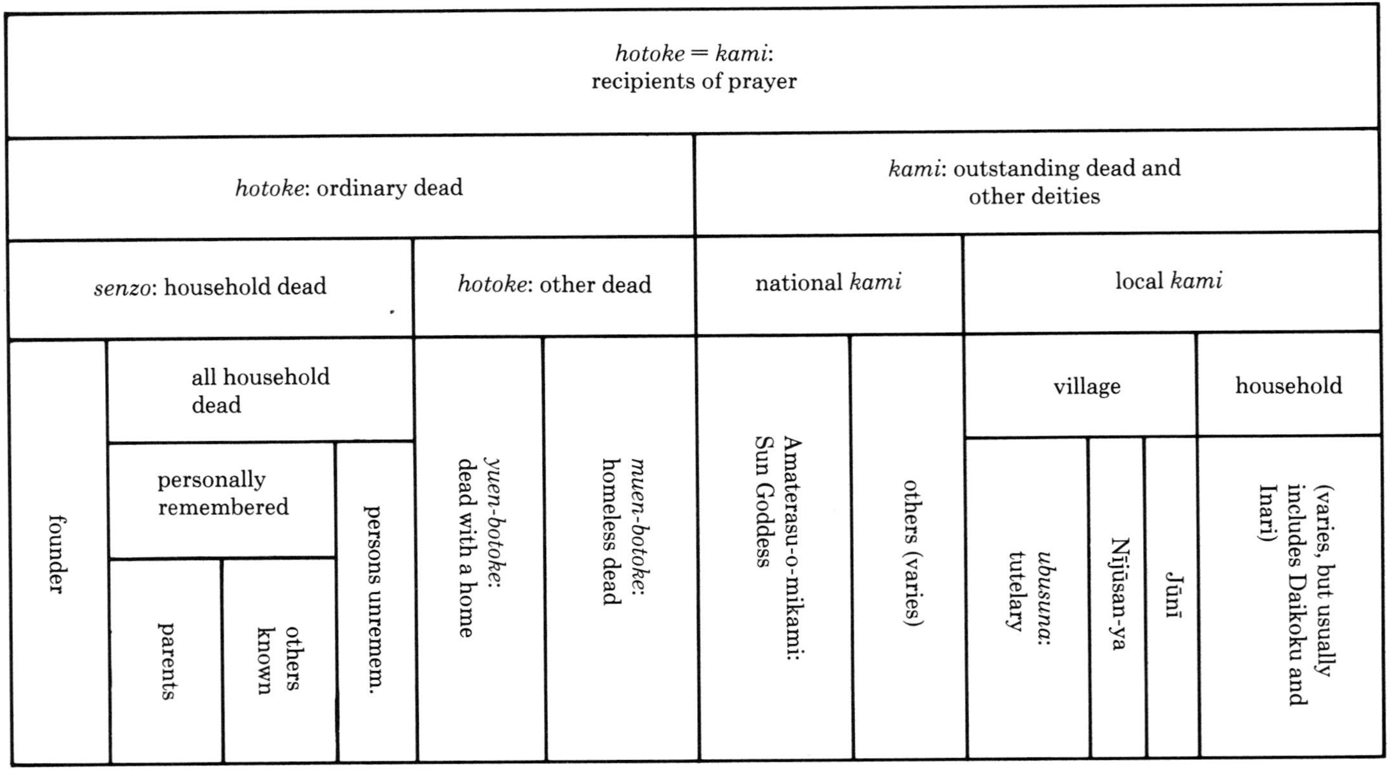

hotoke = kami: recipients of prayer	kami: outstanding dead and other deities	local kami	household	(varies, but usually includes Daikoku and Inari)		
			village	Jūnī		
				Nījūsan-ya		
				ubusuna: tutelary		
		national kami	others (varies)			
			Amaterasu-o-mikami: Sun Goddess			
	hotoke: ordinary dead	hotoke: other dead	*muen-botoke*: homeless dead			
			yuen-botoke: dead with a home			
		senzo: household dead	all household dead	persons unremem.		
				personally remembered	others known	
					parents	
			founder			

Figure 1. Recipients of prayers and offerings in Yamanaka.

have no descendants and thus no one to care for them, no memorial tablets, and no place of their own—can be troublesome. The Kōsei-kai staff member in Yamanaka occasionally is possessed by them, and one or two householders, including the retired superintendent of education, set a placatory place for them at All Souls' Festival.

Within one's own household, all *hotoke* are "ancestors." These may, depending on context, be either all household dead or only the founding generation. Among all household dead, distinction is sometimes made between those whose lives had overlapped one's own (especially one's parents), whom one therefore can remember while praying, and the undifferentiated household predecessors who no longer are personally remembered. It is the collective ancestors who are the usual objects of prayers by the priest, of prayers and offerings by the household, and, for Kōsei-kai members, divination, prayer, and offerings by Kōsei-kai officers.

Activities and Locations

Householders pray and make offerings at their altars, their graveyards, and the temple in daily and yearly cycles and in a linear series after a death.

The altar, kept in the best room of the house,[25] exists to hold the memorial tablets, the household's most cherished objects. ("We didn't even save the tablets" is a set phrase indicating a particularly sudden and disastrous fire.) The tablets are cherished because they represent (and according to a few people, are)[26] the ancestors. Others say the tablets are the principal but not exclusive locus of ancestors, while most people say ancestors are "everywhere." For this majority, the tablets represent ancestors without necessarily embodying them. For everyone, the tablets are the primary focus for prayer and offerings.

Altars vary with household wealth, but most are plain wooden cabinets about 1.5 m tall, with several tiers of shelves. The topmost shelf bears the tablets, and lower shelves bear small containers of food, water and tea, an incense burner, and occasional offerings of fruit or flowers. Below these are several larger shelves enclosed by doors, storing such documents as tax records and birth certificates. Altars are among the better-made pieces of household furniture, but in Yamanaka all but that of the Kōsei-kai meeting place are more modest than those in wealthier areas (Smith 1974); none is lacquered or gilt.

Graveyards are sites of periodic prayers and offerings. They are scattered throughout the hamlet, mostly at some distance (on average, perhaps half the length of the hamlet) from the household to which they belong, although frequently close to some other house. Each grave has an upright stone incised with the dates and posthumous name or names of the dead. Several households have consolidated the remains from all graves in a small vault under a single large stone inscribed with the family name, the phrase "generations of ancestors," and the names of persons interred.

The temple, site of most graves in cities, here has only a few. Since only one household in Yamanaka has graves there, and since only five or six people from the hamlet go to the temple even for important festivals, it is least frequently the place for prayers and offerings.

Most but not all households make a daily offering. After the breakfast rice (or noodles or other staple) is cooked but before anyone begins to eat, a small portion is placed with tea or water on the altar before the tablets. The person placing the offering (usually the wife) says a short, silent or quietly spoken prayer with eyes closed, head slightly bowed, and hands placed palms together in front of the chest. The prayer usually requests a safe day for the household.

The next most frequent performances are those of the yearly cycle of Buddhist holidays: All Souls' Festival (*obon*), Spring and Autumn Equinoxes (*higan*), and the New Year (*shōgatsu*). These are observed even by most households that make no daily offerings.

All Souls' Festival, similar to those elsewhere,[27] is the most important. During its three days, September 3–5, the spirits of the dead are formally welcomed home (though often thought to be there the rest of the year as well), fed, and entertained. Living former members of the household who have moved away, such as younger siblings of the house head, also return to visit, eat, and report to their seniors both living and dead. The festival is thus a household reunion.

Early on the morning of September 3, an All Souls' altar (*bondana*) is built to display the memorial tablets more fully than in their box in the everyday altar. The special altar is a rectangular platform about 1.0 m wide and 70 cm deep, supported about 1.0 m from the floor by a post at each corner. The tops of the posts extend about 1.0 m above the platform and bear a pair of braided straw ropes strung between them and garlanded with several kinds of flowers. Slender leafy sprigs of bamboo are lashed to the front two posts. The tablets are arrayed along the back of the shelf. Before them usually are several framed photographs of the most recent dead. In front of these are a platter of fresh whole vegetables (usually including eggplant, cucumber, and corn), a bowl of water, and a whisk of long-stemmed flowers for daily sprinklings of water on the vegetables. In most houses there is also a "cucumber horse" (*kyūri-uma*) with toothpick legs, on which the spirits of the dead ride to and from the house and the other world, carrying offerings, some say, back to the other world.

After building the altar, several (preferably all) members of the household walk to the graveyard to lead the spirits home. Most households offer incense, flowers, and balls of glutinous rice cake at the graves (which have been tidied, and the grass cut, a few days before) and pour water over the gravestones—to clean them or for the spirits to drink, in two prevalent views. In earlier times people carried lanterns to the graveyards to guide the spirits back, but in Yamanaka no one now does this, although a few households do in nearby hamlets.

In the evening a few tradition-minded households build a small "welcome fire" (mukae-bi) to guide any spirits who have not yet found their way. On the next two mornings, prayers, rice, and tea are offered at the special altar instead of the usual one, and incense usually is burned. At least some meals during the three days are vegetarian and festive.

In the afternoon or evening of the third day people escort the spirits back to the graveyard, carrying the bamboo sprigs, flowers, and vegetables from the altar together with water, incense, and glutinous rice-cake balls. Some build another small dooryard bonfire, the "sending-off fire" (okuri-bi) to light the spirits on their way. Unlike many areas of Japan, people here do not send off the spirits by setting them afloat in special lanterns, although this has recently been brought to the area by Kōsei-kai, which holds a sending-off service on the bank of a recently built reservoir. This ends with a mass lantern-floating in which hundreds of pastel-tinted lanterns are released from rowboats to drift away in the twilight.

In larger hamlets around Yamanaka, as in most of Japan until recently, "All Souls'" dances (bon-odori) are held on the three evenings of the holiday on some convenient open ground, frequently the Shinto shrine. Everyone with the inclination, most wearing the comfortable and traditional light cotton yukata robe, moves in stately (or, in some of the five or six dances of the repertoire, more vigorous) circles clockwise around a pine- and bunting-decorated tower. Atop the tower is a platform with drummers and pipers or, recently, a phonograph. Yamanaka held its own dance until the late 1960s, when declining participation and unfavorable comparisons to bigger dances elsewhere led to its postponement to a diminished performance during the Autumn Equinox Festival. The remaining dozen or so Yamanaka enthusiasts for bon dancing now must walk to the larger neighboring hamlet.

Two other holidays when the spirits of the dead return home are the Spring and Autumn Equinoxes, April 18–24 and September 18–24. No special altar is built, but a special food, glutinous rice cakes coated with sweet black-bean paste, is offered at the usual altar after the spirits have been fetched from the graveyard. At the end of the week they are sent off again as at All Souls', but with simpler offerings of rice balls, water, and incense.

New Year's is a national holiday with both Buddhist and Shinto significance. People in Yamanaka visit graveyards, the shrine, and sometimes the temple. Most make offerings at the graveyard, but the spirits do not come home. Most Shinto New Year's preparations and decorations seem intended more for the Shinto *kami*. The temple holds a service, as at All Souls' and Spring and Autumn Equinoxes, but few people come. The few from Yamanaka make only a short call and leave again.

The other major occasions for prayer and offerings are funerals and the memorial services (again, similar to services elsewhere, with minor variations[28]), which follow funerals on every seventh of the first forty-nine days after death and on the first, third, seventh, thirteenth, twenty-third, thirty-third, and (ideally but infrequently) fiftieth anniversaries of the death. During my first stay in Yamanaka, 1970–72, no funerals occurred, so I recorded short generalized accounts from several residents. During my visit in 1977 there was a funeral, and several features were different, perhaps in part because cremation had begun[29] after a crematorium was built in Ueno City.

According to my informants in 1972, when someone dies, a household member notifies another household in the *kumi*. This household tells the rest of the *kumi*, which in turn notifies the village office, the temple, and the rest of the hamlet. It also begins arrangements for funeral meals, the funeral palanquin, and notification of relatives. The *kumi* also sets the funeral date as soon as possible, usually within a day.

Early on the funeral day the corpse is washed, dressed in white, and placed in an upright fetal position in a cubical coffin. As mourners arrive, each makes a donation, Y1,000 for neighbors and distant relatives and Y2,000 for close relatives, to defray costs. Names and the amounts of donations are recorded by a *kumi* member.

When most of those expected have arrived, the priest chants a sutra before the altar. A small bowl with two piles of powdered incense, one of them smoldering, is handed through the several rooms of the house usually filled with visitors, each of whom transfers several pinches of incense to the burning pile. When the priest has finished the sutra, the coffin is placed in a palanquin and carried to the grave by cousins of the deceased. The bearers wear short white jackets (*haori*) and special straw sandals (*waraji*) and leave the latter at the first crossroad on the way home. On returning home, each mourner throws a purificatory pinch of salt over his shoulder before entering and eats a small serving of fish and sake prepared in his absence. The palanquin is returned to a deserted area of the hamlet, in a shallow cave at the bottom of a steep embankment of the river, well away from dwellings "because of its association with death and its smell of corpses."[30]

At the funeral in 1977 there were some apparent changes (notably cremation and the more leisurely pace it makes possible, and the disappearance of several purificatory acts). Although I cannot say how representative this single event was, it is unlikely to have been aberrant. The deceased, Kimura Ichiro, had been a retired house head in his late sixties, a heavy smoker who had succumbed at length to lung cancer. He had been a moderately prominent man from a household slightly better off than average, so the funeral was slightly more lavish than average (both priests from Eizōji, father and son, came instead of the usual single priest).

Ichiro had died one morning in early August, and when Hideo (the Kōsei-kai staff member and a member of Ichiro's *kumi*) and I arrived that evening, the house was already full of people, a low buzz of talk, and the mingled smoke of incense, cigarettes, and mosquito coils. The sliding panels that partition houses had been removed, as for other large social events, transforming the house into a single large room.

People were largely in three groups. One group was of women, in the kitchen preparing food. A second group, the men of the *kumi*, was in what would normally have been the middle room and was making lists—mostly of people to call—and discussing costs and amounts of food. The funeral for someone else (younger and relatively poor) from the area who had died in a traffic accident had cost ¥30,000. The men of the *kumi* agreed that ¥100,000 would do for now, and the rest could be picked up later. They expected 135 guests but would get food for 150. The third group was Ichiro's close relatives, mostly his grown children and almost all from outside the hamlet. They were conversing quietly in the best, southernmost part of the house, where Ichiro lay stretched out on a bed (a *futon*) and covered except for the top of his head with a white cloth.

In front of him was a low table as a temporary altar, bearing two lighted candles, two vases of flowers, a bowl of smoldering incense, a bowl of fruit, a bell, and a rosary. As each visitor arrived, he lit an incense stick, placed it in the bowl, rang the bell (some did not ring), bowed to the dead man and to his children, and joined one of the groups. After a while the cloth was pulled back from the corpse and its face was washed and shaved by a daughter while the others continued to sit in quiet conversation. When the shaving was finished, the corpse was placed in the coffin, washed from big plastic basins, and covered with a white quilt and a transparent plastic sheet. The close relatives remained all night to comfort the spirit (*tamashii*—not yet *hotoke* even to laymen).

People from the *kumi* and elsewhere in the hamlet, some thirty in all, spent the next day in further preparations at the household. The women again were mostly in the kitchen, while the men, still in informal summer wear, began in the same seated discussion circle where they had ended the evening. The relatives, now in more formal dress (dark pants and ties with white shirts, and dark dresses), again kept apart, mostly in the courtyard. The coffin was in the same place as before, but draped with a white cloth with a shiny white floral pattern and topped with a sword blade "to ward off evil." Before it was the same temporary altar, an ordinary low table with battered formica top and folding legs. On it, in addition to the bell, incense, and candles of the first night, was a tray with cooked food: a bowl with a half dozen small round glutinous rice balls, a bowl of neatly rounded cooked rice with a pair of unseparated, plain wooden chopsticks (the disposable, restaurant kind) stuck vertically into the dome of rice, and a glass of water. A funerary envelope printed with a black "ribbon" faced the coffin. To the right of the table on the tatami were two packages of fruit, formally wrapped and tied with black ribbon.

At nine in the morning five or six male relatives loaded the coffin into a compartment in the back of a bus from the crematorium in Ueno City, and two dozen men and women (mostly relatives but a few from the *kumi*, and myself) and eight children accompanied it to Ueno. Ichiro's daughter-in-law distributed incense sticks, and about half the mourners filed up to deposit them at an altar between the doors to the twin ovens. On the altar were a mandala, candles, incense, fruit, pink rice cakes, a black-ribboned photo of Ichiro, and a large bottle of sake, of which he had been fond, in a white wrapper inscribed "before the soul" (*goreizen*). Two little doors over the dead man's face were opened for a last look, which a few people took, and then closed. The coffin was placed on a steel tray and rolled into the oven, which ignited with a low roar. A few women wept quietly, but otherwise, as in the household, no one showed much emotion. The daughter-in-law passed around cakes, crackers, canned juice, and cold sake in tea cups. A crematorium official suggested that anyone with shopping in Ueno might do it during the hour that cremation would take, but everyone remained in the little hall in the front of the building. When the tray was withdrawn, still glowing red, an attendant poked through the ashes with tongs and had four or five relatives help place them in an urn.

At the house workmen had erected an elaborate rented altar, some 2 m high and wide, to bear Ichiro's urn, photograph, tablets, and offerings, including cut paper and wood decoration made by *kumi* men. The altar was a number of tiers of unpainted wooden platforms, illuminated from inside through translucent pastel plastic panels. When everyone had returned from Ueno, the *kumi* women served a vegetarian lunch.

By the following morning the decorations flanking the altar were complete: five big stands of flowers, over 2 m tall, and four trays of fruit banked out toward the room, wreathed in gaudy "flowers" of aluminum foil and plastic. In the courtyard stood several more wreaths. In the room adjoining the altar were five stacks of cushions for the service, with the names of their hamlet donors under "before the spirit" on big slips of paper.

About eleven o'clock the two priests arrived from Eizōji and began writing Ichiro's posthumous name (determined by the household's status and donation to the temple) on tablets, including one for each son. *Kumi* women prepared another lunch while the men recorded visitors and their contributions, from ¥1,000 for *kumi* members to ¥30,000 for close relatives. After lunch the close relatives sat in an arc in the middle room and bowed to the continuing flow of visitors.

At about one o'clock the relatives put on short white jackets (*hanten*), knelt before the altar, and followed the elder priest in a half-hour chant. The house was now full, and people stood outside. When the chant ended, people moved away from the altar, and a young relative from the hamlet who frequently acts as a master of ceremonies announced to the people outside that there would be a special service sponsored by so-and-so. The priests chanted for about five minutes, and the young man announced further services from individuals. First, the president of the Yamanaka old people's association came into the house, knelt and bowed deeply to the altar, addressed a prayer to Ichiro as a longtime association member, bowed, and went back out. The retired superintendent of education, as another representative of the association, also kneeling and bowing deeply, read in a loud voice from a prepared scroll a brief history of Ichiro's accomplishments and services to the community, including being principal of a middle school and a president of the association. The M.C. called for any other remarks (none came) and then the names of groups that had contributed to the funeral. Next, he called for remarks from relatives. A son stepped down from the house, thanked all for coming despite the heat, gave his father's death date and a few other facts, apologized for his simplicity, bowed, and reentered the house.

The M.C. called everyone who was outside to approach a table at the edge of the room with the altar and offer incense. While the priests chanted at the altar, people filed up in three lines, bowed, offered incense, put their palms together (or not), bowed, and turned away.

A few minutes before two o'clock the priests' prayer ended with gongs. The relatives rose, removed their white jackets, and began low but relaxed conversation. Some people removed the decorations, the offering tray with rice and water, and the urn from the altar and formed

Priests lead relatives in a chant at the funeral of Kimura Ichiro, August 1977.

a procession outside the house. It was led by *kumi* people with decorated staffs, including one, like an umbrella without cloth, that, when shaken, rained colored, gold, and silver paper and coins, which other people picked up.

At the grave the younger priest prayed briefly; the elder had remained in the house. The water and rice tray was placed in front of the stone (a massive one for the collective household dead), and the urn was placed to one side. Everyone then presented two sticks of incense at the stone. The eldest son climbed down out of sight into the vault and deposited the urn to one side, and everyone presented two sticks of incense at the stone. Most of the people returned to the house, where a bowl of purificatory salt now stood on a table at the entrance (though no one seemed to use it) for another service. A few stayed at the graveyard, burning all the decorations and offerings but the water and rice tray and resealing the vault with its heavy stone cube.

The next service normally would have been held in seven days, but it was annexed to the funeral for the sake of the relatives from distant places.[31] It was a short chant led by the priests, and at the end most people left for refreshments at *kumi* households before leaving for home.

The day ended with another meal, this one for the *kumi* people, and a final service. The meal was the first nonvegetarian one, with sashimi, tempura, sake and beer, and noodles as well as rice and other foods, and was a considerable feast. It was followed by the last service of the day, a "prayer to Amida Buddha" (*nenbutsu*), which an elderly lady (Kimura Nami, a hamlet pillar of Kōsei-kai) said was to send the deceased off to the other world "so he won't stay in this one, which would be bad!" The people performing this were virtually all *kumi* women, still in kitchen clothes and aprons. As they waited for a few others to arrive, their talk was lively and relaxed: the tension of the day was over, and they were winding down. Led by a *kumi* woman, they chanted the prayer from syllabary texts, each striking with a mallet a flat bell laid on the tatami and tinkling a small bell in her left hand. Between sections of the prayer came trays of cookies and crackers and general talk and laughter, unlike the earlier sobriety. The service ended in an hour, and another tray with big slices of watermelon was handed around and the flowered fruit stands were removed. On leaving, everyone received a formally wrapped box containing a quilt (the household spends about ¥20,000, according to the owner of the little general store, despite donations) and a plastic bag of rice with red beans (an auspicious food associated with festivals) for those at home.

This funeral differed from those described in 1972 chiefly in using cremation and the resulting absence of the palanquin and in including the service for the following week. No one wore straw sandals or white jackets to the grave or, as far as I could see, threw salt over his shoulder on returning to the household. Nor did anyone mention the raw fish and sake supposedly eaten on returning home, although these were present in the meal for *kumi* members and may have been elsewhere as well. People generally agreed, however, on the traditional aim: to comfort the spirit and to start the forty-nine days of separating it from the body and household and (according to priests and Kōsei-kai) transforming it into a *hotoke.*

On every seventh day until the forty-ninth, household members visit the new grave. On the forty-ninth day the Eizōji priest comes to say a prayer to complete the passage of the spirit from household to grave. Prayers should then be said each month for a year, on the death day.

The first anniversary of the death brings the first major memorial service (three of which I attended). Friends, close relatives, and someone from each household in the *kumi* gather at the household shortly before noon. Each brings a donation in an envelope marked with his house head's name and the amount (Y1,000 for neighbors and distant relatives and Y2,000 for close relatives), placing it on a low altar containing flowers, candles, incense, new memorial tablets, and a photograph and other mementos. Older, more formal people, like the superintendent of education, kneel, pray to the *hotoke,* and light three sticks of incense before joining the other guests in conversation.

About noon, the priest recites a sutra before the altar for about fifteen minutes. The guests circulate a bowl of powdered incense, each taking a formal kneeling position, raising two pinches of incense toward his or her forehead, and placing them in the smoldering pile. When the priest has finished, all visit the grave (where the grass is newly cut and the site tidied), carrying incense and a flower or vegetable offering to place on the grave. They bow and pray. Everyone eats a small round buckwheat dumpling "to prevent colds" and returns to the house for a banquet prepared by the *kumi.* The banquet itself is a service for the deceased because it promotes friendship among the survivors on his behalf. As guests leave after an hour or more of convivial drinking and dining, each receives food, such as a bag of sugar or tea, and a household item, such as a light quilt or blanket cover. A formal minority kneel, pray, and offer incense as they depart.

Similar services are held at the third, seventh, thirteenth, twenty-third, thirty-third, and sometimes fiftieth anniversaries, though the number of guests dwindles with each one. There are also unscheduled occasions for individual prayer. Many people report to the ancestors household events such as journeys, illnesses, and examinations and ask for benign attention. Such reports are made at the altar or, in serious cases, at the graveyard.

Belief and Analysis: Ancestors and Household Continuity

> For children to do as parents did, after all, you know, that's what gives one peace of mind. That's what *obon* is. (Tanaka *sensei*, retired superintendent of education)

> [Religion is] when your parents die . . . a matter of honoring them, a matter of not forgetting them. (Yamanaka lumberman and former Kōsei-kai member)

People in Yamanaka commonly voice the debt of household continuity owed to ancestors by the living but differ about how ancestors exist, about purposes of prayers and offerings to them, and about ghosts, heaven, and hell. In Japan generally (Smith 1974:39–56; Ooms 1976:79–87), as in the West, the popular notion of "soul" (*tamashii* or *rei*, among others) is vague, and few lay people have clear or strong opinions about it. However, the common view of soul in Yamanaka seems to be much like that in the contemporary West: "immaterial essence, animating principle, or actuating cause of an individual life" (Webster 1977:1110).

Like "soul" in the West, *tamashii* individualizes as well as animates: it is the locus of personality, including tastes and preferences. These survive death for some time, probably until the last annual memorial service when the individual soul is assimilated to the collective ancestors. For the first few years the brand of cigarettes liked by the deceased, for example, as well as flowers, fruit, and incense, may be added to the cooked rice and water or tea at the altar. *Tamashii* is not only a general principle of life but also a collection of personal idiosyncracies—in short, the person sans body.

But opinion varies about whether souls in fact "exist" (*iru*), and if so, whether they survive the body. In Yamanaka (in ratios similar to those in the nation as a whole[32]) a slight majority of the twenty-five household representatives interviewed say they exist, a half-dozen are uncertain, and four people, including a former and a present member of Kōsei-kai, deny their existence. One well-liked and respected woman of sixty responded to my question about their existence, "If there *were* souls, I would pray." The other self-declared "unbeliever," the eccentric

Altar for the first-year memorial service for Hideo's father.

Grave visit at a first-year memorial service. Participants were not sure why the water is poured; some said that it is to purify the grave, and others that it is to give the spirit a drink.

Hamlet men share sake at a first-year memorial banquet.

laborer, said vehemently, "That's a bad idea! A superstition!" Of people who say that souls exist, about a third say they cease to exist at death, disappearing either immediately or gradually. To them the soul is an attribute of the living but not the dead. Of people who say that the soul continues after death, about half explain that it does so contingently, through the impression the deceased made on friends and relatives while alive or through descendants and society generally. (Ooms [1976] found similar diversity and ambivalence in a hamlet near Tokyo and concluded that most people there are skeptical of any such existence.)

Among people who affirm the soul's continuity, ideas vary about its location, its experience in the "other world" (ano yō)—most people say they do not know—and its relations with the living. Traditionally it is supposed to stay in the household for forty-nine days after death and then leave, if memorial services have been properly performed. Its destination is not certain—no one in the hamlet seems to take the Buddhist heaven or hell seriously—but it is supposed to go to the graveyard. However, it may also exist in the world at large, and it returns to the household at All Souls' Festival and other occasions.

If there are oversights in the prayers and song of mourning to console it, or if death was violent or unjust, the spirit may be unhappy and fail to "become hotoke" (jōbutsu suru). It may then appear as a ghost (yūrei) making odd sounds, as an amorphous vapor, or with lifelike appearance in a dream. It may also appear as a blue ball of fire (hidama), usually soon after death. It may cause further deaths (chapter 5; Maeda 1976:141) or other trouble. Although most people questioned in Yamanaka are skeptical of such phenomena, several gave first-hand accounts, and everyone knows of people who have seen one.[33]

Still, most people do not believe in them. "Ghosts" are explained as hallucinations or as an invention of authorities bent on improving morals. As my elderly neighbor said, "Ghosts are just to make you be good, to scare you." A woman in her forties said of people who see ghosts, "It's the person's heart (kokoro). If he's done something wrong, he sees the ghosts of his parents." Another declared skeptic said, some-what ambiguously, "If the living do their duty, with memorial services and so on, there shouldn't be any ghosts." The most common response to questions about ghosts was an expression of doubt, frequently coupled with the phrase, "I've never seen one." The prevailing view is that "ghosts" are the result of minor aberrations in people who see them, usually a guilty conscience.

Just as there is little concern with ghosts, there is little concern with heaven and hell or the whereabouts of the spirits of the dead who, if out of place, are ghosts. The spirits are vaguely assumed to be in or around the graveyard or altar, but they may be anywhere. There is wide agreement with my elderly neighbor, who held that heaven and hell, like ghosts, are the "inventions of highly placed priests." Another view, expressed by the younger temple priest, the middle-school principal, and the Kōsei-kai staffer, is that heaven and hell are states of mind in this life. Most people do not know whether the dead are happy or whether the prayers of the living influence or help them. (Ooms [1976] notes that generally both *muenbotoke* and souls that have reached full ancestor-hood with the final memorial service seem to be beyond influence.) People say that the spirits enjoy coming home at All Souls' Festival, that they dislike having to leave again, and that prayers are to console them. But most people seem not to speculate about the afterlife,[34] and if asked, many—even ones who call themselves "believers"—say that ancestors exist only in the minds of descendants. In their evident disregard for particulars of the afterlife, people in Yamanaka are like people elsewhere in Japan.[35]

The fact that there are no clear ideas about the ancestors' location or mode of existence, however, does not mean that they are unimportant to the household or that there is no interaction between them. On the contrary, they are "in unity" (Shibata 1983:41) with the living and vital to their welfare and continuity. As founders of the households or as its stewards, the dead are creditors. They are models for behavior, markers of seniority in the hamlet, and, in a view formerly promulgated by the government, links in a system of kinship that makes a single household of the entire nation. The most recent are particular objects of filial affection. Last, although no one in the hamlet put it in so many words, it seems likely that, as founders and as links to the founders of the household, they provide answers to some "ultimate" questions about personal and household destinies and about the meaning of life.

The living owe their existence to the ancestors, especially to the founding generation, as children owe existence in an unrepayable debt, *on*. This debt is self-evident; not to recognize it is to be not fully human. The legal scholar Hozumi, for example, wrote that "an infant's yearning for his parents is from a natural desire. . . . When one's respect and affection toward his parents are extended to his parents' parents, a greater respect is due to the latter. . . . It is quite natural for the human feelings of the people to revere one's parents" (Morioka 1977:190). Hozumi's opinion is shared in Yamanaka. To quote three people on three occasions: "You've got to be grateful to the ancestors"; "The fact that we're in this world is owed to the ancestors . . . you've got to be grateful for that"; and "It's not as if they owe their existence to us, but the other way around." Fortes's (1976:6) comment that under "ancestor worship" generally "a person's death does not extinguish the contribution he made by his life to the existence of his society—above all of course, through his offspring"—applies here as well.

The ancestors not only are the creators of the household but also ensure its continued well-being, although interpretations of their continuing contribution vary. (Ooms [1976] concludes that people in his hamlet, possibly because of skeptical Confucian influence, expect neither help nor hindrance from ancestors, while Shibata [1983:41] says that people expect "aid and protection.") In one view, the ancestors are sentient and active. They are protective or punitive depending on the ethics, diligence, and attentiveness of their descendants. Several people said that their usual morning prayer is a request for an accident-free day. Since households normally are healthy and prosperous, sickness, impoverishment, or other adversity may show the displeasure of one or more ancestors. For example, the retired head of an old household, a former member of Kōsei-kai, told me that in the previous year he had become ill for no obvious reason. When he failed to recover in a few days, he went to a diviner (reibai) in the neighboring hamlet to inquire why the ancestors were disturbed. The diviner, a blind woman of about sixty,[36] discovered in trance that the old man's deceased father felt neglected and had allowed the illness to occur. The man performed an extra service for his father and recovered.

Persistent misfortune in a household may be caused not only by present misdeeds or neglect of ancestors but also by karma (go) from past generations. According to the Buddhist principle of casual relatedness (innen), no action is without consequences, which, if they do not come in the lives of the actors, will come in subsequent generations. Bad effects may be remedied, however, if their causes are known. Since the actions of ancestors more than one generation removed are obscure and since karma may be transmitted "for any number of generations," a diviner may be required to connect effect and action. In addition to independent diviners, Kōsei-kai now divines for members, but people who engage diviners of any sort seem to be a small minority in the hamlet today. In any case, karmic misfortune does not breed ill will toward ancestors, who remain objects of affection and longing.

To that slight majority in Yamanaka who do not view the ancestors as active, sentient beings, they are nonetheless important (Shibata 1983:36 notes that "even those who claim to be atheists readily worship at their ancestors' graves"). They are examples of behavior and points of reference in viewing the household's past and planning its future. Davis (1977:70) remarks that in Japan before and even after the war, "To honor them was the mark of solid character." In Yamanaka, parents still hold them before children as models: "I tell my children that my deceased husband used to say, 'It doesn't matter whether you're successful or not. All that matters is that you're upright and true.'" Posthumous fulfillment of their wishes is a goal of all good conduct, and it is difficult to distinguish these wishes from household welfare. Explaining the banquet that follows a memorial service, the village postmaster said (as did people at the services) that the banquet is part of the service (*kuyō*) since it promotes harmony and intimacy among surviving friends and relatives, one of the wishes of the dead.

Ancestors are also requisite to household status in the hamlet since seniority is a component of rank. As Bernier (1975:139) notes of Sone in Mie Prefecture, and as is true elsewhere, ancestors are a "pedigree [whose] tablets prove the antiquity of one's family, thus justifying its position in the village." The "generations of ancestors" (*senzo daidai*, a phrase that connotes continuity and accumulation) are markers of seniority. Memorial tablets, in rows on the best piece of furniture in the best room, are visible evidence of the length of a household's presence in the community. Viewed this way, prayer and offerings demonstrate commitment to place in the hamlet. First generation households, including such transient ones as those of the policeman, the middle-school teacher, and the government forester (all routinely transferred), have no memorial tablets, no religion, and little status. Conversely, the oldest households have substantial altars with tablets they willingly display, a commitment to holidays and temple (their heads are the temple officers), and greater status. In households older than a few generations, there is room to display only the most recent tablets on the limited stage of the altar. The rest may be shown to interested visitors (Smith 1974) and at All Soul's Festival. The retired superintendent of education, for example, volunteering "some real antiquities," produced a large box with most of the tablets of thirty generations of ancestors, from over 500 years. These, he said, were the most ancient relics of Yamanaka. Several other old households volunteered similar displays.

Besides being direct or indirect agents of household welfare and prestige, ancestors—at least those in living memory—are foci of sentimental attachments. People mention their gratitude, respect, and affection toward parents and other ancestors as frequently as they mention desires for health, household welfare, or guidance, and gratitude, love, and longing are said to be the emotions of prayer. "Ancestor worship" in general, and in Yamanaka for example, is "rooted in the . . . nuclear filio-parental relationship," and it is intimate and interdependent (Fortes 1976:5). People indicate that one intent of prayer is to console the spirits, but several added that although this is the ostensible purpose, the real purpose is to console oneself.

Witnessing prayer and offerings also has a pedagogical effect on children, who in turn express gratitude to parents by praying to ancestors. These expressions, by any generation, affirm household cohesion and continuity by affirming the parent-child relationship that, in hamlet common sense, *is* the ancestor-descendant relationship.

Plath (1964:307) has noted that

> as a corporation, the Japanese household includes both living and dead members, and both are essential to its existence. All members are responsible for the welfare and continuity of the corporation, and all should be mutually concerned for their co-members. The dead provide a spiritual charter guaranteeing the right of their household line to a separate existence. The living provide the material stuff.

The central place of ancestors in the household and in the relation of household to community is not simply a folk tradition; it has been actively fostered by the state. Anthropologists have often said that "ancestor worship" reinforces the authority of elders, and that elders may use ancestor worship to that end. Japan is a case in point. As Morioka (1977) has shown, the government has frequently and strongly endorsed, through compulsory education, the ancestors as fundamental elements of the household, the local community, and the nation as a whole. It has, at least for the two centuries ending with World War II, repeatedly equated love for parents with love for emperor and state. In this view, the child's love and respect for its parents naturally extend to grandparents, community, and national ancestors.

The state has also made explicit the identity of the parent-child with the ancestor-descendant relationship. Hozumi Yatsuka, as a state ideologist, wrote (Smith 1974:33) in 1897 that "father and mother are ancestors living in the present." Moreover, parents may be identified not only as living ancestors but even as Shinto deities. The Shinto scholar Norinaga Motoori wrote (Smith 1974:25) in 1786, in an admonition used in the school texts,

> Your father and mother are
> The *Kami* of your home
> Regard them as your *Kami*
> And serve them, oh children,
> With heart-felt piety.

Inoue (Morioka 1977:193) equated the roles of family ancestors, village *kami*, and national founders at their respective levels and, like Hozumi, concluded that it is ancestor worship that "unites the emperor and the people into one family." In Hozumi's words (Morioka 1977:190), "an extension of the concept of the family makes the concept of the nation." Similarly, a Yamanaka farm wife of forty-five tacitly linked duty to household ancestors to duty to the hamlet and its *kami*:

> It's the duty of the living to go [tend the graves] no matter how busy they are . . . as on [Shinto] festival days—this is embarrassing to say, but—I clean up the road, by myself, as far as the [hamlet Shinto] shrine, because we're in the neighborhood.

In the view of villagers as well as of scholars, the parent-child, god-human, and ancestor-descendant relationships are basically one and the same. Too strengthen one is to strengthen the others, and to strengthen any is morally good because it consolidates not only household but also community and state. "For the same reason one is filial to his parents and loyal to the throne, and the national teaching which connects these two is the worship of the ancestors" (Hozumi 1897, in Smith 1974:33).

A final suggestion about the meaning of the ancestors in Yamanaka is that they provide answers to "ultimate" questions of origin and destiny, both for households and for individuals. Admittedly, no one in the village other than the young poet and three educators (the retired superintendent of education, the high-school teacher, and the Kōsei-kai professional) seems interested in such questions. But it may be that such questions are infrequent not only because of their difficulty and remoteness from everyday life but also because answers are already implicit in household continuity and in the ancestors.

The answers may simply be that household and individuals originate in the founding ancestors, and these in turn in a divine being, and that their destiny consists in replicating and perpetuating patterns set by the founders. Household founders themselves all ultimately descend, according to myth (and, until the end of the war, according to the government), from the Sun Goddess, Amaterasu-ō-mikami, creator of the Japanese familial state:

> The ancestor of my ancestors is the Sun Goddess. The Sun Goddess is the founder of our race, and the throne is the sacred house of our race. . . . If the ancestors of the house are to be revered, how much more so the founder of the country! (Hozumi Yatsuka, in Smith 1974:32–33)

The myth of descent from the Sun Goddess is known to every villager, and although perhaps no one now takes it literally, it seems still to have a strong appeal. Every household has a Sun Goddess amulet. Here the ancestors are chartered in Shinto idiom, not Buddhist. But Shinto and Buddhism in Yamanaka, as elsewhere, are not competitive but complementary and blend in several places. Household ancestors are addressed in Buddhist idiom, but they differ from community and national ancestors addressed in Shinto idiom only in their lower age, closer relation to householders, and lesser importance to the community beyond the household. Ancestors thus are strands of a fabric comprising household, hamlet, and nation, and prayer and offerings to them are, among other things, affirmations of continuity in several senses.

Continuity does not mean that people in Yamanaka do not admit and even welcome social and material change—witness their criticism of "feudalism" in the social order and "superstition" in beliefs, and their ready acceptance of mechanized farming, instant noodles, and the PTA. They view these changes, however, as superficial. What is important is that household succession—to house, land, place in the community, memorial tablets, graves, and ancestors—remain intact. As Plath (1964:312) has said,

> The ancestors do not demand that life continue exactly as they knew it. What they expect is not so much specific performance as . . . whatever will assure the continuity of the household line.

Ancestors remain not only morally but physically part of the hamlet, in that their graves are everywhere in it. Graves frequently are in cultivated fields and other well-used places. Graveyards frequently have no markers but the headstones to set them off from the surrounding land, with which they appear continuous. Graves usually are within a few hundred meters of the household to which they belong and always are close to some household, and usually to several. Ancestors thus are located in the midst of the everyday world, within sight of their descendants working in the fields, walking along the main hamlet road or on footpaths, or at home. With their graves interspersed throughout the hamlet and their tablets in the household altars, the ancestors are present physically as well as spiritually.

Past and present generations are intimate. There is little evidence of fear of the dead or of death itself.[37] Respect for ancestors is combined with affection and familiarity. When I asked one devout elderly lady

("Obaa," a Kōsei-kai enthusiast) why her *bon* altar contained no cucumber horse to convey spirits from the other world, she laughed and said, "It's the age of the automobile. They can come by car!" And perhaps a more telling expression of the familiarity of living and dead was the relaxed manner of a party of men consolidating the graves of their main household under one large tombstone. Their dress and demeanor were those of any hamlet work party. The task began formally, with a prayer from the younger priest apologizing for the disturbance, but when the men began to dig, they were casual and gently humorous. As they exhumed skeletons and grave goods, they commented freely on bone size, condition of teeth and subsequent improvements in dentistry, and probable age at death, and they generally seemed on easy terms with their ancestors' mortal remains.

On another occasion the village postmaster showed me his household's tablets, counting out their six generations. He continued, in a matter-of-fact way, that he and his eldest son were the (as yet unwritten) seventh and eighth set of tablets, as if they and the ancestors were already a homogeneous group. While death divides people into living and dead in Yamanaka as elsewhere in the world, here the division is not absolute. Rather, there is a strong assertion of continuity,[38] in which, in Shibata's (1983:41) phrase, "death and life [are] intimately related." Prayer and offerings are, among other things, affirmations that ancestors still are household members. As Shibata (1983:43) says, "the co-existence of the living with the dead is alive among Japanese people."

For living members, the observances promise that their graves in turn will be tended and that they themselves will exist, as ancestors, as long as the household does. People find security in this: their "descendants are the staves they can lean upon" (Hirata Atsutane, in Ooms 1976:89). In contrast to the postmaster's assured inclusion of himself and his son in his household tablets, consider the fear and loneliness of the protagonist of Mishima's "After the Banquet," who has no such guarantee:

> There flashed before Kazu's eyes an unvisited grave in some desolate cemetery, belonging to someone who had died without a family. This vision of the end of a life of solitary activity—a lonely, abandoned grave covered with weeds, leaning over, beginning to rot—sent a fathomless dark fear stabbing into Kazu's heart. (Mishima 1963:168–69)

To be a member of a household is to participate in a community that transcends death. It is, more strongly than is descent in the West, a

Grandfather, father, and son show household continuity on Boy's Day. The day's decorations are in the background, beside the altar and under the god-shelf.

vicarious immortality. In the words of the 17th-century Confucianist Itō Jinsai,

> though the bodies of ancestors may perish, their spirits are inherited by their posterity, whose spirits are again inherited by their own posterity. When life thus evolves, without ceasing, into eternity, it may rightly be said that no one dies. (Nakamura 1964:355)

As Ooms (1976:84–85) states, such beliefs give "meaning to mortality, which in itself is merely disruptive and meaningless. . . . Ancestor worship [enables people] to face mortal existence."

Finally, the yearly calendar of Buddhist observances, like other cycles (Kluckhohn 1979), is a model of and for repetition and therefore of security and continuity. All these appear in a description of the meaning of All Souls' Festival, the most important of ancestral observances and a national holiday, by the retired superintendent and his wife:

> S: Nowadays, rather than being a matter of faith, *obon* is more a matter of the schedule in the life of the Japanese . . . it's one of the ceremonies of the year. So, people get in a train in Tokyo and, Zoom! return home. Then, when *bon* is over, they go back to Tokyo. Then, when it's *bon* again, they take presents for home, get in the train—

> Mrs. *K* (breaking in):—and it's a matter of reporting on one's current life to the ancestors— that sort of thing.

> S (continuing):—so there is praying to *hotoke*, too, but in addition to that, it's one of the ceremonies of the Japanese people . . . it's a matter of *bon* coming, and tidying up and making things clean for it . . .

> Mrs. *K* (continuing): It's a matter of cleaning up, of making things look good, something that you don't clean up during the rest of the 365 days . . . so you can give a little prayer in the morning, "Hail Amida Buddha" . . . it's a matter of your own mood, not the *hotoke*, just your own mood; so you put these things out for *obon*, and—

S (breaking in):—That's part of it. The graveyard is the
same, you know . . . you can't clean it up and cut the weeds all
the time, right? But when *bon* is coming, as you saw the other
day, one tidies it all up, cleans, and so on . . . it's in *that* sense
that *bon* is very important. At everybody's house, no matter
where, it's the same . . . as I said before, a crowd of people
comes, to pray to the *hotoke* . . . that is, our children come,
who have a connection with the *hotoke-sama* . . . it's a time
for children and other relatives to gather and report on their
lives, and say, "There's been this, and this" . . . it's a good
opportunity for this. That's why we value *obon*. Otherwise
there's no fixed time to clean up the memorial tables and the
graveyard. And that's so with the great majority of
Yamanaka people. Really, whether there are *hotoke* or not,
and spirit immortality . . . what sort of thing a man's soul is—
that sort of Buddhist doctrine—people don't know very
well. But for children to do as parents did, after all, you know,
that's what gives one peace of mind. That's what *obon* is.

Summary and Implications

Sōtō Zen Buddhism in Yamanaka varies somewhat from household
to household and person to person. This variability, in part a product of
the turmoil and doubt following defeat in the war, has been accompanied
by the rise of new religious movements nationally and of one of them in
Yamanaka. Dismay and skepticism about old conceptions of social and
world orders appear, with the end of government control of religion, to
have opened the way for new views and for variants of old ones.

A gap separates established professional Buddhism and household
Buddhism in Yamanaka, as elsewhere in Japan. Relations between
temple and households are distant and the services of the temple are of
narrow scope. The priests nominally care for parishioners in life, as in
death, with public ceremonies at the temple and with a modicum of
instruction and example. But neither their training nor their personal
inclinations are directly instructive for parishioners. Priests' audiences
are virtually limited to funerals, where they are less instructors of the
living than technical propitiators of the dead and executors of the
change of relation between them and the living. Thus, established
Buddhism often is called the "funeral religion."

Only a small and shrinking minority of households attend festivals
at the temple. Priests and householders agree that most people go for

mere entertainment, increasingly available elsewhere. The intersection of the worlds of priest and layman is narrow, the ideas transmitted few, and their interpretations of Buddhism divergent. Parishioners look for little moral guidance, practical advice, or emotional solace from priests.

Household Buddhism for most villagers consists in maintaining the relations of living and dead and of children and parents, and thus household continuity. Ancestors may or may not exist independently of memories of them, but in any case ancestors and descendants depend on each other. Some people see ancestors as direct and active agents of household welfare, while some think them more removed from events. Everyone, however, recognizes some influence of ancestors in the present as common sense. Whether they are sentient or not, praying and presenting food to them ameliorates karma, expresses filial debt, loyalty, and affection, and affirms household order, solidarity, and continuity. In death as in life, ancestors are models of and for behavior, proved by the very existence of the household. Just as important, they remain givers and takers of affection. In the context of intimate, enduring relationships within and between households, ancestors are good models whether or not they are sentient beings.

But ideas and feelings about the dead sometimes need elaboration and interpretation, which the temple does not provide. Kōsei-kai does provide them, and a community with which to share them. One Yamanaka member—the elderly lady who said the ancestors could come by car—says that its capacity to explain is its main distinction: "Kōsei-kai explains your feelings every month, but the temple priest only at funerals . . . and Kōsei-kai's explanations are more detailed."

Chapter 4
Shinto

Introduction

Objects of worship in Shinto are called *kami*, usually glossed "gods" or "deities." Their nature is problematic, and opinions of Shinto scholars and people in Yamanaka suggest its diversity. The often-quoted 18th-century scholar Norinaga Motoori says that

in principle human beings, birds, animals, trees, plants, mountains, oceans—all may be *kami* . . . whatever seemed strikingly impressive, possessed the quality of excellence, or inspired a feeling of awe was called *kami*. (Matsumoto 1972:37–38)

The 20th-century scholar Ono Sokyō, like Motoori, includes as *kami* beings that in the West would belong to such disparate categories as "man," "nature," and the "supernatural":

In a sense all beings can be called *kami*. . . . Among the objects or phenomena designated from ancient times as *kami* are the qualities of growth, fertility, and production; natural phenomena, such as the sun, mountains, rivers, trees, and rocks; some animals; and ancestral spirits. (Ono 1969:6–7)

Unlike Norinaga, Ono notes that *kami* are not necessarily "excellent." "Not only spirits superior to man, but even some that are regarded as pitiable and weak have nonetheless been considered to be *kami*" (1969:7).

In Yamanaka, the indigent day laborer described *kami* not as beings but as an aspect of human behavior: "Correct behavior is what is called '*kami*,'" and, he says, "*kami* exist only in the human heart (*kokoro*)." Surprisingly, the Shinto priest, like the laborer and several others, says that *kami* exist only in the heart and, moreover, that they are something "created" (*koshiraeta*) by humans. This view, however, should not be taken for skepticism about them.

Although all households with ancestors are Buddhist in that they deal with ancestors in Buddhist idiom, almost all are also Shinto; in Japan, the two religions are not mutually exclusive but complementary.[39] Shinto, unlike Buddhism, primarily concerns the community, not the household.[40] However, households are also individually protected by *kami*, and each Yamanaka household has a "god-shelf" (*kamidana*). Unlike Buddhism, Shinto does not require household ancestors and is observed by new households as well as old ones.

The Tutelary Shrine

Like Buddhism, Shinto in Yamanaka has two levels: the major hamlet shrine and two lesser shrines, on the one hand, and households, on the other. Unlike the Buddhist temple, however, the shrine has an intimate relation with and no existence apart from the hamlet, whose tutelary deity it houses and whose unity it explicitly represents. It was established by the hamlet founders some 600 years ago and is expected to last as long as the hamlet.

Organization and Recruitment

The position of shrine priest (*shintō-san*) is hereditary. The priest is a farmer and earns all but ¥8,000 of his annual ¥60,000 (in 1972) from farming, even though he serves at the festivals of a dozen other hamlets as well. The present priest was trained by his father, but his son has graduated from a Shinto college in Tokyo. Unlike the temple priest, the shrine priest is not an administrator but only the celebrant of festivals, for which he is retained by the shrine parishioners' delegation (*ujiko sōdai*).

The shrine parishioners' delegation manages the shrine for the hamlet. It maintains the building, announces one morning of work (to which each household sends a member) each year on the grounds, takes collections for maintenance and festivals, and pays the priest. It is composed of six members chosen by informal agreement, one from each *kumi*. Each member's main task is to collect funds within his *kumi*. He goes from house to house about ten days before each festival with a donation booklet, in which each donor writes his contribution.

Contributions are public knowledge since everyone reads the booklet as it comes along. Amounts should correspond to household wealth, and they ranged in 1972 from ¥200 (about $0.75) to ¥1,000, with a mean of about ¥300. One household (that of the eccentric laborer) never contributes, but most always do. The total collected before each festival averages about ¥15,000 ($50.00). Timber from a small tract of shrine forest also brings occasional revenue. Most income goes for food and drink for the ceremony.

Building and Grounds

The present shrine building dates from 1927, when the previous one burned down. It is a plain, slightly dilapidated structure of undecorated natural wood in the Shinto style. It is actually two buildings connected by a short vestibule (figure 2). The larger of the two, about 7 m on each side, is an outer hall in which the festival is held. The smaller inner building, about 3 m on each side, contains a mirror called the "body of the *kami*" (*shintai*), representing the enshrined *kami*. During a festival the inner shrine also houses a stick with strips of white paper (*gohei*) cut to form a chain of squares linked at their corners. Both mirror and paper strips (common to Shinto elsewhere) represent purity. The paper is also an offering to the *kami* and an indication that the *kami* is present. During the festival the doors to the inner shrine, otherwise closed, are open, and the "body of the *kami*" may be dimly seen.

The grounds are wooded, as at most shrines, and comprise a rectangle of about half an acre on a slight rise near the southern end of the hamlet. They are entered from the main road through a stone gate (*torii*) that cleanses visitors of anger and other defilements.

Festivals

The shrine has three festivals, in spring, mid-summer, and fall, as do tutelary shrines in most farming villages, to celebrate planting, mid-season, and harvest. The three Yamanaka festivals are similar enough that a single general description can be given.

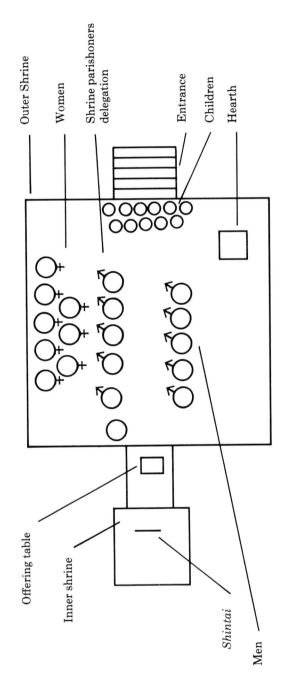

Figure 2. Plan of shrine.

All three nominally begin about two o'clock in the afternoon, but people usually only begin to arrive then. Earlier in the day the shrine has been swept and tatami laid on the floor. Fresh straw rope with paper cut in pendant squares has been stretched between the pillars of the gate and across the entrance side of the shrine building, and tall flags announcing the festival have been erected beside the gate.

At two o'clock both the chief of the shrine delegation and the priest are still making preparations. They place white paper squares hung in bunches on vertical sticks inside the inner shrine and place the usual elements of Shinto festival offerings (dried whole fish, raw rice, sake, salt, and "something green," usually scallions) on the offering table. The priest changes from everyday clothing to festival robes in one corner of the main hall. Children play noisily outside and inside the shrine. People continue to arrive, but over half pay their respects from outside the shrine, with two handclaps and a bow, and leave again.

The festival begins around two-thirty, when either the priest or the chief delegate says that it is time. People take their places, kneeling formally on the tatami. The priest kneels to the right of the vestibule (at "A" in figure 2), the shrine delegation in a row along the right side of the shrine, other men along the left side, women near the right wall, and children near the entrance on the right side of the hall.

The priest notes that the festival has begun and bows. Everyone then bows to the floor from the kneeling position. The priest stands, steps before the offering table, and chants, unintelligibly, for about a minute. He takes a pine "purificatory wand" (haraigushi) from the table and shakes it, in turn, over the heads of the delegation and other people to the right, the men at the left, and the children at the entrance, as each group bows. The priest puts the wand back on the table and returns to his original place.

He takes a folded sheet of paper from his robe, holds it before him together with the mace, rises and moves slowly to the table, and kneels facing the inner shrine. He bows, unfolds the paper, holds it up, and reads the prayer (norito) in a loud, high-pitched chant beginning with the name of the shrine, his own name in a lower voice, and the name of the festival. The chant lasts about ten minutes, ending with the date in a normal speaking voice.

The priest refolds the paper, raises it together with the mace, bows twice, replaces mace and paper in his robe, and claps twice. He rises, takes pine branches (in most of Japan, traditionally not pine but sakaki: Cleyera ochnaces) from the table, and distributes one to each of the men, beginning with the delegation. The delegate nearest the table rises, approaches the table, bows, reverses the direction of the branch so that the stem points to the inner shrine, places it on the table, steps back, bows, claps twice, bows, and returns to his place. The others follow one at a time, varying slightly the number and depth of their bows.

When all have presented their branches, the priest approaches the table again, leads everyone in two deep bows, two claps in careful synchrony, and one deep bow, and returns to his original place. All kneel again and bow facing each other, ending the prayer.

Everyone stands. The men put down long planks on the floor where they had been sitting, and men and women spread on them bottles of sake from the offering table, cups, chopsticks, and such foods as packaged nuts, oysters, pickled Chinese cabbage, and stew. Conversations, muted throughout the prayer, become louder and more general. The fifteen or twenty adults who have stayed sit casually, pour cold sake (*omiki*) for each other, eat, and usually begin to sing. Camaraderie continues for about an hour, and everyone begins to drift homeward in pleasantly inebirated little groups.

Beliefs and Analysis

What does the festival mean to its participants? Views of Shinto scholars and of villagers differ somewhat because of differences between specialists and laymen and because Shinto is regional and heterogeneous. They agree, however, on a number of points.

Four elements said (Ono 1969:51) to characterize Shinto festivals— "purification" (*harai*), "offering" (*shinsen*), "prayer" (*norito*), and "symbolic feast" (*naorai*)—appear in Yamanaka as well. "Purification" occurs when people pass through the gate and building entrance, under the straw rope with white paper (*shimenawa*), and when the priest shakes the branches over them. The "offering" also is twofold: the foods on the table throughout the performance and the branches placed there during it. The "prayer" is given by the priest, and the "symbolic feast" is the informal party after the prayer.

Similarly, some scholars list four common features of *kami*, which seem present here. First, tutelary *kami*, like humans, are essentially benevolent. Evil is not their doing, but an accidental accretion of "dirt" (*gomi*) on intrinsically good humans. This pollution does not permanently estrange people from *kami* since it can be removed by purification; there is no original sin (Ueda 1972).

Second, *kami* are inherent in all things, including humans and all natural phenomena, "animate" or not. As Munakata (1977:6) notes, "There is no distinct boundary . . . between the material world and the spirit world." But some *kami* are more important than others and so are enshrined and have their benefits to humans reciprocated with festivals.

Third, *kami* (at least tutelary ones) are concerned with human affairs, influenced by human communication, and reflect the parent-child relationship. "The relation of *kami* to humans is that of *oya-ko*: the parent-child, or better, the ancestor-descendant relation" (Ueda 1972:15). Hence, the prayer, which mentions the intent of the festival and the name of the celebrant, pays respects, gives thanks, and reports to the *kami* or petitions for more help (Ono 1969:56).

Fourth, since *kami* typically are benevolent, they are pleased by human merriment and conviviality. They (like the *hotoke* at memorial services) are entertained by the party ending the festival.

But this synopsis is simpler, more coherent, and more positive than the views of hamlet people. Asked about the festival, some merely say, "It's the village (*mura*, a vestige of the hamlet's earlier village status) festival"; others, that there is no particular purpose; and others, that it may be reasonable to ask, but they have no answers.

A majority agrees with the priest (and with interpretations of Shinto festivals elsewhere: Hori 1968; Ono 1969; Ueda 1972) that festivals mark stages in the agricultural year, ensure successful crops, and give thanks. "Basically," the priest said of the spring festival, "it's an 'anniversary' [*kinen*] kind of festival; it's to begin cultivation and to pray for good crops." Before possession of weapons was prohibited, it included brandishing swords and firing rifles in order, on one common interpretation, to frighten birds away from the grain. The autumn festival, in the typhoon season, is widely said to be for averting storms. But people attribute no single purpose to any of them.

Most people are equally uncertain about meanings of particular elements, such as a chant that they say distinguishes the autumn festival from the other two: "As for good times in this world (*kono yō no yoi toki wa*)/Let horns grow in rows upon horses (*uma ni tsuno ga oi sorō*)." After presenting the branches, everyone crosses to the inner shrine and marches, chanting, three times around it in single file. At each circling the shrine delegation chants the first verse, and all respond with the second. Although everyone mentions the chant when asked the purpose of the festival, they disagree about its meaning. One view is that it asks that the defeated warriors who settled Yamanaka be able to return victorious to Edo. Another is that it asks for success in horse breeding, once the economic mainstay of the area. Horses were led to market in Ueno, then a castle town, by a "rope" (*tsuna*), later corrupted to "horn" (*tsuno*). A former Kōsei-kai member, cutting brush and weeds at the shrine before the festival, gave still another view: "That's a mystery.

Cows have horns, but not horses . . . the meaning must be, good times in this world are as rare as horns on horses. Times are usually bad!"

One reason for the lack of clarity about purpose, perhaps, is that there is no single purpose, but many. If ritual symbols are, in Turner's (1967:50) terms, "multivocal," whole festivals are multivocal several times over. According to Shinto scholars, festivals have a number of aims, and those in Yamanaka clearly have several. First, despite uncertainty, festivals still have explanatory and practical aims concerning the hamlet's well-being and relation to the natural environment. These aims seem to have dwindled in importance as technical knowledge has grown. According to the superintendent of education and others, fewer people take *kami* seriously than before the war. Some still do, however, and everyone feels that the *kami* somehow represents the hamlet, if not as an active, independent advocate, then at least as its symbol.

These two apparently divergent views of *kami*, as active advocate and as symbol, are not mutually exclusive, especially for people, including the Shinto priest, who believe that *kami* "exist" (*iru*) but in the human mind alone. The priest's assertion that they are created (*koshiraeta*) by humans seems skeptical from a Western viewpoint; otherwise, the man seems conservative and devout. The paradox may stem from the inability to fit Western realism (the view that there are "things" corresponding to sense impressions or, in Kantian terms, noumena behind phenomena) with Japanese phenomenalism. The Japanese are willing to

> accept the phenomenal world as Absolute because of their disposition to lay a greater emphasis upon intuitive sensible concrete events, rather than upon universals. This way of thinking with emphasis upon the fluid, arresting character of observed events rejects anything existing over and above the phenomenal world. (Nakamura 1964:350)

In such a Berkeleyan view, not only *kami* but everything is in the mind of the perceiver.

A few people speak of *kami* as willful entities, apparently somewhat independent, with more or less specific locations. The tutelary *kami* is said to spend the winter in the mountains, descending to the shrine for the growing season. Other *kami*, according to a woman of seventy-two (Obaa, a fervent Kōsei-kai member), "are in the mountains and at the shrine beside the bridge and at the pass." Most people seem to think of *kami* as principles of things, inherent in them like natural law. This view has precedent. Ueda (1972:38) notes that according to Shinto belief . . . all forms of existence are comprehended in religious perspective as spiritual entities. The idea that material objects might exist in and of themselves does not arise. This point is fundamental to Shinto ontology.

The Yamanaka festival similarly is thought of both as recognition and as expression of principles of life and growth inherent in the world. These principles are not precisely formulated, nor are humanlike principles distinguished from unhumanlike ones; Shinto is not science. Nonetheless, like science, it attempts to formulate and act on general conceptions of the world. Despite the erosion of the old world view and of *kami*, the festival is for a few people still a direct means to understand and influence daily life.

A second aim, shared by most if not all participants, is Durkheimian: to express and strengthen social bonds. This seems to be what many mean when they say that they go "because it's the village festival." The middle-school principal—who may have read Durkheim—said that festivals are meant to express and encourage hamlet unity. An elderly farmer probably expressed an older view when he said that the fall festival is to avert storms. Asked whether failure to perform it would bring more storms, however, he said it would not and added that festivals are just something that Japanese have because they are Japanese. This response suggests "custom" as a motive, but it also suggests fellowship, clearly promoted by festivals. People are particularly amicable then, and after they begin to drink, they occasionally put their arms around each other (not daily behavior) and proclaim that the hamlet is a good place to live. Attendance is not only a pleasure but, according to the superintendent of education, a duty (*gimu*) as well. People are expected to come and are considered antisocial if they do not.

Western anthropologists (e.g., Wallace 1966) often have characterized such social purposes (often supposed to be latent or unconscious) as "real" in contrast to manifest but "mistaken" or "irrational" technical purposes. One consequence of this distinction is Beattie's conclusion (1970:252) that religious behavior is "symbolic" and "calls for its own kind of investigation." But Ueda (1972:38) argues that in Shinto, general "human participation in and advancement of this life constitute . . . a realization of the will of these deities"; Yamanaka participants are well aware of the social content of the festival but do not sharply distinguish it from "technical" content. In their view, both social and technical goals are part of "participation in and advancement of this life."[41] The fact that people now find means other than *kami* more effective for most technical ends does not indicate an intrinsic distinction of social from technical purposes, but only a contingent one.

People also go to the festival for entertainment (*goraku*), for each other's company in a setting in which work and conflict are suspended and the enjoyment of food and song licensed under the banner of community and *kami*. Workaday prohibitions of drunkenness and leisure are removed and indeed reversed. One is not only free but positively enjoined to drink and make merry. To pour sake for others and to accept it are here social virtues, points of "human duty" (*giri ninjo*). In the Shinto view, festive inebriation is pleasing to the *kami* because self-possession and self-advancement are forgotten and the original exhuberance of life renewed.

Decline

Despite these reasons for participating, the festival, like Shinto in the home, is in decline. All agree that past festivals were better attended and merrier, and this is not mere nostalgia. Besides slackened attendance, the festival has lost two former performances: a dance (*kagura*) with mythic scenes has recently ceased, and its half-dozen carved wooden masks and robes are lying in a chest, nibbled by mice; and the portable shrine once paraded around the hamlet by the children's association is no longer carried. According to my reflective old neighbor, even those who go to the festival are not necessarily devout. Of ten who go, he said, perhaps five believe (he rubbed his hands together in a gesture of prayer), and the other five are indifferent. "It's just a mental discipline (*seishin shūyō*), a matter of mood (*kibun*)," he said. One festival means much the same as another. "The farmers have a slack period and gather to drink sake and sing songs. That's all there is to it."

The decline of the festival reflects processes common to rural Japan (Morioka 1970–71; Suenari 1972). Depopulation has left scarcely enough young people for a *kagura* dance, and the children's portable shrine is not carried simply because there are not enough children. Hamlet cohesion has diminished as agricultural machines supplant communal labor, cars enable people to commute to jobs, and television brings alternative entertainment.

Asked about *kami* themselves, the focus of festival and household worship, however, people do not mention demographic or economic factors. They say that they now have less interest in *kami* because there are now better interpretations and means of control. As a man in a nearby hamlet said, the silkworm festival there is held "only out of custom" (*shūkan dake de*). In the past, he said, when silkworms sickened and died or failed to spin, farmers had no recourse but to pray. Now, however, there are scientific remedies, and when something goes wrong farmers go to the agricultural specialist. So the festival is not really motivated by faith, he said; only people over seventy still believe in *kami*. My old neighbor gave a similarly rationalistic account of the end, some sixty years before, of the Yamanaka festival for Raiden, *kami* of thunder and lightening. "People didn't know about electricity in the past, so they treated it as a *kami* . . . but that stopped about the end [1912] of the Meiji era . . . now there's no festival, and trees have grown up in the path."

The greatest blow to *kami* was the loss of World War II, which "seemed to remove the whole underpinning of the social order" (Dore 1978:56). The government had said that Japan, as the "land of *kami*" (*shinkoku*), could not lose. Proof was the "divine wind" (*kamikaze*) that had destroyed the Mongol invasion fleet of 1281, an event that several people in Yamanaka used to explain national sentiment about *kami*. Throughout the war, patriotism and courage had been mustered around *kami* (Bunce 1955:62), including the emperor, and the first defeat and occupation in Japanese history discredited them. My neighbor gave his view of the war in a conversation implicitly linking magic, *kami*, and Kōsei-kai. I had asked him about charms against snakes. He said charms were "superstitions of the past" (*mukashi no meishin*) and no longer used, but added,

Well . . . some may still be doing them. . . . During the war people prayed a lot at the shrine and god-shelf for victory: "Let us win! Let us win!" but the war was lost anyway. People lost faith.

G: So people haven't prayed so much since then?

H: That's right. No matter how they prayed, the war was lost. The most important shrine is Ise, Ise Jingu. The emperor went to pray there, but the war was lost anyway. In other wars—the Japanese-Russian War, the Sino-Japanese War, the China Incident—people prayed too, and the wars were won, but it was because we were lucky. But in a scientific war, you've got to be scientific . . . in the Pacific War [WWII], Japan didn't have scientific strength. America did have scientific strength and dropped the atomic bomb . . . the Japanese were holding on to old-fashioned beliefs.

G: After the war, people haven't believed in *kami* so much?

H: That's right . . . well, down that way [pointing south] they're still doing it, nonetheless.

G: At the shrine?

H: At Hideo's [the Kōsei-kai meeting place] and places like that. But as I see it, that's a matter of money making. They gather money and send it on. Actually, if someone's sick, the only thing is to go to the doctor. Instead they're encouraged to pray [rubs hands together] . . . that's wrong, taking money from the poor.

Magic, Shinto, and Kōsei-kai alike are for him bootless appeals for protection from snakes, for victory, or for a cure, addressed (as he said at another time) to nonentities. He feels much the same, if not so vehemently, about the Sōtō Zen temple. More skeptical of religion than most people in the hamlet and more ready to express it, he is not, however, entirely atypical. Most people other than Kōsei-kai members now are probably midway between his skepticism and Shinto and Buddhist orthodoxy. But there are many intermediate beliefs, and even those of a single person—perhaps like all beliefs—vary with time and occasion.

Two Minor Shrines

In addition to the tutelary shrine, two minor shrines in the hamlet have annual festivals.

Nījūsanya-sama

The shrine for the *kami* Nījūsanya-sama is on a little-frequented knoll 100 m above the main road, near the middle of the hamlet. The building is hardly more than a hut, about 4 m long and 2 m wide, with a raised platform and two shelves at the end away from the door, a stoneware hearth, and worn straw mats put down for the performance. The grounds have no gate or other visible entrance or boundaries.

The festival, a "women's and children's festival," is held about the middle of April. The children's association makes the preparations. The boys go from door to door on festival day gathering donations: raw rice or Y100 to Y200 in cash for festive red beans and rice, cooked by the *kumi* chief's household and served to visitors at the shrine. The only other preparation is to beat the dust from the mats and place them on the floor.

As a minor festival, this is performed not by the Shinto priest but by a *yamabushi* ("mountain ascetic"), a hamlet resident and occasional diviner who discovers auspicious times and directions for various enterprises, finds lost objects, and does a "spring purification" (*harugitō*) for a number of households. Eighty-two years old (in 1972; he died in 1977), he is the last *yamabushi* in this area, an occupation that combines elements of Shinto, Buddhism, and folklore and that has virtually disappeared throughout Japan.

The *yamabushi* arrives at the shrine about four o'clock with a pine branch to which white paper wreaths are tied. He places two small piles of red rice on the higher and more recessed shelf and supervises the lighting of five candles on the lower shelf. He puts on a black robe and begins a chant punctuated by a small bell. The boys, the only others present (seven came to the festival I observed), kneel formally along the inside walls. The chant lasts about twenty minutes, ending with a final jingle of the bell and a direction from the *yamabushi* that all clap twice and twice again.

This concludes the formalities. The *yamabushi* leaves and the boys portion out handfuls of red rice and small pieces of paper, for visitors, some children, and some adults, who now briefly visit the shrine. Most clap twice, throw a few coins in an offering box in front of the shrine and leave again. When the last visitor has gone, the boys empty the offering box. Two of them leave with the money (about Y500 or Y600) for soft drinks, peanuts, and rice crackers, shared forthwith in the shrine.

The boys said that the purpose of the festival is entertainment. Adults had varying opinions, as with other festivals. Most said that the festival is for good luck and that the *kami* is the "*kami* of luck." The previous year's hamlet chief said it was the *kami* of farmers, who pray for good crops. The "rock-cliff millionaire" indicated that he did not know but that it was said that if one prays there, he will earn money, and that in the past people had had no other recreation. The young poet said at first that the real reason for the festival was custom (*shūkan*). As we watched the visitors come and go, he suggested others:

1. It entertains the children.
2. It raises money for the other children's association activities, such as a post-New Year's bonfire. These require meetings with soft drinks and crackers.

Yamanaka's eighty-two-year-old *yamabushi* ("mountain ascetic"), the last in this area, divining.

The Nijūsanya-sama Festival, conducted by the *yamabushi* and attended by the children's association.

3. It brings together children from the far end of the hamlet.

4. It enables adults to converse [though they seemed to come and go with minimal conversation], and so is a medium of "communication" [he used the English loanword].

5. Since it is a custom that has always been observed, people would feel something amiss if it were not.

Jūnī-sama

The second minor shrine, for Jūnī-sama, has its festival in the second week of September. The shrine lies among trees near a bridge over the gorge separating the north end of the hamlet from the south end of its neighbor. Like the Nījūsanya-sama shrine, the building is small, plain, and dilapidated. At the end away from the entrance is an alcove with shelves bearing a miniature stone shrine containing two small ceramic foxes, emblems of Inari, kami of rice. During the festival the alcove also contains a cut-paper wand, raw Shinto food offerings, and foods to be eaten. Inside the shrine red bunting with the shrine's name is put up, and outside are two festival flags. Straw rope with white paper is hung over the doorway and alcove.

The performance is by the Shinto priest. He begins about four-thirty, after he has placed the offerings and lighted four candles in the alcove and dressed in a white inner robe, a cream-colored outer robe, and his tall black cap. He claps twice, chants a written prayer, and has the participants—all men—lay branches in the alcove. His performance is shorter and simpler than at the tutelary shrine. When he finishes, the men take the food and sake from the alcove and end, as at the tutelary shrine, in amiable tipsiness. Meanwhile, visitors from most households come and go, each receiving a handful of red rice on a piece of paper. Only the eight or nine men who fit inside, all from Yamanaka, stay from beginning to end. Unlike the case at the tutelary shrine and Nījūsanya-sama, visitors from outside come as well, from the nearest kumi in the hamlet at the far end of the bridge. The atmosphere is informal, as at the tutelary shrine, and there is quiet conversation even during the prayer.

The origin and intent of the festival, as with the Nījūsanya-sama festival, are obscure. The priest said that it is for the kami of the bridge. Another man said it was for a mountain kami, for safety in mountain work. Most seemed only to feel that it somehow promotes hamlet welfare and is mainly an occasion for relaxation and friendly discourse.

Households

Every household in the hamlet, unlike many modern urban households, has a "god-shelf," a plain wooden shelf some 50 cm long and 20 cm wide, hung near the ceiling against a wall, usually in the best room. On it usually is a plain wooden miniature shrine housing one or more talismans (*ofuda*), including one from the Grand Shrine at Ise for Tenshō-kotaijin (or *Amaterasu-ō-mikami*), the Sun Goddess.[42] Occasional talismans are those of the silkworm *kami*, the New Year's *kami*, Inari, *kami* of house and grounds as well as of rice, and Daikoku, *kami* of wealth. In front of the talismans (occasionally simply tacked to the wall above the shelf rather than housed in a shrine) are small dishes with cooked or uncooked rice, water, and on special occasions like New Year's, other foods. Foods are presented with a bow, two claps, and a prayer and should be changed daily; in fact, most householders change them only occasionally. A few people say that although they have the god-shelf, they neither pray nor make offerings.

People in Yamanaka describe no elaborate beliefs about *kami*, whether in the shrine or in their homes. Most simply expect a general benevolent influence. Some pray to the Sun Goddess for the welfare of the country. One or two people speak of *kami* as guides to moral conduct, useful in instructing children. Many, however, seem to regard shelf and talismans as a household accessory like a lightening rod, installed and left alone except for occasional maintenance. Two people said that they do not believe in *kami* at all, and one added that people normally become atheists as they become civilized. But one farmer of fifty-five, who had come to the fall festival drunk and boisterous, said later the belief in *kami* would never disappear. In a Malinowskian explanation, he said,

> As for completely disappearing . . . I don't think it'll ever come to that. People are building satellites and so on, but some-times they fail, and when they do people think there are *kami* that determine whether they fail or not . . . [gives examples of failed rockets and satellites]. Human power and science are still not so great as to do away with *kami* and probably never will be. It's that sort of thing that makes us think there must be *kami-sama*.

A few people said that they pray for the welfare of house and country and make careful offerings every day. In all, attitudes toward household

A neighbor puts up New Year's boughs at his god-shelf, above the altar.

kami, like *kami* of the hamlet shrine, range from rejection of them as superstitious fallacies, to unelaborated acceptance, to explicit belief and daily observance.

Summary and Implications

Shinto in Yamanaka, like Sōtō Zen, is a variegated cluster of beliefs and practices concerning more or less humanlike beings, *kami*, with an interest and influence in human affairs. *Kami* are inherent in all natural phenomena, but not all merit individual attention. Most important for the hamlet is the tutelary deity, addressed at three annual festivals at the main shrine. Like Buddhism, Shinto has a household level as well as a collective one, but Shinto is mainly for the hamlet as a whole.

Festivals seem to have three main purposes. First, they and the *kami* to whom they are directed offer a general interpretation of hamlet life. Their interpretation and influence are global, drawing no distinction between "social" and "technical" matters. But the importance of *kami* for pest control or for averting storms now appears slight, and some people discount them entirely.

Second, festivals express and reinforce hamlet solidarity, as some people explicitly indicate. Solidarity is one of the wishes of the *kami* and evidently what people mean when they say that they go "because it is the village festival." People frequently express communal sentiments at festivals, to which each household should send a member and a little money out of hamlet loyalty.

Third, festivals mark the beginning, middle, and end of the agricultural year with relaxation and entertainment. Within the peaceful, wooded shrine grounds, work and sobriety are temporarily abandoned, pleasurably punctuating the seasons.

In spite of these attractions, interest in festivals, household observances, and the *kami* they address is in decline. The *kagura* and the children's portable shrine have been abandoned, and festival attendance has decreased. A few people no longer pray to *kami* at all. This decline is in part the result of demographic and economic changes: population loss, especially of young people, means fewer active participants; agricultural machines, transportation, and jobs reduce interdependence; and television brings alternative entertainment.

Just as important, the attraction of *kami* for interpreting and influencing natural and social events has been reduced by their spectacular failure in war and by the success of alternative, impersonal scientific principles. The world in which the people of Yamanaka live is less anthropomorphic and anthropocentric than it was a short time ago. Not only moon rockets, but also wind and rain, sickness and health, the germination of rice, and the turn of the seasons now are more provinces of physics, chemistry, and biology than of beings sympathetic to human endeavor.

While science has better keys to natural phenomena than *kami*, one may suspect (although no one said it) that something has been lost. It may be that the world now is not only less personal but also less integrated. Formerly, a tutelary *kami*, with a few fellows, could account for most events of significance to the hamlet. Without *kami*, these events—meteorological, botanical, social, or other—are merely results of innumerable other events, many of them arbitrary from a human point of view. Events still occur according to orderly principles, but with the new models, many events, though orderly, are neither purposeful nor just. Contemporary science now conflicts with "cozy-meaningful" thought (Gellner 1970:40).

Kōsei-kai, however, asserts a universal causal nexus that is not only orderly but unified, purposeful, and just. The postwar decline of Shinto, the concomitant doubt, and the rise of science seem to have left gaps that Kōsei-kai addresses:

> In a mechanical world where man has been reduced to a cog in a cogwheel, new personal problems arise again from the inside of man . . . the more important ones are problems of the "mind." (Risshō Kōsei-kai 1966:137)

Other things as well are reduced to cogs when *kami* and other spirits disappear. Mechanization, which led Descartes to declare the universe a great clockwork, seems to be producing in Japan a scientific but humanistically ambiguous world view, and for some people the ancestors elaborated by Kōsei-kai are taking the ground from which *kami* have been expelled.

Chapter 5
Risshō Kōsei-kai in Yamanaka

Introduction: Arrival, Growth, and Decline

Risshō Kōsei-kai arrived in Kawa Mura in 1947 when Takeda Junko, in her early thirties, returned from Tokyo to Morita, the next hamlet up the valley from Yamanaka. In Tokyo she had been persuaded to join the movement by her older sister, "for no particular reason," she said, "except for filial piety."

No one else in the area joined for three years. Then in 1950, two of Takeda's friends in Morita joined. In 1951 local Kōsei-kai records show that two more joined, and in 1952 two more from Morita and three from neighboring Shirakawa joined. In 1953 six years of rapid expansion began: seventy-four new members in 1953, ninety-one in 1954, forty-six in 1955, thirty-three in 1956, fifty in 1957, and thirty-seven in 1958. After 1958 the influx dropped sharply, to one in 1962. It increased moderately in the mid-1960s and then declined nearly to nothing from 1970 through 1977.

Local Kōsei-kai records do not show termination of membership, and all who have ever joined tend to remain in the books. Thus, it is difficult to estimate the number of active members since 1947. But conversations with members, observations of attendance, and meeting-place dues records suggest that by 1972 half the people who joined had withdrawn or lapsed into inactivity and nonpayment of dues. This proportion was about the same in 1984.

The growth and decline of Kōsei-kai in Yamanaka have paralleled its career in the village as a whole. The first member, later professional, was Kimura Hideo, who joined in 1953. He was followed the same year by eleven others and by six more in 1954. There were no new members in 1955, one in 1956 and in 1957, and two in 1958. Four years followed with no new members, and then one joined each year from 1963 through 1966, two in 1968, and the most recent one in 1969. Of these twenty-nine people, however, only eleven were active in 1972 and 1977. Of the others, two people told me they definitely had quit, four denied ever having joined, four have left the hamlet, one has died, and seven have become inactive.

Organization: Church and Branch

National headquarters in Tokyo administers thirty-three dioceses with some 225 (in 1980; the number was somewhat under 200 in 1972) regional churches (*kyōkai*) in towns and cities throughout the country and abroad. A church has a chief (*kyōkai-chō*), an administrative staff of about a dozen, and an administrative area divided into a small number of branches (*shibu*). Branches each have a chief and treasurer (*shibu-chō* and *kaikei*, figure 3) and are divided into regions (*chiku*). These are further divided into two levels of smaller regions, distinguished from the higher-level region by directional terms and place-names, respectively (e.g., "North Region" and "Yamanaka Region"). The last and smallest unit usually corresponds to and is named for a hamlet. This unit, like each higher one except for the highest "region," has a single administrator, the group chief (*kumi-chō*).

The Ueno Church was established in 1970, when its headquarters were completed near the center of Ueno City, after gradual growth brought promotion of the area from branch to church. Its territory is roughly a third of the prefecture in which it lies and is largely mountainous, with one city (Ueno), three townships, nine villages, and a population of 136,000. Of this population, the church's records claimed 2,260 as members in 1972, divided among three branches: 1,069 in Ueno Branch (Ueno City, two townships, and three villages); 461 in Atama Branch (one township and four villages); and 730 in Kawa Branch (Kawa and Tani villages).

As the direct representative of President Niwano, the church chief, a tall, austere woman in her early fifties, transmits doctrine from headquarters to branch leaders and occasionally to assemblies of lay members. She also maintains the church building, collects and transmits funds from branches to headquarters, maintains connections with local religious, civic, and government organizations, and presides at five monthly services at the church. She occasionally visits local meeting places in branches, counseling members in small group sessions. Below the church chief is an administrative staff (in Ueno, twelve people) divided into four sections for cultural affairs, missionizing, planning, and liaison. An "office chief" (*jimu-chō*) is general secretary, treasurer, and chief bookkeeper.

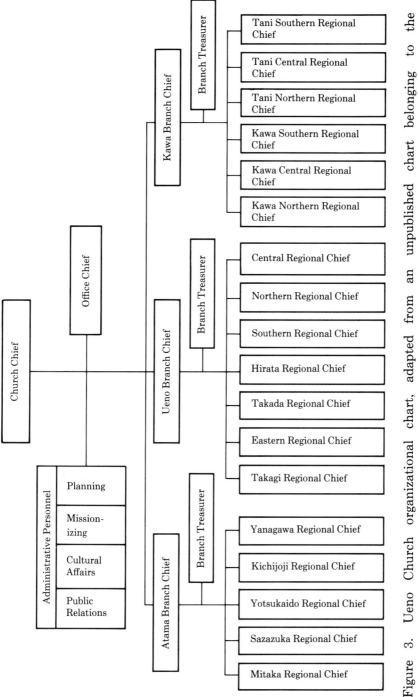

Figure 3. Ueno Church organizational chart, adapted from an unpublished chart belonging to the Kawa Branch chief. Organizational divisions sometimes but not always correspond to towns and villages.

All these officers work in the church headquarters (*dōjō* or "training hall," usually simply called *kyōkai*, "church"). In Ueno this is a modern, two-story, ferro-concrete building with 679 m^2 of floor space. Its attractive, well-furnished rooms include a large hall for worship and counseling, a lecture hall, a small reception and communications office, a drawing room, a bookkeeping office, kitchens, and living quarters for the church chief.

Also below the church chief and nominally based in Ueno, but working mostly in their own branches, are three branch chiefs (*shibu-chō*). These semiprofessional officers, chosen for leadership and teaching ability and given doctrinal training, usually mediate between the church chief and laymen. They are the usual leaders at counseling sessions and are Kōsei-kai's chief representatives to its lay members. The branch chiefs usually attend the five monthly meetings at the church and help administer it. But most of their work is in their branches, counseling at meetings, visiting homes, or consulting with lay officers. The branch chiefs of the Ueno church, one woman and two men, all are gregarious, articulate, and pleasant people in their fifties.

Below each branch chief is a series of part-time, unpaid offices. One treasurer for each branch records and transmits monthly dues and donations to the church. A number (six in the Kawa Branch) of "lay heads" (*shūnin*) of the regions of the branch give advice in the branch chief's absence. Below each lay head are one "general affairs officer" (*shomuin*) and several "group chiefs" (*kumi-chō*), usually one for each hamlet.

Since no one below the branch chief gives official counseling, the official functions of the branch hierarchy are downward transmission of meeting schedules, news of special events, and requests for donations, and upward transmission of funds and requests for counseling and special services. It also transmits personal messages unrelated to Kōsei-kai. In all, however, fewer communications follow the hierarchy than its order and symmetry would suggest. Ordinary members and the branch chief, instead of communicating through intermediate officers, typically talk directly at the meeting place, at members' homes, or by telephone.

Appointments to branch offices below the chief are made at his recommendation by the church chief, with *pro forma* confirmation by national headquarters, on the basis of proselytizing, diligence in counseling meetings, trips to the church and to national headquarters, and donations. The offices carry neither stipend nor great responsibility. Appointment appears to be more a reward for service or an attempt to exploit members' standing in local communities than a means for substantial administration. For example, the Yamanaka group chief in 1972 was a devout but not very active man of seventy. He was appointed, he said, in the hope that the respectability of his old, though now somewhat impoverished, household and of himself as a former community leader would help recruit others.

The Meeting Place

The meeting place (*hōza-jō*) for the Kawa Region of Kawa Branch is in Yamanaka, roughly in the middle of Kawa Mura and near the main road. Until 1968 it had been in the neighboring hamlet of Morita in one room of a small general store owned by a Kōsei-kai member. When the member took a job in the village office, however, Kōsei-kai's requirement that someone always be in attendance at the meeting place (and, another member said, opposition at the office to a village employee's having such a clear commitment to Kōsei-kai) caused him to give it up. It was relocated in Yamanaka, in the house of Kimura Hideo, then one of three members of the Ueno missionizing division.

The meeting place is the main room (*zashiki*) of the house, near the southern end of Yamanaka. The house, typical of older farmhouses in the area, has two stories (the second for raising silkworms) of post and beam construction, with wattle and daub walls. The traditional translucent papered sliding panels (*shōji*) with storm doors account for about half the exterior wall surface, and the 117 m^2 of the first floor are divided by the usual opaque sliding panels (*fusuma*) into seven rooms. These include a kitchen and a large earth-floored room that is the informal entrance and site of the bathtub and such messy work as stripping green beans from their branches. The whole house, like most in the hamlet, is spacious and well worn (when I returned in 1984, the interior had been generally refurbished and a room at the southern end Westernized, with carpet, sofa, two armchairs, and coffee table).

The meeting place is the largest room, at just over 20 m^2. It is used by the household for dining, watching television, and casual entertainment, often simultaneously, as well as for Kōsei-kai functions. Its most striking feature is a Buddhist altar over twice the size of those in most homes, set in the rear wall facing the entrance. It has a veneer of imitation marble, curtains closing it at night, Kōsei-kai paraphernalia, and usually offerings of fruit, vegetables, and flowers. The other major feature of the room is a low, quilted table over the square sunken hearth (*kotatsu*) common to most of northern Japan. In winter the hearth holds a small charcoal brazier that heats the space enclosed by the table and quilt. People sit with their feet on boards in the pit, warmed at least from the waist down, and family, guests, and Kōsei-kai members gather around it for meals, conversation, or counseling meetings. Other furnishings include a television set, usually with an accumulation of small items of daily use and occasionally flowers; a small glass-fronted case with books and household papers; a calendar; and often bedding that has been folded but not put away. There is also a Shinto god-shelf with a talisman from Ise, for Amaterasu, and one from Yasukuni Shrine in Tokyo, for the war dead. In front of the talismans are raw rice, water, and sake in a bowl and glasses, all with the Kōsei-kai crest.

In addition to the altar the contents of the room *qua* meeting place are framed black-and-white photographs of cofounders Niwano and Myōkō-sensei (the latter on the god-shelf); a list of names and dates of ancestors receiving special services, on the wall to the right of the altar; a polished brass incense burner flanked by two brass candlesticks with candles and a bell, in front of the altar; a blackboard at the left of the room with Kōsei-kai branch and church events for the coming month; and a small steel floor safe with the month's collection.

The altar, the most elaborate item in the room, 1.7 m wide and high, occupies almost a quarter of the rear wall. It reaches from the ceiling to under a meter from the floor and is about a meter deep, with three shelves across the bottom third. Its contents, roughly as recommended in a Kōsei-kai diagram (figure 4), occupy positions of importance declining from top to bottom and from center to sides. First is the "principal image" (*gohonzon*), a hanging scroll with a richly painted Gautama Buddha standing among four smaller bodhisattvas, in the center of the rear wall. Flanking it are three smaller scrolls with script but no images: to the left, a scroll with the posthumous name of Myōkō-sensei, and to the right, a scroll for the enshrined dead collectively (*sōkaimyō*) and one for the karma of house and grounds (*takuchi innen*). To the far left is a scroll not specified in the official chart, with a painted Buddha like the first but smaller, the principal image for the household itself.

On the topmost shelf below the scrolls are three sets of plain wooden stands with offerings, usually cooked rice and tea or water, and sometimes sake. On the second shelf (not on the first as in the chart) are two death-day registers (*kakochō*), folding booklets with the posthumous names and death dates of Kawa Region members. Left and right of the death registers are two small brass lanterns with electric lights. On the bottom shelf, near the center, are two small dark-red plastic pedestals with cakes, flanked by two plain wooden stands with fruit on the one to the left and vegetables on the one to the right, and by two vases with flowers. Between these are offerings, on the wooden stands if these are otherwise empty, of first fruits or of gifts of food received by the household. All offerings end on the household table as they are displaced by new offerings, usually after a few days, or sooner if perishable. Curtains close the altar between the last evening prayers and the first morning prayers.

The altar differs in several ways from those of nonmember households. Most obviously, its large size and extension onto the floor by candle-holders and candles, incense burner, and bell distinguish it from altars of nonmembers and of other members as well. A second feature is its repeated display of the Kōsei-kai crest, present to some degree in altars of all members. Third, nonmember altars have no scrolls, although some have a small wooden bodhisattva (usually Kannon) or a photograph of a recent or eminent ancestor. Fourth, death registers are not displayed in nonmember households. Last, sake, normally a Shinto offering, is rare elsewhere, and cakes, fruit, flowers, and vegetables elsewhere are much less profuse and more casually offered, without the stands used in the meeting place.

The meeting place also serves as a shop for texts of the Lotus Sutra, Kōsei-kai sashes, rosaries (juzu), candles, and incense. For its use of the room, Kōsei-kai pays the household Y2,000 (about $8.00 in 1972) a month, about 4 percent of the household's income.

Members in Kawa Region

Even simple statistics about Kōsei-kai members in Kawa Region, such as number, ages, sex, and extent of participation, were hard to get. Inquiries about lists of members, organizational and growth charts, and donation lists met resistance for over a year: the materials did not exist, were outdated, were temporarily with someone else, had been lost in the move to the new church, or would be available in the future. After a year, the branch chief and others gave me some of them, including copies of ones sent to headquarters, and some seemed to inflate membership and activity at the meeting place. A form for "greatest number of people assembled at one time," for example, listed eighty-seven and forty-five for two consecutive months when in fact there never seemed to be more than thirteen or fourteen at once. Reports of paraphernalia sold at the meeting place appeared similarly inflated.

A few weeks before the end of my first stay of fourteen months, Hideo gave me two sets of documents for Kawa Region. One was a set of members' cards (kaiin kādo), one for each member, with name, birthdate, date of joining, and sometimes a one-sentence reason for joining. The second was a booklet with a list of members by hamlet, which differed slightly from the set of names on the cards. These

Figure 4. Outline of altar display recommended by Risshō Kōsei-kai, adapted from unpublished guide for members. 1: "principal image"; 2: scroll for Myoko *sensei*; 3: scroll for the dead; 4: scroll for karma of house and grounds; 5: death registers; 6: cooked rice; 7: water; 8: sake; 9: tea; 10: crackers; 11: vegetables; 12: fruit; 13: flowers.

promised to make it possible to talk with hitherto unknown members. As it turned out, of the twenty-nine people listed for Yamanaka, only eleven were still active in 1972. Two had withdrawn, four had left the hamlet, one had died, seven were inactive, and four said that they had never joined. No active member was listed who had not already been mentioned by others or appeared at the meeting place. By 1977 two more had died and no one else had joined.

In Kawa Region as a whole, about 150 members (roughly 2 percent of the population) of 203 in the annual report are active to some degree. Of these, about fifteen or sixteen, including two regulars from Yamanaka, appear frequently for services or counseling. As in the church and the national membership as a whole, their mean age is about fifty, and about 60 percent are women.

Activities at the Meeting Place

For most members, activities at the meeting place are the greatest attraction. These are chiefly five monthly memorial services: on the fifth of the month for the "Bodhisattva of Space"; on the tenth for Myōkō-sensei; on the fourteenth for the Great Gracious Deity Shichimen; on the fifteenth for Śākyamuni Buddha; and on the twenty-eighth for the Great Bodhisattva Hachiman. Counseling sessions follow these if a branch chief or higher officer is present.

There are less important activities as well. An attendant (in Yamanaka, usually "Obaa," Hideo's adoptive mother) performs a short service morning and evening; individual members occasionally come to pray; and in winter "ascetic exercises" (*reikan shugyō*) are performed on five subsequent mornings, January 22–26. Local bookkeeping and distribution of publications are done here too, and in national election years, posters and other materials for candidates endorsed by Kōsei-kai are distributed.

Memorial Services

The five monthly memorial services are similar except for the presence or absence of counseling afterward, which depends mainly on the presence of the branch chief. Services usually begin about 10:30 in the morning, after everyone expected arrives. People begin to arrive at 9:30 or 10:00. Each first approaches the altar and formally bows prostrate for about ten seconds. He or she then rises to his or her knees, rubs a rosary between open palms for a second or two, and does another, shorter, prostrate bow. Only then does the newcomer greet the others, who have continued in casual conversation, and exchange comments on the weather and inquiries about health. If he or she has brought gifts of food of household or meeting place, someone strikes a flint with an iron before the altar three times and places the food on the bottom shelf.

When everyone (normally six or seven) has arrived, the senior member suggests that they begin, kneels before the incense burner in front of the altar, and lights incense and candles. Everyone puts on a Kōsei-kai sash with the formula, "Glory to the Sutra of the Lotus of the Wonderful Law," diagonally from left shoulder to right hip, takes out the sutra and a rosary, and kneels facing the altar. The senior member leads an initial chant of the formula three times and a chanted rote reading of part of the sutra for half an hour. Divisions of the text are marked by a single bell struck by the assistant and by three repetitions of the formula.

The reading concludes with another three repetitions of the formula and a ten-second prostrate bow, followed by kneeling, rosary rubbing, and another bow. Everyone recites the creed:

> We, the members of Risshō Kōsei-kai
> Under the leadership of our revered teacher,
> President Niwano,
> Recognize the essential way of salvation in Buddhism
> And pledge our best efforts, in the spirit of
> Buddhist laymen,
> To perfect our character and realize in our lives
> the Bodhisattva Way.
> To this end, by improving in knowledge and practice
> of the faith,
> In personal discipline and in leading others,
> We will endeavor to realize a state of peace
> For the family, the community, and the world.
> (Rissho Kōsei-kai 1966:126)

The leader says, "Thank you very much, Mr. President," toward the president's photograph, and all repeat the two prostrate bows and rosary rubbing.

Everyone takes off his sash and puts away rosary and text, and most take a place at the table. General conversation begins. Unfinished business is done, and such church events as charity drives are announced. If the branch chief is present, he asks whether anyone wants "interpretation" (*musubi*).

Counseling

If, as usual, several people want counseling, an hour or more of it follows. Kōsei-kai leaders say that their advise is based on the Four Noble Truths, especially on the concept that all sentient beings have the Buddha nature. The aim of counseling is to "help all the participants reveal their Buddha-nature by working together with compassion to solve the problems of someone who is in trouble" (Risshō Kōsei-kai 1980:10). Problems discussed in Kawa Mura range from lost personal property, high blood pressure, and conflicts with mothers-in-law, to possession by fox spirits.[43] Health problems account for about half of all discussion, followed by problems with interpersonal relationships, but no topic seems to be inappropriate.

The branch chief is a soft-spoken, articulate, sympathetic man and a good listener (the other branch chiefs, and especially the church chief, are more dogmatic, as Dale [1975] notes of *hōza* leaders at the head-quarters). Much of his advice seems common sense. He usually tells people with medical problems to see a doctor if they have not done so.[44] He tells people having problems with other people or with medically intractable sickness to examine their own attitudes and behavior. This self-examination reflects the dominant Buddhist view of suffering, that problem and solution lie within the sufferer himself.

Identifying the problem often requires considering the sufferer's karma, which may mean either results of actions of past members of his household or results of his own past actions. Troublesome cases may require divination, by interpreting the characters of the individual's given name (Dale 1975 reports use of the family name), by his birth date, or by patching together evidence from the complaint that suggests, analogically, an ancestor's grievance. Action to correct the problem depends on the cause, usually neglect of prayer and offerings to an ancestor. To remedy it, prayer and offerings are first given by the sufferer. If this fails, officers may perform services at the Ueno Church, and even at national headquarters.

Although the presiding member (usually the branch chief) bears responsibility for the counseling, other members occasionally contribute a few words either to the branch chief in supplementary explanation of a problem or to the sufferer in encouragement. Both leader and laymen seem sympathetic, but their theme is that the person should improve his or her own attitudes and behavior.

The Kawa Branch chief at home.

Everyone sits close together at the low table or, if the group is too large, in a larger circle beyond it. The group is face to face: the diameter of the circle is under 2 m, less if all are at the table. The leader faces the entrance, his back to the altar (the place of seniority and responsibility, but being in the circle suggests communion as well[45]). Intimacy is encouraged by limiting the circle, officially at least, to twelve participants, and voices are low. People are also shoulder to shoulder and leg to leg, and their physical closeness heightens the emotional closeness produced by verbal expressions of sympathy, understanding, and approval. Intimacy is thus encouraged in a number of ways at once.

Emotions expressed range from those of the complainant, sometimes agitated or tearful (highly expressive in a culture that generally discourages displays of feeling in adults; Hardacre [1986] notes such expressiveness in the New Religions generally), to the milder, usually sympathetic agitations of other members, to the sympathetic but detached calm of the leader, with his steady and measured responses. The leader concludes the session with several minutes of relaxed, confident, and earnest discussion of principles.

When he finishes, everyone kneels toward the altar, recites "Hail to the Sutra of the Lotus" three times, and bows twice, rubbing the rosary. The leader thanks President Niwano again. All exchange bows and thanks, and people with leisure turn to the hearth for green tea and relaxed conversation.

Loose ends and "ties" at a typical counseling meeting. The purpose of a counseling meeting is to hear, interpret, and suggest solutions for members' personal problems. Although these vary greatly, most, as noted, concern health or personal and family relationships. After a member has presented his or her problem, the leader responds with *musubi*, literally a "knot" or "tie."

Kōsei-kai's use of the term *musubi* is unusual and unfamiliar to nonmembers. It means the interpretation given a problem by the leader, who identifies underlying causes or "connections" and tells how to influence them. It suggests the primary purpose of the meetings: to tie together experience by identifying the causal relations behind disturbing events and thus to provide connectedness and meaning. The same aim is also suggested by other terms frequent in counseling, such as *gō*, "karma" or comprehensive causality; *innen*, "fate"; and *en*, "connection." Implicitly and often explicitly, the counselor aims to overcome members' feelings of unconnectedness, dissociation, and lack of pattern. Members' experiences are problems in large part because they are "unattached"; they are loose ends that the leader must tie up. The first and most important step is to show that the problem is the result of a particular

The church chief, center, gives "ties" at an evening counseling session in a Kawa Branch meeting place.

cause, or of several causes. This identification itself brings relief. Moreover, when the cause has been identified, it can be eliminated.

Problems and "ties" presented at meetings reflect, explicitly or implicitly, the major points of Kōsei-kai doctrine (meetings in Tokyo are not so much "counseling" as "teaching" [Dale 1975]). Those discussed at the Yamanaka meeting place one mild December morning, for example, are reasonably representative.

When I arrived at ten o'clock, the service had already been held. Ten people were there, and another arrived an hour later. These were the branch chief, a pleasant and soft-spoken man of fifty-five; Kimura Yūko, seventy-two, the usual caretaker of the meeting place and mother-in-law of the household; Mori Sayoko, a woman of sixty and the other unfailing participant in Yamanaka; Takagi Junko, a woman of about fifty from neighboring Morita who is the distributor of Kōsei-kai literature for Kawa Region; a woman of eighty, also named Takagi, from a hamlet 3.5 km south of Yamanaka; a young woman and her ten-year-old daughter, from the hot-spring spa 3 km north; two women of about sixty-five from Morita; Takagi Sanshirō, a postman of about fifty, who is one of the earliest members and who with Takeda Junko is credited with the original proselyting for Kōsei-kai in this area, from Morita; and Takeda Junko, who arrived from Morita about an hour after the meeting began. The following account is, in condensed but chronological paraphrase and occasional quotation, the discussion from my notes and tapes.

The woman of sixty-five from Morita, the only one present whom I didn't know, made the first request for a "tie." She said that about a month before she had lost a ¥10,000 note (then about $33.00, or about a week's wages for local unskilled work) that she had intended to take to a household to which she was indebted for her son's school lodging. The household member directly concerned, the creditor, had died before being paid, and the woman had intended to pray to her while at the house. Before she went, however, the money was stolen from a parcel that she had put down for a few minutes while shopping. She wanted to know from the branch chief what the ancestors meant to teach her by the theft.

The branch chief replied that it was good that she was not spiteful. But she, too, was guilty for tempting the thief. "Enmity over money" (*kane no urami*) is a bad thing. For example, not long ago someone was robbed of a year's earnings in silkworm money after putting it down in a store, and he was enraged at the thief. After the theft, bad luck came to both households. The thief's household fell on especially bad times: everyone in it died. But bad luck struck the victim's household also: madness, deaths, and other misfortunes (here discussion turned to diverse reminiscences of the event). The curse of money enmity continues through the generations. The person stolen from was a branch household of the branch chief's house. The "tie" for the lady's stolen money, he continued, was that this was a sign from someone who had died and wanted services. The old lady now existed in happiness because of the help of the ancestor, so she must have respect and gratitude for him.

The elderly woman continued her account with earlier recollections. She had lost her father at nine, her grandfather at fourteen, and her mother at twenty. Although her mother had been indebted to neighbors, her mother's siblings hadn't repaid them. The lady always intended to repay the debt. She had married early, to an adopted husband. At that time there was no paddy land in the village, so she used her wealth to build paddy for people. Hence, people could grow and sell rice, at least in her hamlet.

The branch chief said, that's a very good thing, a "charity" (*kudoku*, a frequent term) to them. The benefits of this would continue to spread. It also constituted a service (*ekō*) to the ancestors and would compensate for her parents having died without doing good. Thus, she had taken her ancestors' place in doing good, because she had joined Kōsei-kai.

The woman remarked that some people had opposed the construction of the paddy, so it had been difficult. The branch chief replied that if there are opposing people, it helps one to make up his mind to act, and that it is more virtuous to achieve something against opposition.

The woman continued. While the paddy was being built, she had prayed every day at a *Jūnī-sama* shrine near her house, and often at a more distant *Fudō-sama* shrine about 6 km north. But she missed one night of praying and someone who had been injured building the paddy died; therefore, *kami* do exist. The branch chief continued: as with the Gautama Buddha's attainment of enlightenment, it was precisely because there had been opposition that she had been able to do something good. This experience had been an explanation to her of the nature of buddhahood. Her gratitude was insufficient. There are many people who suffer: people whose husbands die early, who have no children, who die miserable deaths. To enable these people to attain buddhahood (*jōbutsu suru*), she must perform charities.

There are no effects without causes. The theft incident had a cause: that she wasn't grateful. That she had been able to do what she did in building the paddy was due in part to her dead husband. She should accept the following "tie" from the branch chief concerning the theft. First was her lack of gratitude. Also, there probably was an ancestor who wanted more praying. She should think about it. Because the money had a connection with death and ancestors, ancestors probably had to do with its loss. Therefore, someone needed prayers more immediately than did the creditor. She should look again at her death register. At the December joint service she should pray for all ancestors honored by Kōsei-kai.

The next person to request counseling was Takagi Sanshirō, the fifty-year-old postman from Morita. He had recently boarded a bus and immediately had become nauseous although he usually didn't suffer from motion sickness. He had gone to a hospital but was told that his blood pressure was fine. What could it have been?

The branch chief, who had been murmuring understandingly, replied:

> It must be that you don't have enough blood. When a virtuous person eats, all the nourishment goes into his blood, but in your case, for lack of virtue, even if you eat well you don't get the good out of it. In the great life (*dai seimei*) of the universe, one must live a natural life. As you get old, you can't tax yourself with unreasonable activity. A human's body must be in harmony with the universe's great life, but it's difficult to realize that you're part of it. The thing that is sustaining your body is the ancestors, so you have to be grateful to them.

Even he, the branch chief, often forgot this when he was healthy. "The power of living is given by the spirits of the dead, so you've got to be grateful to the ancestors and gather merit by praying . . . that's what you should do." The branch chief's own mother, father, and grandfather had all died of anemia (*hinketsu*), and he felt it might be about his time, too. But he was spreading the teachings of Risshō Kōsei-kai and building up merit so that perhaps he would not die soon after all.

The third and last recipient of advice was eighty-year-old Mrs. Takagi, in apparent poor health, from the hamlet a few kilometers north of Yamanaka. Last month on the 16th, just a month ago, she had gone to visit a town some distance away and had come back the next day. The day after coming back, she had given morning tea to a workman at her house and suddenly had become dizzy. She had tried to go to a doctor but had only gotten as far as her neighbor's house and again had nearly passed out. She managed to support herself by holding on to a large rock. She called her neighbor and was taken to a doctor. She was given an injection and revived. She had long had high blood pressure but had been taking medicine for it all year round, so there was no reason for anything to happen. What did the ancestors mean to teach her with this spell of dizziness?

The branch chief, who knew the woman well, as he does most branch members, replied, "Isn't there something amiss, something you're not doing?" The woman replied that she hadn't gotten along with her parents, so she had concentrated on making her husband happy . . . but perhaps she wasn't doing this sufficiently? In fact, she admitted, she and her husband fought. Another woman asked, "How old are the two of you?" The elderly lady was eighty, and her husband eighty-two . . . her husband was weak and in bed most of the time . . . he liked sake and drank one *shō* (almost 2 l) every three days.

The branch chief suggested that some ancestor might have come for his annual memorial service (*nenkai*) and not have been prayed to; she should look that up in her death register. It was also possible that there was someone "without surviving relatives" (*muen*) who was depending on her for prayer and not getting it; she should have her joint list of posthumous names (*sōkaimyō*) prayed for once. Her attack of dizziness had probably been because she was tired, but behind that probably was her failure to pray enough to the spirits of the dead.

At this, the woman remembered a recent event. Someone (apparently a friend) had slipped in her hot bath, been scalded, and died. Soon after, it was as if the old woman herself had been burned: her skin turned red, broke out in blisters, and itched. She had a posthumous name-slip written by Kōsei-kai and prayed to it at home and was cured. But it wasn't being prayed to by Kōsei-kai officers, so she thought perhaps that was the source of her dizziness. The branch chief agreed.

Analysis: Some themes and assumptions. Most major principles of Kōsei-kai doctrine (most shared by Sōtō Zen in Yamanaka, and some by secular hamlet culture as well) may be found in this meeting. They are comprehensive causality, the need for gratitude to ancestors and for self-reform (Hardacre [1986] sees self-reform as central to all the New Religions), the efficacy of prayer and offering, the interdependency of people, and the need for several levels of interpretation. Some of these are expressed only in passing, and others merely suggested, but all are implicit.

The most general principle is comprehensive causality, or karma, paraphrased by the branch chief: "There are no effects without causes." This is the first assumption upon which counseling, like other action, is based. There are no accidents, no events that cannot be explained.

Unexpected nausea, theft, and dizziness all are explicable in terms of other events; all have meanings. This comprehensive causality is not amoral or mechanistic like the causality of Western philosophical determinism, but moral and personal: the branch chief expects a long life because he is doing good works, and the woman's money was stolen because she was ungrateful to her ancestors. Nor is the causal link between moral action and reward only psychological or societal; it is, rather, built into the world at large. Humans are, as the branch chief indicated, "part of the great life of the universe." The elements of the universe all interact, and human society is continuous with the nonhuman world; they are a single system. Within it, actions such as charitable construction of paddy bring good results, and actions such as theft bring bad ones, to all concerned. If these results do not come directly, they come indirectly.

Comprehensive causality is most frequently expressed in relations of ancestors and descendants, and insufficient gratitude in descendants is the most likely cause of misfortune. Ancestors retain the teaching role they had as parents, which continues to benefit descendants. The woman whose money was stolen and the woman who suffered dizziness, for example, were being taught their lack of gratitude, as was the man with nausea: the "thing that is sustaining your body is the ancestors, so you must be grateful to them."

Prayer is effective partly because it is a means of self-reform and partly because it is desired by ancestors. Not only one's own ancestors, but other spirits of the dead, if they lack descendants, may cause trouble to get attention. The identity of an ancestor wanting prayer may be established by scrutinizing one's death register for neglected persons. If it cannot be established, services may be performed for all spirits of the dead at once.

All people, living and dead, are interdependent, and not merely within a single generation or between two generations of a household. Enmity (or amity) "continues through the generations." Within one generation, theft or benevolent construction of paddy affects not only the principles but people around them as well.

Last, there are several levels of causality. The old woman's dizziness had probably come because she was tired, but behind that was her failure to pray enough. Similarly, the theft suffered by the other elderly lady was caused by her lack of gratitude and also her failure to pray. The man's nausea, since it was not caused by high blood pressure, probably was caused by insufficient blood, inability to get nourishment from food, overexertion, lack of identification with the great life of the universe, and ingratitude. Immediate causes of unfortunate events—as with Evans-Pritchards' Azande—are not ignored, but neither are they sufficient.

Winter Ascetic Exercises

Winter ascetic exercises (*reikan shugyō*) are held each morning at six o'clock from January 22-26. They are intended to strengthen self-discipline and to pay respect to ancestors. More rigorous and ecstatic exercises, for people with stamina and time, are held simultaneously at the church.

In outline the ascetic exercises are like the five monthly memorials, but there are several differences. First are the hour and the cold. At six o'clock it is still dark outside and below freezing. It is barely above freezing inside since the only heat other than the enclosed hearth is from charcoal in a ceramic jar (*hibachi*) instead of the usual small kerosene space heater. It is an hour earlier than most people get up in winter. Second, a longer part of the sutra is read, taking an hour instead of half an hour. Because this part is unfamiliar, most people other than the leaders read in low halting voices and have only the most general sense of the meaning of the text. (If asked, they say that the event as a whole is an ascetic exercise. Hideo said that in principle everyone should stay afterward for an explanation, but in fact, they go home.) The only offerings in the altar are flowers because breakfast rice has not yet been cooked and because this exercise emphasizes the living, not the ancestors.

Activities away from the Meeting Place

Away from the meeting place, members' activities include service before their own altars, visits to the church, trips to national headquarters, charity work, proselytizing, and reading Kōsei-kai publications.

Service at the Home Altar

The service before the home altar can be given adequately by one member of each household. He or she places freshly cooked rice, tea, and water on the altar in the morning and reads the sutra morning and evening. This should take about twenty-five minutes. In fact, however,

Church officers and members, wearing their devotional sashes, chant a sutra to begin winter ascetic exercises in the Ueno Church.

only a few people say that they read the text in full. Most abbreviate it, reciting only the refrain, "Hail to the Sutra . . ." or reading it only once a day.

Visits to the Church

Every member should make at least one trip to the Ueno Church each month for a more elaborate memorial service. Members should also go to the winter ascetic exercise in Ueno (where it lasts all night and often culminates in trance) once a year. However, in Kawa Region only about a dozen people, less than 10 percent of roughly 150 in good standing, go to the church each month, and about the same number go to the ascetic exercises.

Trips to National Headquarters

Every member is expected to make at least one trip a year to national headquarters in Tokyo, where the concentration of wealth, leaders, and impressively large and lavish architecture visibly represents Kōsei-kai's success. Participation in these trips is closer to official expectations than is church attendance. Just over half the active members in Kawa Branch go each year, despite the cost of Y4,000, which is the main obstacle for people who do not.

For those who go, the trip to the headquarters is the high point of the Kōsei-kai year. The six and a half hour journey, made by the entire branch in two big chartered buses in two expeditions each year, is well organized, and people are enthusiastic. The travelers introduce themselves one by one over the bus loudspeakers and sing Kōsei-kai songs. The buses arrive about noon. The next twenty-four hours is a round of prayers, tours of buildings, counseling, inspirational films of lives of members, and lectures, broken only by eight hours of sleep in two communal halls, one for men and one for women.

The visitors' first stop is the "Great Sacred Hall" (daiseido), one of three monumental, ornate buildings[46] in the middle of the headquarters complex. The building centers on a large worship hall facing the "principle image" (gohonzon), a carved and gilded wooden statue, 10 m tall, of Śākyamuni, the Gautama Buddha. The visitors pray a few minutes and hurry on to tour the "Hall of the Open Gate" (fumonkan), an even larger and more lavish building centered on a lecture hall for 5,000. Both buildings are showy displays of traditional Buddhist motifs, modernistic

Inducing trance in "winter ascetic exercises" at the Ueno Church.

aluminum and glass, and technology, including environmental systems run by computer. The visitors spend the rest of the afternoon in counseling groups led by headquarters advisors with expertise sufficient to overcome otherwise recalcitrant problems. They dine in the "Great Dining Hall" of the Great Sacred Hall and end the day in a large opulent bath in the visitors' dormitory.

They begin the next day by reciting the Lotus Sutra from six to seven o'clock in the main worship hall of the Great Sacred Hall, under the great dome. The main floor of the hall is usually filled to capacity by members of ten or twelve churches from various areas of the country. The service begins with quiet drama. Curtains slowly part before a broad, elevated stage bearing an altar and the great Buddha image, revealing a rich tableau of bright and muted colors. Lanterns, candles, and floodlights illuminate flowers, *bonsai* pines, bronze offering vessels, velvet drapes, marble surfaces, and the gilded Buddha. Five officers file to their seats on stage facing the statue and lead a slow, resounding mass recitation of the sutra.

The service ends at seven o'clock, and everyone goes downstairs for breakfast in the Great Dining Hall. The visitors spend the morning and part of the afternoon hearing talks and seeing films in the vast luxurious auditorium of the Hall of the Open Gate. There are newsreels of conventions at headquarters and of President Niwano meeting foreign dignitaries, films of the difficult but rewarding lives of members, and readings, such as a poem in which a young woman recounts her discovery of filial piety through Kōsei-kai. The presentations are multimedia and highly polished. President Niwano appears on the screen and in photographs on the walls, but not in person.

Lunch is followed by a few more talks by headquarters speakers and departure for home at three-thirty. The return, too, is convivial, with Kōsei-kai songs and individual encomiums on the visit over the bus public address system.

Proselytizing, Charity, and Reading

Other activities, none taking more than a few hours a month, are proselytizing, charity collections, and reading movement publications. Proselytizing (*michibiki*, "guidance") officially is one of the most important duties and the principal basis for appointment to office, but most members in Kawa Region have long since run out of fresh audiences. In the mid-1950s, the years of rapid expansion in Kawa Mura, a small core of people were enthusiastic missionizers. In Yamanaka almost no

Members pray at the Ueno Church's first outdoors All Souls' Festival.

household escaped repeated enjoinders from Hideo and his adoptive mother-in-law. These two even now sprinkle conversations with the benefits of membership. However, although every member reports attempting to make converts, most do not like it and say that they have done less in recent years. People in nonmember households also say that attempts to convert them once were continuous, but that most members now had given up.

Although few if any households have escaped proselytizing, some get more attention than others. Households with someone in chronic poor health receive markedly more missionary visits, but almost any misfortune, such as a fire or an auto accident, may be interpreted by Kōsei-kai members as a call for improved ancestral relations. If a household has several mishaps in a row, it is sure to get renewed appeals. Proselytizing also seems more frequent, and more causal, with kin and neighbors than with others.

Kōsei-kai's attention to chronic problems may not extend, however, to chronic poverty. For example, an indigent and distracted woman of about fifty-five, the only person in the hamlet receiving government financial aid, is one of a very few households who seem never to be approached. This seems odd because she is a neighbor of the meeting-place household and, according to Hideo, comes to pray at its altar almost every day (this may have been an exaggeration, as I saw her there only once despite my very frequent presence). Hideo says that she is "uninterested" in joining, but it may be more that Kōsei-kai is uninterested in her. As one elderly member in the hamlet frankly said, "You've got to have money to be a member." Although dues are only Y100 a month, members cannot expect real benefits unless they have memorial tablets made and cared for at the meeting place, at Y1,000 a month. There are other costs as well. My elderly neighbor and the eccentric laborer (both of them out of the mainstream of hamlet life, and particularly plainspoken about religion) volunteered that Kōsei-kai is simply a money-making organization—apparently a common assessment in the hamlet, as it is of other New Religions elsewhere. In any case, although officers speak of taking contributions from richer members and giving them to the poor, I saw no evidence either of conversions or of redistribution among the poor in Kawa Region. Several times a year, however, Kōsei-kai does hold national charity drives, for which members gather money or old clothes. In the fall of 1971, for instance, a drive to collect clothes and funds for war relief in Viet Nam produced several hundred pounds of clothing in the Ueno Church area.

Reading Kōsei-kai publications is the activity to which people in Yamanaka give the least time, although most member households get at

Tug of war, Ueno Church Field Day, Ueno City.

least one of the three periodicals: the *Kōsei Gurafu*, a pictorial monthly, the *Yakushin*, a small monthly with inspirational stories and articles illustrating points of doctrine, and the *Kōsei Shinbun*, a weekly newspaper. These all are aimed at a general audience and discuss such problems of social relations as how to instill filial piety or scholastic discipline in one's children. The *Yakushin* seems generally conservative, and the *Gurafu* liberal, modern, and urban, so between them they appeal to a range of readers and suggest the movement's breadth. Like the headquarters complex, they convey not only Kōsei-kai's comprehensiveness but, by their sheer volume and glossiness, its size, power, and success. Nevertheless, subscriptions, though only about ¥300 a month for all three, appear to be more an obligation than a privilege. No one in Yamanaka except Hideo reads them frequently, and even the Kawa branch chief said that he had not read them regularly for years. Their influence is largely indirect, mostly through Hideo.

At headquarters there are additional activities. Dale (1975) reports that all members living in that area contribute services including cleaning, ushering, and food serving. Headquarters also holds sixteen annual public festivals, including New Year's, the birthday of President Niwano and the Buddha, and the anniversary of Nichiren's death, but members in Kawa Region take little or no note of them.

Summary

Risshō Kōsei-kai arrived in Kawa Village in 1947, and the first Yamanaka member joined six years later, at the start of a decade of rapid local and national growth. In the mid-1960s growth in Kawa stopped and a slight decline began, and membership now is more or less stable.

The mean age in the region in 1972 was about fifty. Sixty percent of members are women, and they are somewhat more active than are men.

Local organization is part of a national hierarchy. Below the Tokyo headquarters are churches throughout the country, including one in Ueno City. Churches are subdivided into branches and three levels of region, the smallest of which are hamlets. Leadership is professional at the branch level and above.

Facilities consist of a meeting place in each of the highest regions in each branch, a training hall at the church level, and the headquarters complex. The meeting place in Yamanaka serves a region with an official membership of 200 and an active membership of perhaps half that.

Most activities are conducted at the meeting place, the church, or the national headquarters. Most important and frequent are five monthly services and the counseling sessions following them. Meetings are held at all three levels, but members from Yamanaka and the vicinity usually go only to the meeting place, rarely to the church or to the head-quarters. But visits to the church and to the grand and imposing head-quarters are strongly encouraged. Trips to the headquarters are made en masse and are well designed to make an impression of organization, wealth, and modernity. Worship at home is similar to that of local Sōtō Zen but uses the Lotus Sutra and some Kōsei-kai paraphernalia.

The services are for Gautama Buddha and four other deities, including the cofounder of Kōsei-kai, and for the household dead, represented by name in a register in the meeting-place altar. Services consist largely in reciting part of the Lotus Sutra, with offerings of food and incense and gestures of respect. Following a service there usually is a counseling meeting at which members describe problems and receive "ties" or interpretations.

Problems usually concern health and domestic quarrels. Inter-pretations usually attribute problems to a flaw in the member's attitude or behavior, and the consequent displeasure of one or more ancestors, and recommend corrective measures. Measures aim at self-improvement, appeasement of the ancestors, and resultant alleviation of the symptom. They typically include increased diligence in prayer, requests to Kōsei-kai officers for services at the meeting place or church, and contributions of money or labor to Kōsei-kai undertakings. Perhaps most importantly, they include reflection upon one's own motives and behavior.

Chapter 6
Six Members and an Interpretation

Of the eleven active members in Yamanaka, six are noticeably more active than the others. They are a reasonable cross-section of the active minority in Kawa Mura, diverse individually and in their relations to the movement and the hamlet. Their participation in the movement ranges from full-time work and the evident commitment of household wealth to it, to occasional attendance at meetings coupled with skepticism of local leadership, to local distribution of its publications as an indication of support for a more active friend and relative. Their participation in the hamlet ranges from acting as hamlet chief, to abdication of a formerly active hamlet role for service to the movement instead, to chronic marginality to hamlet life. Their beliefs also vary, ranging from an interpretation of Kōsei-kai practice as psychological self-help, to belief in a spectrum of spiritual interventions in the affairs of the living.

Six Members

Kimura Hideo

Hideo, Kōsei-kai's first member in Yamanaka, joined in 1953 at the age of thirty-one. The only Kōsei-kai professional in the hamlet, he is important for understanding the movement's relation to its members and to the hamlet. He recruited most of the later members and may be largely responsible for their subsequent departure. Since joining, he has been the movement's most tireless advocate and the most ardent interpreter of its doctrine. He is head of the meeting-place household and during my initial stay was a member of the Ueno Church missionizing department. Just as that stay ended, he was made chief of a new branch, but even before this promotion he was pulled by loyalties to Kōsei-kai, on one hand, and to his household and hamlet, on the other. By my return in 1984, he had retired from Kōsei-kai work and was busying himself with four new grandchildren.

Vignette. Hideo, fifty at my first stay, is a vigorous man of medium height and powerful build, with wavy hair and an alert, wry, and self-deprecating humor. He is a published poet in two languages. He was a key informant, who spent perhaps more time with me than did anyone else, and in practical matters, such as papering the inside walls of our somewhat run-down house or digging out its toilet, he was unstintingly helpful and genial. Nevertheless, our relationship remained somewhat formal, and he remained somewhat guarded about his role in Kōsei-kai. His reserve was probably in part a result of my own ambivalence about Kōsei-kai, which, as I made known, was only one of the foci (if the chief one) of my study, and in part a result of his position between church and hamlet.

Hideo was born in 1922 in Morita, the hamlet immediately north of Yamanaka. He was the second son in the old and established household of Takada Tarō (Hideo's present surname, Kimura, is that of his adoptive household). His father was prominent in village politics, becoming chief of the village council in 1956 and mayor in 1960, and again in 1964, and receiving the Order of the Rising Sun from the emperor in 1967, shortly before he died, for his work for the village.

Hideo's schooling ended at sixteen when he was sent to Japanese-occupied Manchuria in an agricultural settlement scheme. He stayed for six years, learning Chinese well enough to publish poetry in it. In 1944 he was sent as a medical corpsman to the South Pacific, where he served mainly in Palau. He escaped being wounded, he says, by praying daily, and after the war returned safely to Morita. In 1948 he married into his present household in Yamanaka as the adoptive groom of a woman whose first husband had been killed in action a few weeks after her marriage.

His new household, according to other villagers including his son and mother-in-law, was of relatively low standing. It was new, having been founded three generations before as the only branch of another Yamanaka household of modest means and social position. It was plagued by bad luck, including physical and mental illness, and disasters. His wife's father had gone mad in 1926 and in 1932 had set fire to the house, burning it down and accidentally igniting the neighboring house of the now retired superintendent of education. The superintendent's house burned to the ground, and in trying to rescue its contents, his brother and two volunteer firefighters were killed. The arsonist was hospitalized and died in 1935. His sister, who remains in the household, has ever since been mute and semicompetent. His three sons and older daughter's husband were killed in the war. The daughter returned home and later married Hideo, who succeeded to the household. After the birth of the new couple's only son in 1949, she contracted peritonitis and was disabled by pleurisy for three years. At the same time her mother had severe asthma. According to another Kōsei-kai member in the hamlet (in an unconfirmed report), Hideo himself was troubled by excessive sexual desire.

In 1953 a school mate and friend (the postman who had complained of nausea at the counseling meeting) from Morita, the second person in Kawa Mura to join Kōsei-Kai, persuaded Hideo that the household's troubles stemmed from its immorality, principally that, in the words of another member, "they didn't have faith in (*shinkō suru*) the ancestors." The entire household joined and, on the independent accounts of Hideo, his wife, and her mother, took a rapid and lasting turn for the better. His wife recovered from her pleurisy, and her mother's asthma disappeared. Within two years Hideo was elected the first hamlet chief of Yamanaka under the democratized postwar village administration.

Hideo and his mother-in-law became the most ardent advocates of Kōsei-kai in Yamanaka and between them recruited most of the other twenty-seven people who joined. Hideo began to ascend a series of local Kōsei-kai offices: in 1954, *kanbu* ("leading member"); in 1958, chief of the new Ueno Branch Youth Division; in 1959, treasurer of the *hōza* (then equivalent to the present "branch") and first treasurer of the Ueno Branch; in 1961, again chief of the Ueno Branch Youth Division; in 1962, branch delegate to the North Kanto chapter of the Association of New Religions; in 1963, Youth Division delegate to national headquarters; in 1964, national headquarters' delegate from the Fourth Ueno *hōza*; in 1968, one of several administrators of the Ueno Branch; and in 1972, chief of a newly created branch of the Ueno Church. These posts varied in importance, and only the last two were paid. But Hideo took each seriously, as shown by their prominence in his yearly review of events in the household, hamlet, village, nation, and world, written (uniquely, he says) on the back of each year's Sun Goddess talisman when it is replaced by the next year's talisman.[47]

For ten years Hideo's religious career was accompanied by moderate success in secular hamlet affairs. As noted, he was first hamlet headman (not a powerful post, but still one requiring the confidence of the hamlet) two years after joining and was reelected in 1963 and 1964. He also served two terms on the board of the agricultural cooperative, a more powerful post than headman, and was an administrator in the village office.

After this, according both to him and to people in other households, Hideo's duties in Kōsei-kai began to pull him away from the hamlet, particularly since his appointment in 1968 to the Ueno administrative staff, when he began to spend most of his time out of the hamlet. At the same time, defections from Kōsei-kai in Yamanaka and an increasingly widespread view that the interests of hamlet and movement were in opposition led people to criticize Kōsei-kai and its alienation of Hideo from his duties as householder, *kumi* member, and hamlet member. Some say that Kōsei-kai is simply a money-making organization and that Hideo, though not a bad man, has been taken in by it. Hamlet criticism, perhaps intended to draw him back, seems instead to have been a wedge. His 1965 term as agricultural cooperative director was his last public post except for the minor one of *kumi* chief. During my time in the hamlet he was rarely home except for such labor-intensive occasions as rice transplanting, and in 1971 he came to only one of the three Shinto festivals. He spent even his nights more frequently at the church than in Yamanaka.

His son, with whom he is close and friendly, said that although some people know his father to be an idealist (*risō ka*), more people probably think that he's just a paid employee of Kōsei-kai, in it only for a wage. He felt that their household was not well spoken of: everyone comments favorably when another household repairs or replaces its roof, but when they did theirs, no one mentioned it. His father's father had been mayor of Kawa Mura, but people seemed to have forgotten that as well.

Beliefs. In Hideo's view, Kōsei-kai doctrines are rational and scientific, and when discussing them with me, he emphasized their similarity to natural law.[48] Of karma, for example, he said, "If you do something good, the result will be good. Good brings good; evil brings evil. I think that's the same in any country. It's like Mendel's law: red peas will produce red peas, white peas, white. One can think the same way about ancestors." He likened a Kōsei-kai system used to discover an individual's inherent traits from the syllables of his name and the names of his ancestors to the ABO blood system: personality traits, like blood types, are discrete, heritable, and subject to systematic investigation. (Hardacre [1984:92–93] notes a similar equation of karma and blood types in Reiyūkai.) When I asked him his opinion of the fireballs (*hidama*) some people still say manifest the departing soul after a death, he said, in a similarly secular vein, "Fireballs? They exist, all right. I've seen them myself. But they have nothing to do with spirits. They're just the gas given off when the body decomposes."

His accounts of why people join Kōsei-kai, and his eschatology, are also cast as much in a rather secular psychology as in theological terms. People join, he said, because of personal unhappiness and the realization that lasting happiness can be found only in helping others. People who join are concerned with suffering in human affairs. The solution to suffering, however, is in reform of self and society, not in another world. Indeed, there probably *is* no other world than the present one. Ancestors exist only subjectively: "After death, the spirit is in the hearts of the survivors . . . I don't think the spirit continues to exist out there in space, but only as an influence on the minds of the living . . . yes, one prays to the dead, but only to affect one's own spirit." Another time, when I asked what happens to the soul after death, he said, "They dig a hole and put you in it." He closed his eyes, tilted his head forward, and folded his arms across his chest in the old burial position. When one dies, one dies, and that is all. He added that this was still quite a way off, and laughed.

While Hideo stresses Kōsei-kai's concern for daily life rather than for an afterlife—in which he says he does not believe—he nonetheless gets occasional communications from the spirits in a way that suggests their separate existence. Once in the early 1960s, according to his son, he was cutting mulberry branches (for silkworms) in the field below his house and accidentally beheaded a snake. Soon after, his wife fell ill. He went to a medium in Morita to discover the cause of the illness and learned that it was the spirit of an old woman who had lived in the house down the hill and across the road, who had recently died. Her spirit had been in the snake he had killed and was now in a crow, flying restlessly. To cure his wife, he must plant a tree in the field in order to give the crow a perch. He did, and his wife was cured. Subsequently, he began to receive spirit communications directly. In another incident recounted by his son, Hideo was reciting a Buddhist prayer when he fell over in a swoon and began speaking in another voice. The voice belonged to a seventeen-year-old girl of a neighboring hamlet who had been raped and made pregnant; she had then committed suicide. Her voice named the rapist. After this there had been many such communications.

Hideo readily confirmed these communications, although he was reluctant to add detail or to assign them much importance. He said they occur about once a year. He has no forewarning, but they occur only when he is reciting the Lotus Sutra. Then he falls over senseless and the spirit speaks through him. The identity and message of the spirit, heard by whomever is with him, are difficult to interpret, but usually it is a friend or relative of the household. One was a member of the household: as a soldier he had been killed and had come to talk through Hideo to his mother. The mother (Hideo's mother-in-law, and with him one of the two great enthusiasts of Kōsei-kai in Yamanaka) was present when he and his son told me of this visit. Although no one seemed certain of the content of the communication, she clearly was happy with it.

Hideo represented himself as passive in these events since he can neither predict, control, or remember them. To illustrate, he threw up his hands suddenly, closed his eyes, exclaimed, "Whoops!" (*gaaa to!*) and fell over backward on the tatami. He sat up again with a smile and continued: there is no "religious" meaning in these communications; they are simply something that happens. However, it seems likely that they show him, to himself and others, as a privileged interpreter of the karma of other members. His access to the spirits may be modeled (as Earhart, personal communication, has suggested) on the trances of Myōkō-sensei. Although Hideo bases most of his interpretations (at counseling meetings or house calls) of members' troubles on doctrinal principles rather than on personal experience, he, like Kōsei-kai leaders elsewhere, makes no sharp division of principle and experience.

He also has such intuitive experiences as dreams, which are less than outright visits from spirits but more significant than waking thoughts. In the winter of 1972, for example, his mute, eccentric aunt and fellow householder was struck and injured by a car while walking on the highway at dusk. His mother-in-law told me that he dreamt the following night that the cause was neglect of the aunt's deceased former husband. On rising in the morning, she said, he had made a new memorial tablet for the husband and presented it with flowers at the altar of the Ueno Church. As a result, the aunt was making a good recovery. His capacity, then, for interpreting untoward events is not limited to doctrinal exegesis, on the one hand, and spirit possession, on the other, but is more general.

Hideo's ideas are complex. As noted, he thinks that the spirits of the dead exist only in memory, but he involuntarily receives communications from them as though they existed separately. Moreover, his interpretation of such events as illnesses and traffic accidents seems to vary with his audience. For example, when I asked why his aunt had been struck by the car, he said merely that she had been working late in the fields and had been tired. When I said that his mother-in-law had thought it was a matter of bad karma (a view she had attributed to him), he brushed the suggestion aside: "Well, that's the way grandma thinks." In general, interpretations he made to members seemed more extravagant and couched more in terms of ancestors and less in terms of natural science than those he gave me.

His professional relationship to Kōsei-kai seems complex as well, and difficult to assess. Although he is paid by it, he says that he also contributes to it, usually about ¥10,000 a month, or almost a quarter of the household's income. Since this income is barely adequate for the household budget without such a deduction, it is possible that he was selling household land, as rumored in the hamlet. His contributions have been partially offset by the ¥2,000 he receives monthly for supplying the meeting place and, more importantly, by ¥20,000 a month to defray travel and other working expenses. But this was insufficient for a living wage, and his household evidently was meagerly sustained by silk farming and his wife's seasonal work at a hotel at the hot-spring spa.

Then in January 1972 he was appointed chief of a new branch of the Ueno Church, with a monthly salary of ¥50,000. With this appointment it appears that his formerly straitened finances were bolstered to the point at which he could spend almost all his time on movement matters. This may have been his goal since he began in the mid-1960s: to transfer time, energy, and evidently a considerable part of his money from household and hamlet to Kōsei-kai. Some people in Yamanaka give this interpretation both to his activities and to Kōsei-kai professionalism generally. My elderly neighbor referred to Hideo as a "salaryman," or career white-collar employee, of Kōsei-kai even before his promotion to branch chief made this description financially plausible. Another resident, the eccentric laborer, refers to the movement as "Risshō Kōsei-kai, Incorporated," adding that like a corporation, it requires an investment from members before it pays dividends. In Kōsei-kai, he said, the dividend on a sufficiently large investment is that the member can become a salaried professional.

Some other people, however, have more benevolent views of Hideo and his relationship to Kōsei-kai. The man who likened it to a corporation added that Hideo was not at all bad but merely taken in. A Kōsei-kai member and hamlet resident, though critical of Hideo, sees him as altruistic if not quite willingly so, citing his extensive donations and inadequately compensated services. Most important, his son, who knows him well and seems objective enough, says that his father really is an idealist although many people do not know it.

Hideo himself explains his commitment as he does that of others, in terms of service to other people and the betterment of his own character. His statements about it seem carefully orthodox. He does not speak of money, either of his donations or of compensations for his work, although he once or twice alluded to his impoverished state. "Being of use to people," he says, "is the only way to real happiness." He says that his personality has improved since he joined: he used to have a bad temper and become angry on little provocation, but now he is even-tempered. He owes this, in a phrase he often uses, to Kōsei-kai's "magnificent teaching" (*rippa na oshie*).

Kimura Yūko: "Obaa"

Kimura Yūko, seventy-two, is Hideo's mother-in-law, adoptive mother, and fellow householder. She too joined in 1953, immediately after he did. "Obaa" ("Granny," to her household and to us), like Hideo, is vigorous and humorous, but unlike him she is blunt and forthright and seems to have a simpler relation to Kōsei-kai. Together they are its two loyal enthusiasts in Yamanaka.

Vignette. Obaa came to Yamanaka in 1917 as a bride of seventeen, from a village 20 km away. She soon had two sons and a daughter. Her ensuing life in Yamanaka was full of misfortune (partially described above for Hideo). Ten years after she came, her husband, whom she describes as suffering an "excess of righteousness," went mad. Six years later, when she was thirty-three, he burned the house down by setting its thatch afire. This ignited the neighboring house, burning it to the ground and killing the householder's brother and two hamlet firemen as they sought to save valuables. When she was thirty-six he was hospitalized; he died a year later. One of her husband's sisters had come home from an unhappy marriage and has been mute and chronically disheveled since the catastrophic fire. Obaa's sons all were killed in the war, as was her daughter's husband. Obaa herself began to suffer from asthma. Her daughter remarried (to Hideo), suffered a miscarriage, gave birth to a son, and contracted peritonitis and pleurisy, which lingered for three years. Obaa's only grandson suffers a chronic liver ailment.

Obaa says she joined Kōsei-kai because of her asthma. She had gone to a doctor without success, "So I thought I'd have to cure it by faith." Tenri-kyō, an older, Shinto-based New Religion to which she had belonged for fifteen years, had also failed her. "It's not a bad religion," Obaa says, "but they don't *understand* things. Kōsei-kai understands. If it's asthma, they can look at a person's heart (or spirit: *kokoro*) and understand the cause of his sickness." Persuaded, like Hideo, by the postman to try Kōsei-kai, she joined in the spring of 1953. By fall she was cured. "So I'm grateful. That's why I pray, might and main, every day. I really feel *very* grateful."

She is the usual keeper of the meeting place although Hideo officially is responsible. She spends half an hour morning and evening reciting the Lotus Sutra before the altar, arranges the offerings of fruit and vegetables, and is present at almost every meeting. She leads the chant in the winter ascetic exercises. With her unfailing good cheer, deep confidence in Kōsei-kai, and blunt candor, she is perhaps its most valuable proponent in the hamlet, at least since Hideo has withdrawn to the Ueno Church.

Beliefs. Obaa views joining Kōsei-kai, particularly Hideo's conversion and subsequent work, as a turning point in her own health and in household fortunes generally. "Our luck used to be bad," she said, listing their many misfortunes. "But now we're really happy. Papa [Hideo] has changed our luck by always doing things in Kōsei-kai . . . because he does Kōsei-kai work all the time, we're very fortunate now."

Obaa bundling rice seedlings for transplanting.

Hideo and Obaa chant an evening service at the meeting-place altar.

Obaa's belief in prayer and offerings to the ancestors is literal and untempered by the scientism that makes Hideo explain karma in terms of Mendel or limit the posthumous existence of souls to descendants' memories of them. Her world is full of ancestors and *kami*, which she says are the same. She is a repository of charms and incantations (*majinai*) for warding off snakebite, toothache, burns, and skin eruptions. Her incantation against snakebite, for example, is spoken before entering woods:

Kono yama ni
nishiki madara no
mushi araba
kaya tatsu
hime ni meguri aobeshi.

If on this mountain there are
any two-colored dappled vermin,
cut a miscanthus
and one may see
a princess.

Ancestors, although insubstantial, are for Obaa otherwise similar to living humans. For them to hear prayer, for example, it must be said slowly and clearly in a loud voice, as they may be distant. But their location cannot be specified because they are everywhere. "They're all over Japan, all over the world . . . in the air . . . they *are* the air. So they're in everyone, when you breathe. The one who discovered that was Śākyamuni, who taught us Buddhism and the Lotus Sutra." Although they are everywhere, the ancestors are concentrated in their memorial tablets. They are there year-round, she says, although some people think that they come home only at All Souls' Festival. They are also especially at the graveyard, where she visits them without fail on All Souls', New Year's Day, and the Spring and Autumn Equinoxes.

Her visits are more assiduous than those of other people. Early one New Year's morning, Obaa, Hideo, his son, and I were walking home in the dark after a bus had brought us from a midnight service at the Ueno Church, when Obaa suddenly disappeared. Then we heard her away from the road, stumbling through snow over a plowed field to the household graveyard to give the spirits a New Year's greeting. Hideo and Masatarō laughed sympathetically and said, "That's Obaa— diligent!"

Kimura Nami

Kimura Nami, a woman of sixty-five, joined Kōsei-kai in 1954, one of ten who joined within a year of Hideo and Obaa. Nami is head of the household from which Hideo's and Obaa's household had branched three generations earlier. She is a close friend of Obaa's, kindly and humorous like Obaa but more diffident, perhaps because of her near deafness. Our second nearest neighbor, she visited us almost daily with presents of food, usually a sample of something cooked for her own household. Her household is small, with only her unmarried son and senile father-in-law (the "mountain ascetic," chapter 4). Her husband died a number of years ago, and her daughters have since moved away.

Vignette. Nami, like Obaa, came as a bride from outside the hamlet. The household into which she married is in its eighth generation, but despite its respectable age it has no relatives in Yamanaka other than its single branch, the household of Obaa and Hideo. Moreover, it is said (at least by another Yamanaka Kōsei-kai member and by a member of its own branch) to be of low standing because of dissolute gambling two generations ago by the then head of the household, who lost most of its fortune. Although he tried to recoup, he had been unable to muster loans because he was not trusted by anyone in the hamlet.

Nami's household, though not as unfortunate as Obaa's, continued to have troubles in the present generation. Her husband suffered bad health and back pains for a number of years before he died in his mid-forties. He had first tried to find relief, on the advice of a local diviner, by sending the household's image of the fox god Inari-sama, who cares for house and grounds, to a major Inari shrine at Kasama to be prayed for. This was ineffective. Next he was persuaded by Hideo to join Kōsei-kai. He was diligent, prayed morning and evening, and stopped using abusive language, but his health did not improve. He died in 1955, a year after Nami joined. The children were still small. Nami too was weak then, although she is now strong enough to work long hours in the fields. Though not given to talking about herself or complaining, she says quietly that in those years she "really suffered, I tell you." Her health is better now, but she still feels the frustration and boredom of deafness, and concern for her son, twenty-seven, who suffers from boils.

Nami is not only nearly deaf but also illiterate, rare in the hamlet. She did not graduate even from primary school. Her hearing has been poor since childhood, when she says her ears hurt constantly and she cried all the time. Now there is an operation for it, but the doctor says it is too late because "it's all turned to stone in there." In her youth she

Nami feeds mulberry leaves to silkworms.

had tried another remedy: like others with ear problems, she pierced a hole in a shallow sake cup (roughly the proportions of an ear) and offered it with raw rice at the little shrine of a deafness-curing *kami* in the mountain above the hamlet. This had not helped. Later she joined Kōsei-kai, at her husband's request and in the hope of curing her asthma, and had asked their advice about her ears. They suggested a solution, but, she said wryly, being hard of hearing she could not understand it.

Beliefs. Nami's attitude toward Kōsei-kai, quite unlike that of her close friend Obaa, is noncommittal acceptance with occasional irreverence. She calls herself an "unbeliever" (*mushinjin*), apparently meaning indifference as much as disbelief. But she feels that Kōsei-kai has a good effect on the personality of members, making them kinder˙ than other people. It is also good for one's health: "If you follow Kōsei-kai, your body will be sound . . . Tarō [her son] has never even had a cold."

Nonetheless she never goes to meetings, to the Ueno Church, or to the Tokyo headquarters, though she otherwise spends a great deal of time with Obaa, the meeting-place keeper. She does not go to meetings because: "If you're meek (*sunao*), and say 'yes, indeed,' and so on, it's fine . . . but I'm not meek and don't have the time and money." She does not even perform the basic service, reading the Lotus Sutra before the household altar. Instead, she serves Kōsei-kai members in Yamanaka by distributing the weekly and monthly publications, which she gets from a distributor for the district. And, despite the lack of apparent benefits, she pays Y500 (then about $2.00) a month in dues and contributions. This seems to be continued gratitude for the curing of her asthma some twenty years before, an investment in future health, and, just as importantly, support for her good but more devout friend Obaa.

Nami, then, though she is considered and considers herself a member in good standing, is really committed neither to doctrine, to ritual, nor to counseling sessions. Rather, her dues and distribution of Kōsei-kai materials seem to be a means of showing solidarity with her branch household, her only relatives and closest friends in the hamlet.

Mori Sayoko

Mori Sayoko, a woman in her early sixties at my first stay in the hamlet, also joined Kōsei-kai in 1953, less than a year after Hideo and Obaa. She and Obaa are now the two people from Yamanaka who unfailingly attend meeting-place functions.

Vignette. Like Hideo, Obaa, and Nami, she is not a native of Yamanaka but came to the hamlet as a young adult. Unlike them, however, she is not married to a native. Her husband comes from the nearby hamlet with the hot-spring spa and, unlike most Yamanaka people, is not even a part-time farmer. For several years he was an unskilled worker for Tokyo Electric at several small hydroelectric plants in the area. After the war he became a taxi driver in the larger hamlet of Morita. The household's status in the hamlet is thus thrice prejudiced, by being outsiders, by lowly occupation, and by the location of their work outside the hamlet.

For forty-four years the Moris lived in Yamanaka in a small house rented from the communal property association. They saved their money, putting nothing into the somewhat ramshackle house, and late in 1970 moved (which fortunately left the house available just as my wife and I arrived) into a new house of their own in the nearby hamlet, near its border with Yamanaka.

The new couple had no kin in Yamanaka or neighboring hamlets, other than the husband's parental household in the hamlet with the spa. This was unusual: the only other households in Yamanaka without kin in the hamlet are those of the policeman and forestry officer, who are rotated from area to area. The Moris' lack of kin apparently was uncompensated by close relations with people in their *kumi*, although they were at least admitted to it, a status withheld from new households for a generation in some areas. The only households with which they seem to have become friendly in forty-four years are those of their fellow Kōsei-kai members Obaa and Nami.

Their evident lack of close relationships in the hamlet may be attributed in part to being outsiders without kin, in part to Mori's low-status work outside the hamlet (only people who work within it, preferably as farmers, are considered to participate fully), and in part to their reticent and unobliging manner—perhaps an effect as well as a cause of their situation. In any case, Sayoko, much the more active of the two in Kōsei-kai, is dour and says little except within the circle of members. Among members, however, she is talkative and even dogmatic.

Sayoko says that she was converted by Hideo. She had rheumatism (she also called it "nervous rheumatism": *shinkeitsu ryōmachi*) at the time. "I couldn't move my legs, and I couldn't move my hips—so this group—I was told to join it by Hideo's household—and now I'm like this [i.e., cured]." Before joining she had gone to a doctor. "But I didn't get any better. Then the Instructor [Hideo] told me that since there was this group for praying to the ancestors, if I joined it and prayed to the ancestors, I would get better, so I joined." Her rheumatism

Sayoko and another Kawa Branch member polish candlesticks as a "service" (*kuyō*) at the meeting place.

soon disappeared. At the same time, however, she had heart, liver, and gall bladder trouble: "I was *totally* sick!" Her illness lingered for seven or eight years, and she was hospitalized three times. She finally recovered thanks to the combined efforts of doctors and Kōsei-kai.

Beliefs. The "blessings" (*kudoku*) she has received are global, including benefits to health, family relations, personality, and miraculous avoidance of accidents. All these begin with good relations with the ancestors and depend on understanding their messages. Her blessings include being able "to hear what the spirits of the dead say, to live happily without fighting with my husband, and having sickness cured." When Sayoko counts her blessings, her reticence disappears.

Our household has really received a lot. About the time I joined, my husband had a car that he used to take along the old road. But one day the car just wouldn't move. It had gas and it had oil and there wasn't anything wrong with it at all, but it just wouldn't go. So he came home, and another person took the car and went—and ran over a child. The car my husband was supposed to take wouldn't go, so he gave up, and another person took it and ran over somebody with it. So the ancestors—from the point of view of Kōsei-kai—when my husband—it could be anyone, but since *he's* praying—the ancestors had said, "It's dangerous to go today, so you mustn't go!" You can't hear the ancestors speak in words, so they gave him the message by keeping the car from going. If the car had gone, my husband would have had the accident. We receive a *lot* of things like that.

And then—nowadays, it's done with chain saws, but in the past, my husband—now we have electric hearths like this, but then, great big hearths made a lot of business for wood-cutters, you know. So people had to go to the forest to cut wood. And he cut wood for a number of people. The trees were really tall and big around, and there was no way to pull them back that way, so they were slid down from above. So they'd be slid from point to point on the mountain. My husband and the others, as soon as they'd pitched one down, would call, "Watch out!" And no sooner than one had been pitched than it would come flying, they say. So if you had bad luck, you couldn't dodge and protect yourself. Against an accident, you know? There was no way to escape. So when my husband goes to a place like that he makes sure to pray at the bottom of the hill. So even though he goes to such really dangerous places, he's always saved by that. We've received *that* kind of blessing, too.

But not only that, but having money, or anything, is the same way. But really, that time with the car . . . So our household . . . really . . . the ancestors averted my husband's disaster by preventing the car from moving. Instead of my husband's doing it, another person in his place did it. There are lots of things like that. So people in Kōsei-kai, on average, get a *lot* of blessings. There are so many one can't even know them all.

I joined Kōsei-kai in Shōwa 28 [1953] and received the collective death register, where the souls of ancestors of the Mori household are put, from headquarters. I put it up. Nowadays, to make a "visit of thanks," it's fine just to go to the Ueno Church, but at that time you had to go to head-quarters. At the time, my husband said, "You should go to headquarters to give thanks." But I'd never been to a place like Tokyo, so I couldn't go alone. My own home was in Murano, you know. Our [daughter] Ake-chan was about to become a first-grader and I was going to buy her book satchel, her knapsack, in Fukuoka, so my father said, "Come home." So instead of making a visit to headquarters, I went to my own home. At that time I was carrying our [son] Masao. Well, I came back from Murano really loaded with the knap-sack and shoes and clothes and stuff bought for me, and my stomach was hurting and hurting, so that I couldn't even move like this. So I went to have the doctor have a look at it. He said it was an extrauterine pregnancy. He said it would require an operation. Well, that would have cost ¥3,000— ¥7,000 . . . I tell you, Mr. Guthrie, it would have been terrible, in those days when the yen was worth what it was. So I went running over to the house of the present Instructor. When I did, he said, "Mrs. Mori, why don't you always come over here?" So I said, "Well, I don't always come over here, but my husband told me, 'Go give thanks at headquarters'; but I couldn't go to headquarters by myself, and since my father said, 'Come to Murano and we'll buy you some things' . . . so, well, I went to Murano." "That's it!" he said. "It's because you aren't grateful to your forebears. Really, headquarters, more than Murano—you should have gone to your own home on your way back from headquarters. Instead of going to headquarters, out of your own desire—because if you went to Murano your parents would buy you things—to your forebears—you didn't have gratitude. So because you weren't grateful to your forebears the baby didn't enter the place it was supposed to but came out as a misfortune." That's what he told me, the present Instructor, you know? I thought, "That's it, I'm really sorry." And I prayed, "Forgive me." And when I did, Mr. Guthrie, the pain in my belly stopped. And then I went to the doctor and had him look again. And he said, "Auntie, it's really strange, but now there's nothing wrong at all."

That sort of thing happens, you know . . . and the child was born perfectly satisfactorily. He only weighed half an *ikkanme* . . . just 500 *me* [just over four pounds]. So his head, or his face, was *this* small. But, Mr. Guthrie, he graduated from school without ever *once* going to a doctor. Even though he was such a small child.

So . . . well, people who don't believe in the Law may say that's stupid talk, but for people who do believe in the Law, in fact, there are many things of that sort, certainly.

For Sayoko, self-help by reforming one's own attitude and character are as important to happiness as prayer. Reform often means self-abnegation.

For instance, someone says, "We're always having domestic quarrels. What should I do?" She'll be told, "It's probably because you're hard-headed [*tsuyoi*, 'strong'] and don't yield to your husband. Your husband is master of the house . . . as the bread-winner, he's the master. You've got to yield to him in everything whatsoever, or it's no good."

Sometimes the person hears the advice and still doesn't like it, and it's no good . . . but generally, if you follow it, it will change your mind. In the case of hurting legs, they'll say, "You don't use them enough . . . they're there to be used. You should walk on your hurting legs to the houses of believers and do something to make them feel happy." It's the same for hurting hands: "You should use them and join hands with believers."

Analysis. Sayoko's account shows four typical Kōsei-kai assumptions: that there are communications from ancestors, which require identification and interpretation; that these often are warnings and punishments, especially regarding obligations to ancestors; that warnings protect against accidents and illness; and that every event has meaning. Because "you can't hear the ancestors speak in words," you must look at all unusual events for messages. The car's failure to start was not only a means by which the ancestors could divert an accident but also a message that driving would be dangerous. The extrauterine pregnancy was not only a punishment but also a notice that she was lacking in gratitude. As long as one is virtuous and careful to remember the ancestors with prayer and offerings, one will be protected. No sickness or mishap simply "happens."

These themes are those most frequently repeated at counseling meetings: ancestors have an active interest in descendants; they manifest it in observable events; and all events have meaning. To discover the meaning of personal or household problems, one needs the Law, and having discovered it, one needs to act. Action both reforms one's own attitudes and helps others; both aims satisfy ancestors, whose help depends in part on self-help.

Sayoko, perhaps more generally than other members discussed so far, bears out my original expectations about members, with her poor health, lack of kin, and low status. She is very active in Kōsei-kai, present at virtually every local meeting and the treasurer for the meeting place. Most of her friends are members. Through the movement she finds not only health and friendship but also pattern and meaning in the world at large. Even in such seemingly impersonal events as a car's failure to start, she sees the ancestors at work.

Matsumoto Masao

Masao, seventy and in poor health during my first stay in Yamanaka, was persuaded by Hideo to join in 1960, after his wife's death. He died shortly before my return in 1977. He contrasts in a number of ways with the other members described.

Vignette. No newcomer to Yamanaka, Masao belonged to a household that is either the oldest (on his account) or the second oldest (on the contender's account) in the hamlet. In either case, his household is one of the four founding households and has been in the hamlet for sixteen generations. It has connections of marriage or descent with most others in the hamlet and many in neighboring hamlets. Its status seems fairly high, even though it is now of modest means and though Masao's eldest son, already head of the house in 1972, is not a full-time farmer but a driver of a lumber truck.

Another contrast is that Masao, although formally educated only through primary school, was impressively well informed. He was conversant with local, prefectural, and national politics and experienced in a number of village administrative posts. He was a good conversationalist, being a careful listener and an articulate and open speaker. He was also better traveled than most members, having traveled widely within Japan and once or twice abroad.

Masao also seemed atypical in his relations with other members. As group chief (*kumi-chō*) for the hamlet, he nominally was the principal administrator in Yamanaka, but he had little to do with other members and rarely came to meetings. Although he said that he went to the meeting place once a month for the memorial for Myōkō-sensei, I never saw him there; perhaps he came and left very early. He went occasionally to the Ueno Church and to the headquarters, but he seemed aloof from members in the hamlet. His aloofness may simply have reflected his personal and social differences from them, but perhaps it also reflected the mild dislike of many people for Kōsei-kai. Masao was made group chief, he said, in the hope that as a community leader he would attract new members. This was not successful. Instead, his friends told him that they could not understand his joining and urged him to quit. Unlike the members described above, he was not joined by the rest of his household. His son, thirty-seven at the time of my first stay, his daughter-in-law, and their two small sons remain members only of the Sōtō Zen temple.

Masao was reticent about his reasons for joining. He related them in general, abstract terms, first as a capsule history of Japanese Buddhism and of Kōsei-kai, stressing social service.

> Well, it's this way. Kōsei-kai's methods, you know—the forefather in Japan came from China—there was Śākyamuni, you know? Then Buddhism came over to Japan. And gradually—it's a small country, but gradually—Japan developed it. People today are free to misunderstand it, and since the war they have failed to look back to *kami* and the ancestors, around here. But after all, in this country, in order for everyone to live in a spirit of cooperation, no matter what, it's not good to forget parents and it's no good to forget the nation. So because there was such imbecility, President Niwano wondered what he himself could do to keep parents in

mind and generally what would be good for society. So with
that in mind, first of all he went around here and there,
joining different groups. But as it turned out, there wasn't
anything like Kōsei-kai then. There are seventy-four
religious organizations in Japan. Among these Kōsei-kai is
the truest. So thinking this, he created Kōsei-kai's way of
doing things and has been spreading it throughout the
country. So when I found out about its creation and heard
talk about it and thought, "Well, Kōsei-kai's way is pretty
good, isn't it," I joined too. It's definitely not a bad thing.

Masao here echoes Kōsei-kai's view of itself as not new but a
revival of fundamental Buddhism.[49] He mentions Buddhism's arrival in
Japan to suggest Kōsei-kai's historic depth and to contrast this with the
secular postwar period. The social goal he cites, "for everyone to live in
harmony," also is official doctrine.

Beliefs. Pressed about his reasons for joining, Masao said he joined
to serve his ancestors. Asked whether he couldn't have served them
through Eizōji, the established temple, he said,

From Kōsei-kai you can get explanations about disciplining
one's spirits. But from Eizōji it's only when somebody dies, at
the funeral, that the priest gives explanations. Kōsei-kai
gives explanations month by month. That was what made me
think it was a good thing at any cost, to start my mental
discipline by serving the ancestors.

Asked the kinds of explanations, he said,

It's a matter of household tranquility. To have harmony in a
given household, no matter what, if there's not just one
person who is the leader [evidently a reference to conflict with
his daughter-in-law] then in everyday matters day after day,
if your attitude isn't right, there won't be harmony. In
explaining things like that, Kōsei-kai is more precise than the
temple priest.

What Masao wanted, then, was advice on self-reform for domestic tranquility. "Serving the ancestors" was a means to self-reform, and in turn
domestic tranquility is pleasing to ancestors.

Although Masao felt that he was getting the benefits he expected and that Kōsei-kai's teachings are "true," he was openly concerned at the expense of membership (a complaint often made about other New Religions as well[50]). In agreement with the hamlet's critics of Kōsei-kai, he says that its requirements for money are the chief reason for its decline.

Problems. A few weeks before my departure in 1972, Masao talked about the problem of money and Kōsei-kai's local fortunes in several long discussions of a local leader, Matsumoto Fusao, and his precarious position. He expressed several common assumptions and attitudes about Kōsei-kai's place in the hamlet and about the officer's predicament. One assumption is that real piety is not an obstacle to household prosperity but a means to it. Martyrdom for faith is not expected. On the contrary, personal or household failure are signs of impiety, or piety misconstrued, since the blessings of a true teaching (*tadashii oshie*) are tangible as well as spiritual. Masao thinks that people are empirical about Kōsei-kai: they watch member households to see whether members prosper and decide accordingly whether or not to join. Fusao's household did not prosper, and this in part accounts for Kōsei-kai's decline.

Unlike nonmembers, however, Masao blames Fusao's problems not on Kōsei-kai's demands for money but on Fusao's failure to recognize his own limits. The faith (*shinkō*) of Kōsei-kai is powerful and rewarding but also demanding, especially of its leaders. A leader must be a person of strength, of "learning and experience" (*gakushi keiken*), and of some financial means as well. Ambition without these is arrogance and will meet with failure. Ominously for Fusao, there seems to be no turning back for him, in Masao's view. Once one has become a leader, his course is set. Fusao would like to step down, Masao said, but is not allowed to by the headquarters, which warns of worsened karma if he quits.[51] I had begun the discussion by asking what effect joining had had for Fusao.

> To tell the truth, their wealth has dwindled away. Because they don't have the income, after all. This Risshō Kōsei-kai thing, you know, when you really come to believe, the money they collect comes to quite a lot. That's why so few people join. When you get to be an officer, it's unbearable: "Now, there's such-and-such, so pay so-and-so much; now there's such-and-such, so pay so-and-so much." It comes to this sort of thing. So if you have the income for it, you can keep on. But no matter whose household it is, if you're just doing physical labor, you don't have the income. So if it's a

household with property, they sell the property and they pay. *That's* unbearable, really.

At the [Sōtō Zen] temple, once a year there's a report of the balancing of the books; for maintenance, costs are collected from everybody, and it's no trouble. But with Kōsei-kai it's every month, every month. So it's mainly a matter of collecting money all the time, you know.

G: And the money is—

M: Sent to headquarters. Unbearable.

G: So Fusao sold his property, and the money—

M: Sent it to headquarters.

G: Do even ordinary members have to do that?

M: Yes. Yes . . . demands come, you know! They come, but look: any money that's left over after securing one's own life, I'll give it; but if it unsettles one's own life, I can't. So over there [at Fusao's] even though they believe, if they don't watch out it'll be bad. As for me, in my heart I have exactly the same faith, but . . . when it comes to sending money to headquarters beyond one's income, it becomes an impediment to one's life. So finally people with property have to sell it. Therefore faith is really troublesome! It's all right to have faith as long as it doesn't upset one's own life, but . . . And now, in order to have something to send to keep headquarters from complaining, if there's no income, in order to pay a household with property has to sell it and send the money. That's why that person is in a serious way. If he could become an officer with say ¥40,000 or ¥50,000 a month, he'd be okay, but officers below that are in trouble. If he could produce it without resorting to *that* [selling property], it would be all right in the long run, but no one at all is capable of that. That's why everyone says that household's in trouble.

G: About how much have they paid?

M: Well, let's see . . . it would have been about ¥300,000 that he's sent to headquarters, wouldn't it . . . it seems he paid quite a bit, three or four times. Someone like the Kadoya [gas station] household, they've paid about ¥300,000 too, but they have the income for it. So since they have the income, there's some left over from living expenses, and they pay with the excess, so it's not the same; they're not in trouble. If it's the average farmer, it's very—it's impossible.

Fusao, you know, only makes ¥20,000 a month, definitely . . . and it's a little expense here and a little there . . . so it's not enough. It takes ¥10,000 for Kōsei-kai. And in addition, quotas come from headquarters: "Now, you've got to do such-and-such." So in all, they're having trouble making ends meet.

 G: So he doesn't mean to quit?

 M: No—once you've started, you can't stop. When you've got to that point, you can't quit.

 G: Why can't he quit?

 M: He's not permitted by headquarters. Wouldn't be allowed to. So it's really bad.

 G: But—isn't one free in that sort of thing?

 M: One may be "free," but if he quit, far from profiting, things would get worse with him—that's what they say.

 G: What would get worse?

 M: His life. "It will get even worse!" they say.

Here I asked the difference between Kawa Region and the neighboring region, where membership was still growing.

 M: Well, now—it'd be bad to say to Fusao—but . . . Fusao's leadership is, you know . . . inadequate.

 As I was saying before, it's money, money, every month, every month. Because it's that way, everyone quit . . . to keep saying "money, money" doesn't lead to faith, in my opinion. Really, he can't say that sort of thing to people like me. So there are hardly any households now—Kadoya and myself— at Kadoya's, it's two people, isn't it?—and after that, it's just [Nami's father-in-law's] household. All the others quit. Just before I joined, they'd been joining right along.

Here we listed, together, seven former member households including four farming households, a tatami maker, and a truck driver.

 M: They all quit. So Kōsei-kai's showing here is really bad. It's in trouble. There have even been various warnings from headquarters.

 So that's why this way isn't bad, either: the prescribed amount is ¥100 a month, and then ¥100 for good measure, and then, even if a quota comes, only if you feel you've got an excess, it's all right to pay. Doing it that way, and *not* quitting, is best. So that's why in my case, if we don't have a lot of money and if what we have is necessary for the household, if I insisted on paying it, there'd be trouble with my daughter-in-law. That's why it's no good when he says things like, "The superiors—they say it's bad if we don't recruit more people." He says, "This and that is good, it would be good if you join, so join! Join!" Instead of that, if one just let people look and think, "Yes, indeed—that household joined Kōsei-kai and they got better," and understand that way, it would be good.[52] But if after joining, one gradually gets worse and worse, no one will want to come and no one will join.

That's what I meant when I said his leadership is bad. When things are like this, it's necessary to follow the ancestors, but I can only do as much as possible. It's not necessary to go to unreasonable lengths. "Don't strain yourself"; "Just this much money, just this much"; "If it's spare money, give it"; "Don't give to the point of having to borrow; don't do that sort of thing; only give what you can"—that's what the upper-level leaders say. Yes, at headquarters. That's why it's bad that I haven't been going to headquarters much. You're supposed to go all the time, again and again, they say. But I haven't been going much, and that's why Fusao has been after me; but though he's been after me, it's not right. Getting yourself into trouble—one doesn't have to go *that* far. So that's why if it isn't someone of adequate learning and experience, this faith can be very troublesome. To be in it. Really! If it isn't someone who knows his strength, to join it can be bad. If you do, it will use up your wealth. If you use up your wealth, people will think, "Oh, awful!" and get out.

That's why it's bad if you don't have the strength to use the power of the faith and make a livelihood *and* provide leadership for people. So if you don't know where your strength and learning and experience lie, and yet you try to lead people, they'll all leave. It's a big problem. That's what people like me have been telling Fusao, but when we do, he just says, "That's no good."

When you join the leadership, it's really troublesome, you know.

G: And he's been warned by headquarters?

M: Yes, yes. It's no good.

G: Will it get better now that he's been warned?

M: I hope it will, but . . . his way of doing it wasn't good from the first, you know.

G: But didn't quite a few people join?

M: The people who joined—the way it is, you pay ¥100 and the ¥100 dues, each month—they stopped paying it. Those people Fusao converted—when they stopped, he wasn't able to report it to headquarters. If he had, his record would have been bad. So without saying anything, he sent the money himself to headquarters.[53] So since he's paying people's money, he's in trouble. If he hadn't, and had sent a report that the number of members had dropped off, the position of leadership that he'd risen to so far would have been lost. Then his relation to headquarters would've been pitiful. But though headquarters has the names of those members, those members don't give anything. That's the way it is. That's why he's in trouble. He's suffocating, and things are bad. . . . He has risen steadily . . . now, take the Ueno Church, if he were first in command there, it would be all right. Then, if people didn't pay, it would be taken care of by headquarters. And then he'd be getting ¥50,000 or ¥60,000 a month. And Ueno—in Ueno there are the branch chiefs. It would also be all right if he just became one of them. But he's below that in rank.

Analysis. In Masao's view, Fusao has overreached himself. Kōsei-kai is a power to be used with caution and knowledge of one's capacities. It may make demands that the member is not able to meet, and the member must know when this is the case: "if it isn't someone who knows his strength, joining can be bad." Headquarters may also exacerbate a member's fears with threats of karmic retribution ("if he quit . . . things would get even worse") for inadequate performance. Dale (1975:44–45) has noted the same tactic in Tokyo: "Sometimes there is a veiled threat that evil will befall the member if he fails to be diligent in propagating the faith," and some means of maintaining participation "smack of coercion" (1975:57).

But Masao thought Fusao simply aimed too high, having neither the judgment to limit requests for contributions, the strength to admit to headquarters his loss of followers, nor the income to sustain his contributions. Having failed, Fusao's household was declining, which frightened others from the movement. The failure was not Kōsei-kai's fault, however, but Fusao's, for his misjudgment.

Masao appeared satisfied with his own situation. He knew his means and was resolved to stay within them. He was chagrined at Kōsei-kai's local decline and the disfavor with which his friends and family regard it but found its counseling and means of worship valuable enough to continue to defend it to occasional critics, pay his dues, and make occasional trips to headquarters.

Kadoya

"Kadoya" ("corner store") is known in the hamlet, as shopkeepers often are, by the name of his service station. He joined in 1960 at the age of twenty-six and was thirty-eight at the time of my first stay in the hamlet.

Vignette. Kadoya is a small, energetic, and somewhat pugnacious man with a brusque, straightforward manner and slightly slurred speech. During my first stay he became hamlet chief, and his successful service station was bringing his household the highest income in the village, a great improvement over his lot as a taxi driver in Morita when he joined twelve years before.

Kadoya's conversion was gradual. It was opposed by his parents, and he joined secretly:

> The reason I became a Kōsei-kai member was that I was renting a taxi office at the Kadoya [a shop in Morita] in front of the elementary school. I used to talk to Mr. Kimura, who was one of the owners and had a wrapping-paper store. I thought Kōsei-kai was very interesting. I wanted to join, but my parents didn't want me to . . . my parents didn't know for five or seven years that I was a member. They found out when I rebuilt our house.

He eventually was persuaded to join by Takeda Junko, the first member in the area, despite his personal dislike of her. His poor health and Kōsei-kai's expertise in direction lore led him to the decision.

> [When I talked to her] it was always like quarreling. Our personalities didn't mesh. But I had a reason for joining—I had ulcers, twice. When I was working on the gas station, I built a toilet in a bad direction. I didn't notice it then, and I wasn't feeling well and had a checkup for ulcers or stomach cancer. I was told I had an ulcer and had to be hospitalized. I

came home a month later. Then I built another garage wrong but I didn't know it this time either, even though I'd heard about this sort of thing. When I was in the hospital, I read all the books, so I started to read an Ise almanac at last. I found out that I built those buildings in a bad direction, which caused the stomach trouble. I asked Mr. Kimura, Mr. Kaguya, and also Mr. Akagi, who lives in Tokyo now and was a [Kōsei-kai] chief of this area in those days, to interpret the almanac for me . . . I don't know *how* many people I asked.

As I was a taxi driver then, I played around a lot. I was told it is a sin even if you just think of it, or you just make someone think about it. In an extreme case it's a sin even if you just say the person is nice, and that was about all I heard about it.

After I studied the almanac, I found out I was building houses where it said I would have stomach troubles. I thought this was pretty odd and talked to Mr. Kaguya and the hamlet chief, and they said it was true. I gradually understood it better, but still couldn't completely understand Kōsei-kai because of my personality. Finally, I was in St. Luke's Hospital in Tokyo, and I started to think the Law was good. I had already joined, but when I got sick, I started to believe in it. I thought, it'll be easier to study because I can ask questions frankly and they can answer me frankly . . . if I could study, there is nothing I couldn't understand. So I suggested everybody in our household should join.

Kadoya says that Kōsei-kai has helped his ailments, but only partially. His family goes to the medical clinic much more frequently than do others, and he still is preoccupied with health.

Beliefs. Kadoya's beliefs are manifested in comments he makes throughout the discussion.

I'm sure that good things come back when I do work service (*mi no fuse*) and money service (*kane no fuse*). When I came back from the hospital, the church chief didn't have a car. One time we went to the church in Mitaka City in my car. There was a lecture for Kōsei-kai staff, and he was going as the Kōsei-kai educator. I didn't know if I could really drive that far—to Tochigi Prefecture—since I had just come out of the hospital. I had a bad intestine. I sat there and listened to lectures all day long. I learned that I have to do such-and-such and I have to have this kind of relationship with people. And when I thought about it and agreed with it, all the gas in my intestine came out. Until then I had felt bad.

Kadoya says that not only his health but also his personality had benefited: "After I started to follow the teaching, my personality started getting better. My frustration and short temper disappeared. I'm becoming a more amiable person." He says that this improvement is not completed and that he still has problems, but he is confident that they will be solved.

There's an obvious difference in my feelings when I go to the church and the counseling meetings. . . . They get better and better the more I go. My karma (*innen*) comes apart. If I stay away from the church and meetings, my own nature comes out. It shows up when I talk to my customers. My customers say whatever they feel like, so I sometimes have little arguments with them. It would be better if I could laugh and forget what they say, but my own nature comes out when I stay away. I don't think it's good. When I go to the church and the counseling meetings once a week or every five days, my learning increases and I change . . . and when I stay away, my karma comes out at bad times, when I don't think I should show it.

The improvement in his personality had been what impressed him most:

Here's the answer: it's that my bad qualities have been getting better since I joined. Of course, I don't mean *all* my qualities have gotten better, because everybody has a lot of bad points, and I'm one of them! But even though I have a lot of bad points, I'm getting better. That means that the teaching is good.

Many effects of Kōsei-kai activities on Kadoya's personality and health are immediate and personal and sound familiar from psychosomatic medicine in the West and elsewhere, like a stomach ailment cured by his charity:

> When various difficult problems came out, I asked Mr. Okada to give me a "tie," and he explained them to me. "Whatever it is, make a building contribution [*kensetsu*] of Y100,000 [then about $330]," the previous church chief said. "It would be better to make a contribution of Y100,000 and to be better and feeling good than to pay it to a doctor." So I made the building contribution. People said all sorts of bad things about it: "It won't work!" But it's all right to do it for yourself even if people do talk. After I did, it got better, and my stomach doesn't hurt at all now. And what I was worrying about was greed. There's a saying, "the stomach is greed."

However, the benefits he has received are not only physical and psychic but extend to business as well. His shop's welfare reflects virtue, or lack of it, in his behavior elsewhere, which he explains in karmic terms.

> When I was asked to take [the chief to Mitaka] the next time, it was Sunday. I told him I'd take him, but he'd have to excuse me for not staying because I'd be very busy that day. The business goes much better when I'm going to the counseling meetings.
> *G*: What goes better about it?
> *K*: Sales. When I go to the meetings, my sales increase. So I came back. I'd told the church chief, "Please excuse my just taking you and leaving, because my business is busy today." So I just took him and came back alone. I thought that day that the shop would be busy. But it wasn't busy. And when I *had* taken him before, it was Sunday too, and sales had increased by three times!
> So it's good to listen to the Law and do some work service too. I see clearly that if I do the work service, it'll come back to me. I have to do it, and I really became willing to do it then.
> *G*: What relation did giving the ride have to sales?
> *K*: The Teaching says to help people. When one is having a hard time, others have a hard time too, and we have

to help each other in our society. If I'm asked to go, I can't
say no as long as I'm a Kōsei-kai member.

    The Law will be ours if we study it. And not for
others. As soon as I studied it, it became mine and bloomed. I
mean, it got better. And I just took him and came back,
which meant I did only half the work service and didn't listen
to the teachings, so my sales dropped to less than a third . . .
even my sales!

Karma, then, works immediately on sales and not merely through better
customer relations. The favorable results of good behavior go beyond
the need to "help each other in our society," to Law as a causal scheme
on a larger scale. This scheme includes a comprehensive, balanced
ledger of merit: "If I do the work service, it will come back to me."
Although improvements in Kadoya's personality helped customer relations, the effect of staying or not staying at the lecture also came
directly.

    Kadoya's ideas about karma, *kami*, and ancestors, like those of
most people in the hamlet, are not fully systematic. Some familiar principles emerge, however, in his account above. First, like everyone (even
such declared atheists as Gosaburō) in Yamanaka, he assumes that
direction lore is valid. Like most, he does not know its details but thinks
that people fail or succeed and are well or ill depending on their orientation to stars and planets. This must be interpreted by professionals with
almanacs (*koyomi*), for which he first turned to Kōsei-kai.

    A second principle, karma, is to a degree like direction lore in that
it is automatic and largely impersonal. But its causality is also morally
informed, not neutral like that of orientation. Every human action is
morally either good or bad and has a good or bad effect that ultimately
returns to the actor. This Buddhist idea is generally accepted in the
hamlet but gets special emphasis from Kōsei-kai, which claims to show
exactly how to improve one's karma by improving one's behavior. As
Kadoya said of his improved sales, "I see clearly that if I do the work
service, it will come back to me."

    A third principle is still more humanlike: the spirits of the dead
themselves. For Kadoya (as for Mori and Obaa but not for Hideo or
most nonmembers now), they *are* humans (*ningen*) and are independent,
sentient, and active. They do not exist merely in one's heart or mind,
but in the world. For Kadoya one of the virtues of Kōsei-kai is that it
makes plain the importance of the spirits and their existence, even in
fetuses:

Most people don't understand, but I think people who join Kōsei-kai and study the Law understand. For somebody who has a miscarriage and doesn't pray for it, results will come out somewhere that the person doesn't know. They're usually bad: someone gets sick or loses money or the business doesn't go well, and so forth. Most people don't realize that fetuses are humans too, and that they are spirits (hotoke-sama). But Kōsei-kai members know that they are human beings but just couldn't come out into our society, so we have to pray for them.

The traditional notion that the spirits of the dead exist in one of two states—either buddhahood, in which they are benevolent toward the living or simply inactive, or in the limbo of nonbuddhahood, in which they are unhappy and actively malevolent—is implied by Kadoya's answer to a question about the existence of souls after death:

I think that's true [that they exist]. For example, there were some accidents above the Kubota Falls, where some people fell in from the rocks above the falls. It happened again on the third and seventh anniversary. So I think they couldn't attain buddhahood . . . if we held a memorial service for them, they wouldn't pull the next person into the falls at the same place. Every third and seventh anniversary something always happens at the same place. They can't attain buddhahood, so if we had a service for them on the same day of their death, we could prevent the next accident. Even if they attain buddhahood, we should pray for them, at least on the day of their death, every month . . . there's no connection between our household and the people who died, but everybody wants to stop that accident always happening at the same place. I think we should have memorial services for them at Kōsei-kai.

Problems. Despite benefits received and his willingness to give money, Kadoya is unhappy with some officers over personalities, "fallacies," and mismanagement of money. He dislikes several officers and said that a conflict with one of them on night-watch duty at the Ueno Church recently led him to a threat of violence.

There are two duties every month, and whenever I go I'm criticized, and I'm fed up. The other day I went a bit crazy and said I was going to hit him with an axe . . . after this quarrel, people say he's gotten better. He used to complain about every little thing. For example, when we gave tea at the altar, wearing the sash, he said I put the cup the wrong way and one flower was facing the wrong way. I was trying my best not to make any mistakes and feeling afraid he was going to say something. Now I feel I don't want to do it. I think it's stupid; it's much better not to do it.

Since then, Kadoya has stopped going to the church for any duties at all.

Kadoya is also annoyed by the dissemination of what he sees as the false doctrine that prayer alone can solve material problems such as sickness and accidents. He attributes this "fallacy" to inadequate learning in some older leaders and attributes the present loss of members, in turn, to the fallacy.

[The loss] may be because of guidance staff members get from the old Kōsei-kai staff. The old staff never changed. Ten or fifteen years ago they were teaching that you would recover if you pray, that no weeds would grow on your farm if you pray, and no bad accidents would happen if you just become a member and pray to Buddha. And they didn't say this just to members. When they talk about this sort of thing, if it's somebody who knows the Teaching very well, that won't happen, but if it's somebody who doesn't know the Teaching very well, his story won't follow the original, and it will lose members. About ten or fifteen years ago Kawa Mura had a lot of members, and Shirahata [the next village north] had just a few, but now Shirahata has more. It's all because there were some members who didn't know the Teaching very well. It's wrong to say things will be better if you just pray. Things won't get better by prayer alone.

Some staff were badly trained. They listened to half and didn't listen to the other half, so they don't know the real Teaching. For real problems, problems you can't solve yourself, it was wrong to teach them that if you pray, the problems will be gone. By your will—even if you don't pray, but you do some of the Teaching *without* saying anything and do other things while speaking of it—that's one method. I don't mean

Kōsei-kai is wrong. But I guess that's why they're losing members.

Kadoya says that Kōsei-kai also has made the community hostile with aggressive claims that households with misfortunes aren't praying enough. His account recalls Masao's description of Fusao's overzealousness:

> People often say that because a household didn't join, somebody in it got sick.[54] Among old people. I don't think this bothers Kōsei-kai members so much, but it gives nonmembers a bad impression. For example, when some non-Kōsei-kai family gets sick or has an accident, if they're told by a member that if they were members and prayed, it wouldn't have happened, the family won't feel good. If you were a member and had some instruction and were told the same thing, you wouldn't be so angry if you thought you had a "tie" and were told the truth and were taught by it. But if a nonmember is told, he gets angry.

(Nonmembers, including the chronically frail wife of the superintendent of education, described similar proselytizing by Hideo whenever there was an illness or accident in their household.)

Kadoya's most serious complaint is that unnamed local leaders had mismanaged money. He had been talking about his enthusiasm for Kōsei-kai and his five or six visits to headquarters:

> I felt deeply at headquarters. It convinced me. I was also convinced many times at the Ueno Branch. It would be good if I could go more often, but I can't. I can't visit Mr. Kimura [Hideo] so much since I'm busy these days. I used to go visit him at night about twenty times a month, but then he went away to the Ueno Church.

Then, it emerged, some officer had borrowed money from him:

> Even a man who's received a mandala has some points where he's wrong, even though he's been doing it [following

the Law] for twenty years. When I had to follow the Law, and
I've been doing it quite a long time, I started to have my own
ideas and sometimes thought that he makes mistakes even
though he's been doing the Law so many years. I haven't gone
since then.

If you borrow something, you have to return it. If you
borrow a book, you have to return the book. If you don't, it's
not the Law. For example, you can't return a book after
tearing the cover off just because you like the cover. It's like
that. I may be wrong, but I don't like to get my book back
with some pages torn out. If I told the church chief about this,
he'd [the person in question] be warned, and by the office
chief, too. "Pay what you should pay" [a folk aphorism]. If I
want to give it away, I'll give as much as I can. . . . It's that
kind of mistake. I think it's the way *some* of the staff think,
not all of them.

They wanted me to lend Kōsei-kai some money for a
funeral, and I said I would gladly, especially to ease somebody's sorrow. They didn't ask me to lend all my money—but
if they ask me to lend a certain amount, I will. And then they
returned the money, taking some from it and saying I should
give that amount to the funeral or whoever was unhappy. I
don't mind giving money for the funeral, but I think it's more
reasonable to bring back the whole amount and let me decide
about what I give. So I think some people are doing this sort
of thing . . . maybe a few. If I told the church chief and the
office chief about this, they'd be angry.

I wouldn't ask for interest. I'd lend money, if they can't
collect it, even if it were ¥200,000 or ¥300,000, but I don't
think it's the Law that they give me back the money after
taking some themselves to give to the funeral. I was planning
to give some, but if they do that, I don't think I'll lend any
money the next time. That's what I meant when I said they
make mistakes. I don't think the church chief, the office
chief, or the Teaching are wrong; I think a few of the staff are
wrong.

That happened last year and the year before. Each
branch gets a quota, and we usually can't collect the amount
of the quota, but we have to give the allotment to headquarters, so we have to get the difference somewhere . . . I'm
not against Kōsei-kai, but the ideas of a few of the staff are
wrong, and I'm getting hesitant to go to counseling meetings.

Maybe it depends on my attitude too: if I think, "When they're having a hard time they need help," and vice versa, it doesn't make me angry. It depends on how you look at it; maybe it's partly my fault. Maybe theirs, maybe mine. But I can't ask Mr. Kimura for the "tie."

Analysis. Kadoya's account suggests, among other things, that loyalties and antagonisms within Kōsei-kai locally are to local persons, not to the movement as a whole. Although he feels that the borrowers' behavior is malfeasance and that this and other aspects of local administration are harmful, he did not report them to the church chief because the person responsible would be "warned."

Such personal relationships constitute one limit to "instrumental" behavior in Kōsei-kai and are part of what Horton (1970:160) calls the "mixed motives" that, with other features, may distinguish "religious" behavior from more circumscribed and rationalized "scientific" behavior. On the other hand, science too may involve personal entanglements. Moreover, much of Kadoya's relation to Kōsei-kai is explicitly instrumental. He lists benefits to health, wealth, and personality that he has sought and received from it, and also lists his dissatisfactions. His attitude toward Kōsei-kai, like Masao's, is not one of global acceptance or rejection but of separate scrutiny of separate experiences.[55]

Kadoya's rationality, or at least his rationalism, is fairly representative of the attitudes of Kōsei-kai members in and around Yamanaka. They have an explicitly unified model of the world, centered on the ancestor-descendant relationship and applicable to all social relations and indeed to all human experience. With this model they can explain and control otherwise (and to the outside observer) diverse phenomena of health, personality, social relations, business, and the failure of automobiles to start. They can account even for the growth of crops: when two peripatetic Kōsei-kai instructors, quietly enthusiastic women in their forties, visited the Yamanaka meeting place, they spoke of, among other things, being rewarded for meticulous prayer with a remarkable crop of carrots. Their world view fits well with Tylorean rationalism: all experience can be explained. In Kadoya's words, "if I study, there is nothing I cannot understand."

Dimensions of the Hypothesis

At the beginning of this study I had hypothesized that members of Kōsei-kai would have been, at joining, sicker, poorer, less educated, less prestigious, and with fewer kin. I expected that they would have joined in a deliberate attempt to alleviate their condition and that they would, to some extent, have an empirical attitude: they would scrutinize themselves and others and evaluate Kōsei-kai accordingly. How far were these expectations borne out?

Much of the available evidence is subjective, consisting of individual perceptions, sometimes difficult to check against independent evidence of health, wealth, and so on. Where these perceptions are memories of household harmony or even wealth, as they were when Kōsei-kai came to Yamanaka twenty years before, they are subject to the additional distortion of time. On the other hand, independent sources often concurred. If members of a household reported, for example, that they had been chronically ill before joining, this often was said of them by several other households.

Objective measures of the circumstances and aims of people in Yamanaka who joined are of limited significance for Kōsei-kai as a whole because of the small number of people and because of their location in a single village and (largely) a single hamlet. Still, there was rather general agreement about their reasons for joining and for leaving, among members in Yamanaka and in Kawa Mura and among nonmembers throughout the area, and these agree with accounts from elsewhere in Japan.

Health

Almost all members and nonmembers agreed that poor health was the primary reason why people joined. All but one (Masao, and even he mentioned that his health was poor—and he has since died, in 1977) of the six members whose profiles were given gave this as their reason, as did members from other hamlets. Most people in Yamanaka who joined but quit also had joined either for their own health or for that of someone in their household. Almost all nonmembers who would comment on the motives of members said the same thing. There are no village health records for the early period, but the clear hamlet consensus is that households that joined had been sicker than those that did not. Members still seem preoccupied with health, the major topic at counseling meetings, both for "ties" and for casual conversation.

Communal Relations

The second most widely cited problem was social relations, particularly household relations. People occasionally mentioned these in conjunction with health, as though they were linked to it. Almost half the members interviewed, both in and out of Yamanaka, mentioned household quarrels (katei kenka) and the goal of household harmony (katei enman). Nonmembers, on the other hand, never suggested that people were moved to join because of household quarrels. This difference may well reflect Kōsei-kai teachings, not well known to most nonmembers, about the importance of domestic relations and their connection to health.

Independent evidence about relative household harmony is elusive, but other kinds of communal relationships, such as kinship and membership in common-interest groups, are more easily assessed. Of the six active Yamanaka members, one, Mori Sayoko, has no kin at all in the hamlet outside her own household. Hideo and Obaa in one household and Nami in another are related only to each other, a situation almost as uncommon as having no kin. The other two active members, Kadoya and Masao, belong to two of the oldest households in the hamlet and are related to many others, but relations between these two men and their kindred households do not seem close.

Participation in common-interest groups such as the fire-fighting association and the women's association correlates inversely, as predicted, but weakly with membership. Hideo, the person most active in Kōsei-kai, has withdrawn from the fire-fighting association and often is said to have withdrawn from hamlet affairs altogether, but withdrawal seems to have been more a result of his membership than a cause of it. Masao seems to have been even more active in hamlet affairs. Obaa and Nami are members of the women's association, the communal property owners' association, the old people's association, and several others. On the other hand, Mori Sayoko and her husband belong to none of the common-interest groups and seem to have served in no hamlet posts. Members of Kōsei-kai in other hamlets vary similarly in their membership in common-interest groups.

Wealth and Income

The mean tax-assessed real estate holdings of the five active households, at ¥600,000, are 20 percent above the mean of ¥500,000 for the whole hamlet.[56] The holdings are as follows: Nami, ¥1,060,000; Kadoya, ¥937,000; Hideo, ¥731,000; Masao, ¥211,000; and Mori, ¥1,000. They thus range from 2 to 200 percent of the hamlet mean. Although these holdings are the major form of wealth, however, they are not the only one. Nonfarming households, such as the Moris, usually have a bank account or other savings. As the Moris have just built a substantial new house, their income evidently has been more than adequate to their needs for at least some time. Mori Sayoko mentioned no economic benefits from Kōsei-kai, though she spoke of many others.

Members' incomes appear about the same as those of nonmembers. My questionnaire included household income, but only toward the end, when I usually felt hesitant to ask my (sometimes weary) respondents another intimate question. Thus, I asked for and got figures for only twelve households. These included four of the six active members. The mean annual income the twelve households reported was Y1,000,000, while the four member households reported Y1,112,000. The income for members is probably skewed, however, by Kadoya's income, the highest or second highest in the hamlet, in a very small sample. In fact, the mean income of members is probably about the same as that of nonmembers and certainly is not much less.

Since no tax figures were available for the 1950s, when most members joined, I have no firm independent evidence of change in landholdings or income after they joined. Hideo says that his income has declined slightly, while Kadoya says that his has increased greatly and that Kōsei-kai definitely has helped him make money. No one, however, suggested money as a reason for joining (unlike its fellow Nichiren movement and major rival, Sōka Gakkai, Kōsei-kai seldom promises monetary rewards); nor were there any very poor members. This contradicts not only the economic aspect of my hypothesis but also the views of nonmembers in the hamlet, who often spoke of members as being poor. But requirements for dues and donations mean that really poor people cannot afford Kōsei-kai, whose demands for money were the usual reason for quitting. Kōsei-kai appears to make little effort to recruit the poorest despite its voiced concern for charity and equality.

Education

Education was a fourth way in which I had thought people might have hoped to improve themselves by joining, but, as with the other possible motivations excepting health, the evidence is mixed. No member was among the most educated people in the hamlet, yet all but one had graduated from primary school, and two from middle school, average for their generation. Most members seemed no more or less concerned with education than other people. On the other hand, a key figure, Hideo, explicitly says that his work for Kōsei-kai as an instructional officer is an important opportunity to continue his education, and he frequently remarks that he is "fond of studying." He has, as noted, published poetry both in China and in Japan, and his son also is a published poet. He typically responds to an obscure question that his "study of the matter is inadequate," implying his intent to pursue it in the future.

Status

Last, I had thought that people might have joined in an attempt to improve their social status. This may have been true in several cases, either when the household was of low standing or when the person who joined had failed to meet the standards of his ancestors. But the evidence here depends on complex and subtle information about people's perception of themselves and of their place in the hamlet, and interpretations can only be tentative.

For example, the household of Hideo and Obaa, although about as wealthy and educated as the hamlet average, is new at three generations and is a branch of a household that itself is of modest status. In the last generation it lost much of the confidence of its neighbors when the head of the house set the fire in which the nearest house and three lives were lost. But Hideo was twice elected hamlet chief in the mid-1950s, so if he personally is now mistrusted, this must stem from some time since he joined Kōsei-kai. Hideo's own standing may objectively gain from his father's fame as the widely acclaimed first mayor of Kawa Mura and the recipient of an award from the emperor, but if he measures his own status against his father's, he must find it wanting.

Pride in his father's achievements is evident in several framed photographs of his father in formal clothing as mayor and in a copy of the award from the emperor, all on the walls of Hideo's adoptive home. Normally the only ancestors represented in a household are its own, not those of an adoptive groom, but Hideo's father evidently has outweighed custom. His distinguished career was one of the first topics of Hideo's conversations with me, and it came up more than once. The dates of his father's elections are also among the half dozen events in several of Hideo's year-end summaries on the backs of talismans. If, as seems likely from much of his behavior and from comments by his son, Hideo compares himself to his father, it is possible that he feels a need to excel and that Kōsei-kai provides the opportunity. His father also had been a Kōsei-kai member and had been opposed for it, so filial piety may also play some role.

The circumstances of other households similarly are complex and ambiguous enough to prevent ready conclusions, but a desire for status may well have led some to join. Nami's household, though a generation older than Hideo's, is still relatively new, and its founder was a widely distrusted gambler. At least since her husband died, Nami, an illiterate and nearly deaf widow with few kin, has been inactive in hamlet affairs. The Mori household also is of modest status, as a first-generation household with no kin and the low-status work of taxi driver. The household is virtually without connections in Yamanaka and, as we arrived, was in fact moving after forty years to another hamlet. Masao's household dates from the founding of the hamlet, and he represented himself as having been a pillar of village life in his active years, but there is some reason to doubt the extent of his work, and his household now is somewhat impoverished. Last, Kadoya, like the Moris, had low occupational status and seems to have felt it when he joined. Since, like Masao, Kadoya belongs to one of the oldest households, he might be expected to have had more than the average share of land and influence in the hamlet. In fact, however, he was a taxi driver and worked not in the hamlet but in a neighboring one.

In sum, the evidence of greater than ordinary problems and of consequent dissatisfaction among people who joined is mixed. However, one problem, health, is clear. Most members were sicker than average, as members and nonmembers agree. Next most important was household relationships. Five of the six members described, and many members from other hamlets, mentioned household strife as a reason for joining. Low status in the hamlet may have been a reason for joining, though no one said it, and a gap in education was a factor in one case. Poverty, on the other hand, has little or no correlation with membership.

Articulation of Discontent

A view of religion as at least moderately rational and aimed at particular ends implies that people who joined would have expected to solve some problems or achieve some goal. They would have, and could to a degree articulate, an instrumental attitude toward Kōsei-kai. For at least the salient problem, health, this proved true: almost every member said that he or she had been sick and had joined to get well.

The second most widely cited goal was household harmony, the benefit now most frequently specified in Kōsei-kai literature. It appears that there has been a shift, in the hamlet as elsewhere (Morioka 1979), in Kōsei-kai's emphasis from health benefits to social and psychic benefits. This shift may have resulted from improving public health care. In any case, good social relations and the associated peace of mind now appear more important to members than they did.

People generally joined, they said, for specific goals. In addition to these they may have had others, including less specific ones. But they present themselves as having had clearly in mind what they wanted, and this usually was measurable in some way.

Empiricism

The last of my original questions was whether or not people would be empirical about Kōsei-kai. If they had expected certain results, they would know whether they had achieved them and would judge Kōsei-kai accordingly. There is good evidence that such an empirical attitude does exist, not only toward Kōsei-kai but also toward established religion. (Notably, Hardacre [1984:4] also has found a strongly empirical attitude in Reiyūkai, whose "members demand that it produce results. . . . In matters religious, all Reiyūkai members come from Missouri . . . they demand proof.")

Many people, like Masao, speak of Kōsei-kai as though its efficacy can be tested or at least observed:

> If one just let people look, and think, "Yes, indeed—that household joined Kōsei-kai and they got better," and understand that way, it would be good. But if after joining one gradually gets worse and worse, no one will want to come, and nobody will join. . . . If you use up your wealth, people will think, "Oh, awful!" and get out.

Obaa listed her earlier misfortunes and concluded, "Our household's luck used to be bad . . . but now we're really happy. Papa has changed our fortune by always doing things in Kōsei-kai." A man in his mid-forties, from a neighboring hamlet, also seemed empirical when he tried six different religious movements and several doctors seeking a cure. Similarly, in a story recounted by Masao as well as by an official biography, Niwano, the founder of Kōsei-kai, had tried a number of religious groups in different regions of Japan before founding his own.

Kōsei-kai's effect on one's fortunes is not merely general and diffuse. Specific acts can be linked to specific results, as Kadoya discovered the day he came home from a service early, expecting the increased business he had had after the previous week's service. "But . . . I did only half of the work service and didn't listen to the Teachings, so my sales dropped to less than a third." Again, Sayoko's tubal pregnancy was caused by her failure to go to headquarters and rectified by her apology. Even the skeptical Nami said, "If you follow Kōsei-kai, your health will be good . . . [my son] has never had a cold." Every member has similar stories of the connections of actions to results. Of course, these enthusiasts choose their evidence to support their interpretations, but so, necessarily, does everyone who interprets experience. My point is not that their arguments are valid or their conclusions correct, but that they assume that tangible evidence is available.

People may similarly either doubt or confirm the existence of such "theoretical" beings as *kami*. In the counseling meeting described, for example, the old woman interrupted her narrative to say that when she had neglected to pray at a shrine during construction of paddy, a man injured in the work had died. Therefore, she concluded, *kami* do exist. Granted, she came merely to an orthodox conclusion, using evidence that would not meet strict standards, but it is significant that she mentioned the existence of *kami* as an issue, and one to which evidence could be brought. She feels, as do others in the hamlet (unlike Western positivists concerning, e.g., the existence of God), that religious questions are empirical ones, not metaphysical ones about which nothing further can be said.

Nor does all the evidence confirm the reality of the *kami*. A man from a neighboring hamlet told me that his grandmother, on hearing that an American rocket had reached the moon, declared that she would no longer celebrate the moon *kami* festival since if that *kami* had really existed, the rocket could not have landed. Her reaction is similar to those of other people, such as the farmer who said that there will always be belief (though he seems not to share it) in *kami* since science will always have limitations, such as the failure of rockets. When failure occurs, it will be attributed to *kami*. Similarly, Japan's defeat in the war is cited by people of his generation as the cause of their skepticism about *kami*. *Kami*, then, despite being "traditional," are subject to evidence. They are also subject to logic, as when the younger Buddhist priest said, "They don't stand to reason . . . they don't make sense." If the "closed circle" (Marwick 1973) of traditional thought ever existed in Yamanaka, it does not exist now.

Kōsei-kai is as susceptible to scrutiny as are *kami*. Even active members such as Masao and Kadoya, not to mention those who have quit, keep a critical attitude toward it. Twenty-nine people in the hamlet originally joined, but only eleven remain and only six are active. Thus, most may be said to have joined provisionally. In contrast to accounts (e.g., Cohn 1970) of zealotry among religious converts elsewhere in the world, converts in Yamanaka are exploratory and pragmatic, not absolutely committed. Their attitude, in fact, is in part explicit cost accounting. They joined to be cured or to cure someone in their household and quit because the money required became too much. People seem simply to have weighed Kōsei-kai's costs against its benefits, and many, after experiencing both, found the ratio wanting.

Of course, members, like other people, are not exclusively rational, nor is their cost-benefit balance limited to money and health. For members, as for people who continue to deal with ancestors by established means, more is involved than instrumental activities and specifiable goals. At counseling meetings and elsewhere they give and get sympathy, warmth, and support. Relations with each other, as with ancestors and living parents, are diffuse. On the other hand, even these diffuse relationships are explicitly part of Kōsei-kai's calculus since social harmony and mutual support both within and outside the household are among its chiefly stated aims.

Kōsei-kai explains (successfully, members say) phenomena comprehensively: it claims to explain all major events in members' lives with little more than models that people already have for understanding their own households. The central model is the parent-child relationship of dead and living. Children owe their existence to their parents, whose nurturance and guidance, according both to traditional hamlet thought and to Kōsei-kai, do not cease when they die any more than when they are temporarily absent while alive. The social principles that they embodied, too, persist and pervade experience: seniority, filial piety, maintenance of household continuity, and concern for others. Violators of these principles inevitably suffer.

If the influence of parents and other ancestors strongly and pervasively survives their death, one may ask just how it does so. Hideo and many others give Berkeley's answer: ancestors survive insofar as they are perceived by the living, in memory. Other people suppose that ancestors exist even apart from perceptions of them. In either case, the dead are inalienable from the living. Just as beneficent behavior survives death, so, in Kōsei-kai's view, does maleficent behavior. Like physique or blood type, it is transmitted from generation to generation.

There are no accidents. Although experience may appear to have loose ends, Kōsei-kai shows that ties can be found. There are neither meaningless events nor events that cannot be explained.

Summary

As members in Yamanaka understand it, Kōsei-kai doctrine shares much with Sōtō Zen. Ancestors and the social relations and moral obligations for which they stand are part of a comprehensive, universal causal order of all events impinging on human life. The principles of the parent-child relationship (debt to seniors, concern for juniors, and the transmission of ethical, adaptive behavior among other necessities of existence) that operate in household and hamlet also operate in the world generally. Causality in the world is not divided into human and nonhuman realms but is uniform and comprehensive.

The immediate agents of this moral order are ancestors, after death as in life. Since people who have died cannot speak in words, their guidance must be divined in such events as the failure of a car to start, a sudden illness, or a road mishap. But although changes both in body and (more slowly) in personality occur at death, which turn living household members into ancestors, change is less important than continuity. There is nothing "supernatural" about ancestors. Their comprehensive influence on descendants is as natural and as regular as (in Hideo's image) the color transmitted by Mendel's peas.

Kōsei-kai's assumption that ancestors exert continuing influence on households is shared by Sōtō Zen and even by the more agnostic villagers. The fact of ancestral influence is common sense in hamlet life, and Kōsei-kai doctrine differs from this common sense only in degree and emphasis.

Within Kōsei-kai, opinions differ concerning the power of prayer. Some people say that prayers must be accompanied by actions and interpret prayer itself as acting reflexively. Older members, including the branch chief, however, say that prayer is effective because it is heard and acted on by the ancestors.

The attitudes and motives of Kōsei-kai members in Yamanaka about the movement also are diverse, although all hope to use it to please ancestors and improve themselves. The most active member, now retired, seems to have improved his education, salary, health, and domestic tranquility. The least active of the six members discussed, on the other hand, seems to remain a member largely out of sympathy for her branch household. Most joined to be cured of a physical ailment. Most who quit say that the fiscal responsibilities had grown too large. All who remained cite a cure and usually other practical benefits. In addition, membership provides an emotionally supportive community, an official as well as an individual goal. Counseling meetings are opportunities to express fears and sorrows to a sympathetic audience and to get professional advice. Friendships established at meetings continue away from the meeting place. Members not only do Kōsei-kai ritual together but spend more time visiting than their kin and neighborhood ties would suggest.

Since Kōsei-kai thus establishes new connections, it competes with kin, neighborhoods, and hamlet for its members. This competition brings hamlet antagonism toward the movement. Nonmembers say that it exploits members' loyalty, time, and money.

In addition to outside antagonism, there are local disputes within Kōsei-kai. Some concern a professional leader, Fusao, who has concealed a local decline in membership from headquarters by paying the missing dues himself. He is said to have been in financial trouble for some time and to have sold household land. Some members think his troubles result from personal inadequacy, but nonmembers think that he has been exploited by Kōsei-kai. His difficulties appear to have caused continued decline in local membership, in contrast with continued growth in the adjacent region and in the nation as a whole.

Chapter 7
Summary and Conclusions

I have described why some people in a Japanese hamlet joined a religious movement and the results joining had for them, and I have suggested how religious thought and action are similar to secular thought and action, here and elsewhere. On their own accounts, people joined mostly to cure illness, promote household welfare, improve their personalities, and please their ancestors. Members and nonmembers alike think that pleasing ancestors is good and beneficial, and many think that this is because ancestors are interested and influential in household affairs. Ignoring them may lead to illness, accidents, or financial loss. Moreover, maintaining relations with ancestors maintains a framework of meaning with a place for everyone.

These views contradict prevailing Western beliefs about sickness, accidents, and ancestors and contradict the beliefs of a few villagers as well. How should we interpret them? Should we take people at their word about what they believe, or do they somehow not mean what they say? If they do mean what they say, are their beliefs plausible and even reasonable, or do such questions miss the point?

In the 20th century, anthropologists influenced by Durkheim and Freud have supposed that religion does not really concern such natural phenomena as it seems to address but only social relations, of which deities and apparent concerns with nature are symbolic projections. What appear to be cosmological statements about the world at large are really sociological statements in disguise (as Horton [1970:152] puts it, sophisticated anthropologists assume that "things-are-never-what-they-seem"), and even if people really believe what they say they do, religious thought and action are nonetheless irrational, emotional, or "symbolic" and sharply different from secular and scientific thought and action.

In my analysis, religion in Yamanaka in some ways reflects and controls society and in some ways is emotional, irrational, and symbolic. However, these aspects neither exhaust nor characterize it.

Economy in the Religious Model

Religion in Yamanaka manifestly and overtly concerns social relations, but it also manifestly concerns natural phenomena, such as storms
and droughts, and phenomena that are partly "natural" and partly
"cultural," such as car accidents and irregular pregnancies. In short, it
concerns all manner of experience. Characteristically, it attributes to the
nonhuman world such human features as language, ethics, and contract.
Crops, health, and weather, for example, may be influenced by prayer
and offering.

Science now persuades us that such models are mistaken. Why,
then, do so many people use them? To answer this we need to recall how
and when they are used and acquired.

First, religious models are similar to other models in aim and
acquisition. They aim at understanding and are acquired by experience,
largely with other people who already have them. All knowledge of the
world consists in possessing models for interpreting phenomena; models
necessarily are hypothetical and analogical; and science and religion
therefore are on the same epistemological ground (chapter 1). Like
models generally, both science and religion attempt to reduce complexity
to simplicity and chaos to order. They attempt to explain and control.
They differ mainly in that science emphasizes self-criticism and self-
testing while religion celebrates tradition; that science identifies
knowledge as its primary aim while religion combines this with such
practical aims as salvation or longevity; and that science eliminates
humanlike elements from most models while religion centers upon them.
Science and religion otherwise are similar in being schemes for interpreting events, and doing this as economically as possible.

In this view, to show why any particular model is used instead of
another is in large part to show how it is, in its context, more
economical: how it orders a broader range of phenomena or uses fewer
principles. Since order is not so much evident in phenomena as
discovered, and since meaning is not so much intrinsic as imposed, there
is no *a priori* ground for distinguishing phenomena for which a humanlike model is appropriate from those for which it is not. This distinction
is an empirical, not a logical, problem. Until a phenomenon has been
better accounted for by an unhumanlike model than by a humanlike one,
there is no good reason not to use the latter.

In traditional Japanese thought (Munakata 1977:6) the "natural
world is where the gods live," and "there is no distinct boundary . . .
between the material world and the spiritual world." Especially in a
small, closely knit hamlet with a relatively simple technology, humanlike
models appear to account for a great deal, competing unhumanlike

models are relatively scarce, and religion appears grounded in experience.

Hamlet conceptions of household and ancestors make them economical models for experience generally. In Yamanaka as in traditional Japan everywhere, the household is the basic social unit. It is residential and corporate: its members live together and remain together after death, and they share economic and other rights and obligations. Each household exists because someone with material and social means was able to transmit them to succeeding generations. A household endures through continuing efforts by succeeding generations to preserve what they have received: not only house and land but also social relationships and principles. Each generation owes all it has and is to every preceding generation.

Everyone not only should but wants to ensure that the household continues because everyone, living or dead, is cared for by it. Everyone with a place in the hamlet has it as a member of a household. The household's fortunes are the individual's fortunes. For living members it is the source of shelter, food, human companionship, and hamlet rights. It is still the source of these for members who have died. Ancestors, through their tablets, receive shelter, food, and verbal communications. They are received at All Souls' Festival, for which they, like living former household members who have moved to the city, always return home. They maintain their place in the hamlet physically by their gravestones as well as by their tablets. Perhaps more than living former household members, they retain their accustomed social relations.

The prosperity and continuity of the household are part of everyone's debt to ancestors. One owes one's existence to them, a debt that cannot be repaid. Yet one can make partial repayment by helping fulfill their greatest wish, that the household be perpetuated. For people who feel that ancestors are sentient beings, it gives ancestors pleasure and spares them loneliness to receive food, greetings, and celebratory reunions. In the perhaps more recent view that they exist only in the traces of their past influence on the living, especially in memory, commemoration gives ancestors existence itself. In either case, the living practice commemoration as a duty and expect it after their own deaths. It sets the conditions of whatever immortality is possible.

Although ancestors thus depend on the living, they also have power over them. Even people who think that ancestors exist only in the influence of actions they took while alive think that this influence is perpetual. Through genes, landholdings, and social relations a household passes from generation to generation. Some continuities, such as the name given a child or some secret misdeed, are subtle; none is without effect, however, whether immediate or not. If ancestors are sentient and active, they intervene in household affairs, punishing vice and rewarding virtue. "Misfortune" therefore reflects misdeeds, and "good luck," merit. Failure of present good deeds to produce corresponding benefits in a household reflects misdeeds of an earlier generation.

Sentient or not, ancestors thus provide a scheme for interpreting and influencing household events. They retain the characteristics they had in life: concern for household welfare and hence for morality and harmony among heirs; seniority and hence power and authority to sanction their wishes; and an expectation of deference from juniors. Even if they are thought to cease to exist as separate entities, the same debts are owed them, and the principles of social relations they represent are still at work.

Individual characteristics gradually disappear as each person is assimilated to the ancestors. Personality, like the body, is perishable, and memorial services stop at the fiftieth year or sooner, when, in my elderly neighbor's words, "human bones have turned to mud and the human form has been lost." After individuality is lost, the principles of social existence remain: ancestors represent (as exemplars of, and by requiring) selflessness, charity, industry, and harmony. They are thus models for behavior, since one should do as they did, and models of events generally, since they explain what happens when they are not followed. They have the characteristics of all models: restriction to a limited set of relevant features (here, features of social relations), increasing abstraction with increasing distance from the original phenomena modeled (individuals and their relations within a household), and increasing power to account for diverse phenomena as the models become increasingly abstract.

The continuity of the parent-child relationship in the ancestor-descendant relationship is economical in two ways. First, change at death is limited, not absolute. Although the body dissolves, the spirit loses only idiosyncratic and selfish features. Its essential feature—its participation in the household—persists. The doctrine that it does persist is as economical as the doctrine of conservation of matter and energy; it avoids the radical change from being to nonbeing.

A second economy is that the parent-child model covers all events affecting households: relationships of living individuals, relationships of all ancestors to all descendants, and hence the relation of all behavior, past and present, to household welfare. At its most general, the parent-child relation yields universal ethical retribution: all good actions return good to the actor, and bad actions return bad. As ethical or unethical action within the household causes good or bad to the household and especially to the actor, so also in the world at large: the universe is a moral system within which the actor exists, just as in the household, as a node in a network of causal relations.[57] Ethical actions are those that increase harmony in the network; the principles of the household order are also principles of the world order. Kōsei-kai's use of the parent-child relation as a model of and for the world is still further economical in that it is shared not only by Sōtō Zen but by Shinto as well: "The relation of *kami* to humans is that of *oya-ko*: the parent-child, or better, the ancestor-descendant relation" (Ueda 1972:15).

Religion in Yamanaka thus has rational interpretive aims, but it certainly expresses and manipulates "diffuse" social relations as well. People often explain their relations with ancestors in emotional terms and use ancestors as moral examples for children. Such social suasion and such expression of emotion often have been taken by anthropologists to be "truer" functions of religion than are explanation and control of nonsocial and natural phenomena. These anthropologists think that religious interpretations of natural phenomena are based on mistaken belief and hence are aberrations, confused with real social aims, or are real social aims in disguise. These "real" aims are then said to be disguised by the rationalizations of believers, who for some reason wish to think they are controling something external, such as crops or ghosts, not merely themselves. How important are social control and emotional expression in Yamanaka, and how are they related to a rationalistic view of religion?

Many people speak of their relations with ancestors in terms of their own feelings: they pray or make offerings because it makes them feel good (*kimochi ga ii*) and because they feel respect, gratitude, or loneliness. To the extent that expression of emotion is a dominant motive, one might hold that this behavior is an end in itself and therefore by definition nonrational. However, if people seek not merely expression but also explanation and control, their concern with emotion, too, may be instrumental and rational. As doctrine, the "primitive Buddhism" (the core of early thought common to all later schools and sects) fundamental both to Sōtō Zen and to Kōsei-kai is in fact explicitly concerned to explain and control emotion, particularly the pangs of rage, fear, lust, and grief. The first of the Four Noble Truths that are the doctrinal cornerstone of Kōsei-kai and other Buddhism is that existence is suffering. The subsequent three truths explain suffering and how to subdue it. In this sense Kōsei-kai and Sōtō Zen both are directed very largely to explicit goals, a central condition of rational action.

Some Benefits and Problems of Membership

"Magic," in Wallace's words (1966:vi), "does not make the rains come. The gods do not win battles at man's request." What I take to be the central proposition of religious belief, that crucial aspects of the world at large are humanlike, seems mistaken. Nevertheless, using humanlike models for the world as a whole has benefits that for some people outweigh its problems.

Benefits

Benefits, or "charities" (*kudoku*) as members know them, may be described in cognitive, emotional, and practical terms. Cognitively, members of Kōsei-kai enjoy a unified world-view. In its comprehensively causal universe there are no unaccountable experiences. The movement satisfies members' desire for order and system (what Wittgenstein called "our craving for generality") by accounting for disturbances—sickness, mishaps, death—that threaten "bafflement, suffering and a sense of intractable ethical paradox" and "chaos—a tumult of events which lack not just interpretation but *interpretability*" (Geertz 1966:14). It does this by supplying, confirming, and elaborating models of disease and misfortune and how to avoid them, and generally how to conduct oneself in life.

Suffering stems from ignorance; from past misdeeds of, or present inattention to, one's ancestors; from one's own misdeeds; and generally from inadequate understanding of the universal Law (principally the Four Noble Truths) regulating all events. Ultimately it is to the failure to understand the Law that Kōsei-kai attributes all suffering. No line can be drawn between moral and natural law; they are one and the same—an identity implicit in, for example, the branch chief's admonition to the nauseated postman that he must live in harmony with the great life of the universe. The movement's explanations thus are universal and comprehensive.

Durkheim, Freud, Malinowski, Wallace, and others might object that Kōsei-kai's explanations often are fallacious and that explanation as such therefore cannot be its real aim. Several replies can be made. First, not all endeavors succeed at their real aim. Many human efforts—to build enduring dynasties, to change lead to gold, or to fly—have chronically failed or only recently succeeded, but failure has not meant that their "real" aim was something else. It is one of the fallacies of functionalism to suppose that the aim of action can reliably be inferred from what the action accomplishes.

A second reply is that explanations are based on models, which produce various explanations, some of them true by other models and some false. Models often are better evaluated as more or less economical, productive, or adequate than simply as true or false. Although we must always choose some explanations over others, the choice is based on the general adequacy, in context, of the underlying model. But because our knowledge of reality is contingent, and because its context shifts, assessment of models is as much empirical and contingent (cf. Kuhn 1970 on scientific revolutions) as logical. To assess a model is, in practice, not so much to ask whether it exactly represents reality as whether it is better than some alternative. Its worth may, to a degree, be measured by the relative success of some user.

A third reply to the charge of fallacy is that the model elaborated by Kōsei-kai is better than others for some people, though not for all. The fortunes of some member households in Yamanaka clearly have improved, and their attribution of this to Kōsei-kai seems reasonable. Even members whose fortunes have, by objective measures, not improved say that they are happier than before, a test whose empiricism, given Kōsei-kai's aims, is above reproach.[58] People who found they did not benefit from Kōsei-kai left it. Their decision to leave is thought reasonable even by loyal members, who expect benefits in practical terms. Even people who left did not reject the model so much as the movement's claim to best interpret it.

Kōsei-kai's model is not only practically productive but also economical in its simplicity and in the range of phenomena for which it accounts. It consists of a few ethical principles, most of them elements of the parent-child relationship, embodied largely in a human form, ancestors. These principles are thought to obtain in the world at large as they do in the household. Although they do permeate the world, they are clearest in the relation of descendants and ancestors. Ancestors want the household and its attentions to them perpetuated, and descendants want to repay their debt of existence to ancestors and to keep ancestors' guidance and benevolence. This is the relationship between parents and children.

As ancestors gradually lose individual characteristics, they come to consist of little more than the ethical principles of social relations that, among other things, they represented to their children in life. Particularly, they represent austerity, debt, gratitude, and filial piety. These ensure household welfare. According to Kōsei-kai they are instances of the more general principles of Buddhism, especially of comprehensive moral causality. This most general principle itself fits a persistent Japanese theme: that persons exist not as individuals but as nodes in a network of social relations.

Last, one may suggest that even such emotional attitudes as gratitude, respect, and affection, expressed in prayer and offerings, are not necessarily "nonrational" since the model explicitly stipulates them

as a means to well-being. Kōsei-kai enjoins deliberate cultivation and
expression of such emotions toward ancestors and others as instruments
of harmony and hence of personal happiness. Kōsei-kai's model, then,
may be said to be, within limits, cognitively adequate and economical. It
is adequate and economical largely because it is an elaboration of a
model already important in Yamanaka, as in Japan generally.

The model is also affectively appealing as it claims that death does
not sever the bond of parent and child or other household relationships.
Children communicate feelings and household events to deceased
parents and expect communications after their own deaths. People are
not cut off from households by death but continue as members. The
household provides a single sustaining network for both living and dead.
Although the frequency and elaboration of these relations are reduced by
death, the relations are by no means dissolved. As Fortes (1976:5) says
of ancestor worship generally, people in Yamanaka assume that "death
does not extinguish a person's participation in the life and activities of
his family and community." Fortes supposes that this view and the
actions that embody it result principally from a "deeply felt abhorrence
of the possibility of a person's total extinction by death" (1976:6).
Malinowski (1979:45) similarly notes that

> the existence of strong personal attachments and the fact of
> death are perhaps the main sources of religious belief . . . all
> forms of assistance given to the departed soul . . . are acts
> expressing the dogma of continuity after death and of
> communion between dead and living.

Ooms (1976:84), writing of Japan, cites Malinowski and adds that

> ancestor worship in its cognitive aspect is an answer to a
> fundamental human problem: death. It gives a meaning to
> mortality which in itself is merely disruptive and meaningless.

Whether or not "emotional" attachments to the dead are the main
sources of religious belief (I have tried to show that in Yamanaka they
are not the only ones), they do play a role in Kōsei-kai, as in Sōtō Zen, in
the hamlet. When people say that they joined out of filial piety or to
worship ancestors, or that they visit household graves out of gratitude,

they indicate such attachments. Kōsei-kai encourages these attachments. As Ooms (1976:83–85) remarks of members of Kōsei-kai and
other Nichiren-based movements, "The reality of ancestors has become
loaded with more precise meanings"; ancestor worship generally
"provides man with a frame through which he is able to face a mortal
existence."

Such responses to death are not unique, however, but only the most
poignant moments in the broader human quest for meaning in the face
of anomalous experience. Kitagawa (1971:39) argues similarly that "the
significance of the new religions [is that] they claim to offer a coherent
meaning for life . . . to people who feel lost because they sense an abrupt
rupture with the old and familiar world," and Hardacre (1984:220) notes
that Reiyūkai members "want to act in a world regulated by proven
ethical principles."

Most broadly conceived, the affective benefits of membership are
inseparable from its cognitive benefits. As Wittgenstein, Geertz, and
Fernandez among many others have remarked, humans need a sense of
order, pattern, and purpose, and need it urgently. Almost every
commentator on the New Religions (Earhart 1980a and Hardacre 1984
are important exceptions) has attributed their rise principally or solely
to crises in recent Japanese history, and almost all (Blacker 1971 and
again Earhart and Hardacre are exceptions) have seen them as offering
nonrational or irrational, nonempirical, emotionalist escapes from
uncertainty and hardship. But if a need for a comprehensible,
systematic, and intellectually satisfying world, ordered by uniform
principles—in short, a need for meaning—is as real as any, and if social
crises bring not just physical suffering but also the suffering of pervasive
ambiguity (most writers have called the postwar Japanese condition
"anomic"), then the most general emotional benefit would stem from a
scheme for interpretation. Writing of the New Religions, Earhart
(1969:245) notes that "socio-economic crises do not merely threaten the
social and economic order; they threaten the meaning and order of
human existence," and Blacker (1971:564, 567) repeatedly points out the
ambiguity inherent in Japan's "rapid change, invalidated tradition and
mass insecurity" and in "baffling internal changes."

The challenges posed are simultaneously and inextricably
emotional and intellectual. The schemes with which Kōsei-kai and other
New Religions have met them are not clearly less reasonable, or more
emotional, than are scientific revolutions as described by Thomas Kuhn:
results of persuasive compounds of assumption, interpretation, and
argument. The new movements, too, are such compounds. They are no
mere emotional opiates but have, as Blacker (1971:600) puts it, "taken

shrewd and energetic steps toward rational adaptation." Their members, as Hardacre (1984:4) says, "demand proof."

Finally, the model, as elaborated by and incorporated in Kōsei-kai, has observable practical results. Most generally there is adaptive change, as Kōsei-kai claims, in the behavior of members. Doctrine and practice give them reason to think that they have control over and responsibility for their actions and the course of their lives. Kōsei-kai recommends principles for successful life and specific behavior embodying the principles. Insofar as it specifies individual reform, it might as well be called "applied psychology" as "religion," and insofar as it specifies ethical conduct and proper social relations, it might be called "applied sociology." In any case, every member in Yamanaka claims reformed and redirected behavior based on greater knowledge.

A second practical benefit is a social network of communal relations that supplements networks based on neighborhood, kin, and common interests. Local members look to each other for material aid, sympathy, advice, and encouragement in difficulty. Members also have a place in a social framework that extends far beyond the hamlet. They are part of a large, powerful, and materially prosperous organization comprehending not merely the hamlet but the nation and the world. Through its hierarchy they can influence the wider world, whether by collecting clothes for Vietnamese or by campaigning for a candidate for the Diet. Such influence is promised in the last lines of the creed, repeated at every meeting:

> We will endeavor to realize a state of peace
> For the family, the community, the country, and the world.

The size, opulence, and modernity of the national headquarters, its location in Tokyo, and the movement's glossy, stylish publications are evidence to members that their organization not only is successful but also is in the vanguard of contemporary society. Through it they are not merely isolated residents of a rural hamlet but participants in the nation and the world as well. For ambitious members the hierarchy provides a lofty framework within which they may, to the limits of their ambition and talent, attain power and esteem denied them in society outside.[59]

Problems

The varied benefits of membership are offset by varied problems, now reflected in the end of Kōsei-kai's growth in Yamanaka. Most obvious is the demand for money, mentioned by continuing members and by most people who quit as well as by nonmembers. Constant requests for donations have led many to view Kōsei-kai as a commercial venture that exploits the gullible (a judgment extended to most of the New Religions, here as elsewhere in Japan).

A second problem is that Kōsei-kai's assertions of the efficacy of prayer and offerings in curing sickness and obtaining material ends are increasingly faced with alternate, impersonal models such as those of contemporary medicine. Improved medical resources have undercut a major motive for membership, and the movement's old claims of cures now seem superstitious or fraudulent to many nonmembers. The world view of most people in Yamanaka is increasingly secular as secondary education and mass media bring popular science into every household.

Kōsei-kai has tried to adapt to this secular trend (Putnam 1977:57 has noted Kōsei-kai's "openness to change and its continuing concern to make Buddhism relevant to modern man") by claiming to be scientific,[60] by a show of technology in its architecture, and by mechanistic metaphor:

> If all people worked only for their own interest, the world would become impossible to live in like a machine running short of oil. The machinery of society itself would explode through overheating or wearing out. (Niwano 1968:90)

Despite such impersonal metaphors, however, prayers and offerings are still basic practice, and ancestors and karma are basic theory. Kōsei-kai doctrine has fundamental conflicts with modern nonhuman models. Nonmembers in Yamanaka call it "superstitious," a view that is now increasing.

A third problem for members is conflicting loyalties to the hamlet and to Kōsei-kai. In the Kōsei-kai view there is no such conflict since members' service to society includes service to their local communities. But in fact its Tokyo headquarters competes with Yamanaka's shrine, fire-fighting association, and other groups for labor, money, and senti-ment. In the extreme case, that of Hideo, the talent and wealth of a householder at the peak of his abilities were shifted from hamlet to Kōsei-kai. Until his recent retirement, Hideo spent most of his time away from the hamlet, mostly at his office at the church. His case brought the greatest criticism from other hamlet residents, who felt that his household was lost to the community, but it is different only in degree from those of other members.

Corollary to material losses to the hamlet is a sense that Kōsei-kai members' sentiments have been alienated and that the hamlet social order has been undermined. In and around the hamlet, Kōsei-kai members constitute a new common-interest group with diffuse communal relationships. These supplement hamlet relationships based on neighborhood, kinship, and common-interest groups. But relations within Kōsei-kai seem to go beyond most of those within other groups in frequency, intimacy, and overt expressions of solidarity. In these qualities, relations between local members resemble relations within households; members use, for example, the familistic terms "parent" and "child" for a recruiter and a person he brings into the movement. Kōsei-kai also fosters group feeling with its creed, beginning "We, the members of Risshō Kōsei-kai . . .," and its crest, prominent in the altars of members as well as in the meeting place. The community of members, then, parallels and competes with older hamlet organizations at levels from the household to the whole hamlet. In creating new bonds it has weakened old ones and aroused hostility in that majority who have not joined.

Conclusions

I began this study hoping to shed light on several general questions about religion, principally the question of its relation to secular thought and action, by characterizing members of a religious movement in one community and discovering their reasons for joining. I supposed that members would be, in some way, relatively deprived and that they would have joined to change their lot. This supposition was borne out. Members and nonmembers alike said that people who joined were at that time sicker or in some other way worse off than others and that they joined to improve their condition.

But this result, though interesting, is not the most important one. Just as interesting is evidence contradicting the assumption (still frequent, though waning, among social scientists) that religious beliefs in small, relatively traditional, culturally homogeneous communities are themselves homogeneous or uncritically subscribed to and that their principal purpose and result is to reinforce the social order. Instead, there is diversity, skepticism, and inquiry both in the established religions and in the new one, and social division, not solidarity, as a result of the new religion.

Most interesting, however, is that in Yamanaka "religious" and much "secular" thought and action share a major model and some major principles. The model in question is the set of social relations—primarily the parent-child relationship—of which the household is supposed to consist. The principles include economy, coherence, and, most broadly, unity. There is no evident break between ordinary and religious life. "Religion" as the people of the hamlet see it consists simply in assuming that the household, by persisting, transcends death and that neither the social relations nor their human nodes simply cease to be. Seen this way, belief in ancestors is neither irrational nor cognitively gratuitous but an economical assumption of regularity and continuity in social relations. With this belief, death entails an adjustment but no cessation of relations, either between living and dead or among the living.

Belief in ancestors is economical regarding assumptions about individual existence as well. In the traditional view, living and dead alike consist primarily of the set of social relations in which they participate. For individuals, existence begins and ends not with birth and death but with participation and nonparticipation in relationships. Like Berkeley's sense objects, persons exist not in and of themselves but as they affect other persons. This relativity of existence is the reason that it is no heresy for Hideo to say that ancestors exist only in the hearts of survivors or for the Shinto priest to say that *kami* exist only in human minds and even that they are "made" by humans. Again as with sense objects for Berkeley, ancestors and *kami* exist to the extent that they are perceived or remembered or in some way interact with other persons. As Niwano (1968:136) said to Myōkō at her funeral, "Even though your body passes away, your soul is living forever within our minds." It does not diminish ancestors to say that they exist only in their influence on living persons since it is in such influence that living persons also exist.[61]

Some people think the ancestors and *kami* somewhat independent of the living, but no one thinks them completely independent since an ancestor without connections would be a contradition.[62] But a living person without connections—without relations to others—is equally a contradition. In traditional Japanese thought, commonsensical and scholarly, the individual never exists independently but always in a network. To exist is to have connections. To be lacking sufficient connections is to be curtailed or impaired. Physical illness, among other things, may result from hiatus in social relations. Kōsei-kai aims to identify the flawed or broken connections indicated by illness, quarrels, or other symptoms and provide the means to mend them. Identification of the problem in itself provides a connection, literally a "tie." Establishing this tie is the first and most important step in restoring the diminished person to the full set of relations of which he consists. Actions then taken—prayer, offerings, social work—are concrete means to reintegration.

The view of the world that Kōsei-kai affirms and elaborates is unified, with "no effects without causes." Taking as elements of its model the ethical relations of the household, it reasserts the traditional assumption that these relations obtain not only in human society but also in the world at large—that is, in all experience whatsoever. By this assertion Kōsei-kai establishes comprehensive pattern and meaning in the world.

Mary Douglas (1968:340), among others, has noted the human "urge to unify experience to create order and wholeness" and suggests that "our [Western] culture has largely given up the attempt to unify, to interpenetrate, and to cross-interpret." She adds that actually the attempt to unify has not so much been given up as consigned to natural science. Both of her formulations seem correct. Natural science *has* taken over the attempt to unify, but with markedly reduced ambition. It has, in Levi-Strauss's (1966:11) phrase, given up the "imperious and uncompromising demand" for determination. More radically, but perhaps as a corollary, many Westerners are now pessimistic about finding *any* intelligibility or meaning in human existence. The pessimists include anthropologists, professionally concerned to find unity in human existence, among others. Rodney Needham, as noted, writes (1972:244):

> I am not saying that human life is senseless, but that we cannot make sense of it. If only it were at least a tale told by an idiot, we might arrive at some coherent meaning, but the metaphor presupposes criteria of intelligibility and sanity that we do not possess except by convention.

Kōsei-kai members, in contrast, have not given up the attempt to unify experience. They think neither that life is senseless nor that we cannot make sense of it. For them as for Evans-Pritchard's Azande, there are no mere accidents, no events without meaning. Most members are "relatively deprived" in some way. More important, they are determined to find meaning in their deprivation, and elsewhere as well, and thus to grasp their lives. Though deprived, they share Kadoya's confidence that "if I study, there is nothing I cannot understand."

Notes

[1]See, e.g., Basabe 1967 and 1968, Norbeck 1970, Suenari 1972, Earhart 1974a, Smith 1978, Davis 1980, Murakami 1980, and Nakamaki 1983. Smith (1978:5), for example, says that in the village of Kurusu "festivals have been almost completely abandoned." In 1951 Kurusu's rice seedbeds were "still adorned with offerings to Jichin-san, the hamlet's tutelary deity" (1978:89), but in 1978 only one farmer put up such offerings.

[2]General introductions to the New Religions include McFarland's (1967) *The Rush Hour of the Gods*, Norbeck's (1970) *Religion and Society in Modern Japan*, and Arai's (1972) "New Religious Movements." Recent accounts of individual New Religions are Davis's (1980) *Dojo* and Hardacre's (1984) *Lay Buddhism in Contemporary Japan: Reiyūkai Kyōdan*. Hardacre's (1986) *Kurozumikyō and the New Religions of Japan* combines an account of a single movement with an excellent account of the world-view shared, in her view, by all the New Religions. The standard Western-language bibliography is Earhart's (1983) second edition of *The New Religions of Japan*.

[3]Hori (1968:218), for example, says that the movements are a response to the "acute anomie into which the Japanese people were thrown by defeat and occupation." Thomsen (1963:12 and 236) refers to "poverty, illness, powerlessness, and confusion of values," and to "disprivilege and frustration." Norbeck (1970:38) writes that the "great majority . . . were converted because of the promise of cure of sickness or recovery from other misfortune." Arai (1972) mentions illness and the alienation felt by those who left old religious ties in their villages when they moved to the cities, and Morioka (1979:248) writes of "anomie and social disintegration . . . disease, poverty, hunger, and anxiety." Earhart (1980b:xii) refers to the "religious and moral vacuum" after the war, and Murakami (1980:146) mentions the "desolation and poverty" of the Occupation. Davis (1980:9) cites the "immiseration of the population, the humiliation of military defeat, and the anxiety that resulted from . . .

207

radical demographic dislocations." Dale (1975:16), in one of the few Western-language monographs on Risshō Kōsei-kai, also refers to the collapse of the government and its restrictions on religion, and again to the "desperate economic, social, moral and spiritual situation" of the nation. In short, as Hardacre (1984:30) notes, "Studies of the Japanese new religions have relied almost without exception on the notion of social crisis."

[4]In a striking parallel, Hardacre (1984:22) notes that the great earthquake of 1923 "precipitated a situation of general crisis and ushered in an era of suppression," contributing to the conditions for the founding of the parent movement of Kōsei-kai, Reiyūkai.

[5]Crapo (1982) has called attention also to White's (1969) related view, which, however, seems less firmly grounded than Horton's (Guthrie 1982).

[6]Shamanism has had an enduring place in Japanese religion, and Kitagawa (1971) traces its amalgamation with folk Buddhism to the 8th century. Hori (1968) describes its place in Japanese folk religion generally, and Davis (1980) gives a detailed account of it in a particular New Religion.

[7]The official importance and the popularity of Kōsei-kai's *hōza* contrast with the situation in its parent movement, Reiyūkai, where Hardacre (1984) describes *hōza* as strained and unpopular. For an account of Kōsei-kai *hōza* as held at headquarters, see Dale (1975).

[8]Dale (1975) reports much the same emphasis in solutions heard at the Tokyo headquarters, based on the doctrine that suffering is the result of one's own actions and that its cure lies in reform of one's own character and behavior—a doctrine that Hardacre (1986) finds central to all the New Religions.

[9]See Plath 1964, Beardsley, Hall, and Ward 1965, Fukutake 1967 and 1974, Befu 1971, Smith 1978, and Dore 1978.

[10]This is the eccentric day laborer, a moody and by turns garrulous and taciturn man. When I asked about him, several people said that he is "perverse" (*kawatta*) and "untrustworthy" (*shinyo dekinai*), refuses to pay taxes and make festival contributions, and should be avoided. When I came to know him, he made it clear that the aversion was mutual. He

said that other villagers are uneducated and unimaginative and think him and his schemes (including a man-powered airplane, for which he had carved the propeller, and devices to make ships as fast as airplanes) insane. He alleged that another villager, whom he named, had murdered his own wife but somehow had gone unpunished. He said that his relations with other villagers are so bad that in the event of a fire or other emergency, he could expect no help at all.

[11]Several people told me this story independently. When the retired superintendent of education told it, he added that the man's illusion of being surrounded by a sea was probably caused simply by seeing the river from the unusual vantage of the tall tree.

[12]The assumption that behavioral traits are heritable results in the common practice of investigating the mental as well as physical medical history of the family of a proposed spouse.

[13]A similar decline has been noted elsewhere as well (Ooms 1976:86; Maeda 1976:143; and Murakami 1980).

[14]Gōrai Shigeru (1984:26) notes similarly that "many Japanese participate in temple worship and depend on the temple for funeral rites, but do not even know to which Buddhist sect their temple belongs."

[15]These are: January 1–3, *Tendoku daihannya* (Reading of the Sutra of the Great Wisdom); January 26, *Kōso kotan-e* (Founder's Birthday); February 25, *Nehan-e* (Buddha's Nirvana); March 18–24, *Haru higan-e* (Spring Equinox Service for the Dead); April 5, *Segaki-e* (Mass for the Dead); April 8, *Butsu kotan-e* (Buddha's Birth) and *Daihannya* (Sutra of the Great Wisdom); September 3–5, *Urabon-e* (commonly called *obon* or *bon*: "All Souls' Day"); September 18–24, *Aki higan-e* (Autumn Equinox Service for the Dead); December 8, *Jōdo-e* (The Buddha's Enlightenment).

[16]This seems to have been the case for the last several centuries at least, during which Buddhism is sometimes said to have become "fossilized" and to have preached, at most, "resignation" (Tsukamoto 1974:215). Of Buddhism in the 20th century, Tsukamoto (1974:215) says that "no attempt was made to preach any doctrine of awakening or advancement." Dore (1978:261) comments more generally that the "connection between religion and ethics has been an off-and-on thing in Japan."

[17]He seems to be sounding a theme now familiar to anthropologists: that religious conceptions have an "aura of factuality" and seem "uniquely realistic" (Geertz 1966:4).

[18]Gōrai Shigeru (1984:26–32) gives a brief but interesting recent look at the "dichotomy between the 'official' Buddhist teaching and popular faith."

[19]For divergence from this pattern, see Nakamaki 1983. Most people in the hamlet assume that "religion" (shūkyō) is equivalent to "Buddhism" and that all religions have the same purpose, namely, to remain in touch with the household dead. Asked the meaning of the term "religion," people typically replied, "Do you mean praying to the dead?" or "Well, when your parents die, it's a matter of honoring them, a matter of not forgetting them." Smith (1974:164) also confirms the "common observation that the emphasis on memorial rites has long since overwhelmed all doctrinal and sectarian diversity" in Japanese Buddhism. Shibata (1983:39) notes that Japanese "accept ancestor worship as . . . encompassing all religions [and] immediately and instinctively think of the term sosen sūhai (ancestor worship) when they hear the word shūkyō (religion)." Gōrai Shigeru (in Shibata 1983:47) says that "contemporary Buddhism in Japan is funeral Buddhism and ancestor worship."

This situation suggests that Fortes's (1976:12) question, whether ancestor worship should be thought of as a religion or as an extension of social relations, makes a distinction without a difference. On the other hand, Fujii (1983:40), well acquainted with the Japanese material (though from a Christian viewpoint), seems to make a similar distinction: "In Japan Buddhism . . . became more a deep-rooted ancestral cult than a religion in senso strictu."

[20]Smith (1974) gives an excellent, thorough account of terms for (and treatment of) the dead in Japan generally. See also Takeda 1976 and Offner 1979.

[21]The independence of biology and ancestry may also be inferred from the adoption and succession practices mentioned under "The Household" above, as well as from Smith's (1974:183) finding that of ancestral tablets fully 25 percent were those people who had died while still children and who therefore were "ancestral to no one." This among other evidence weakens Fortes's (1976:5) claim that "tautologous as it seems, it is a point of importance that the attainment of ancestorhood

and the ritual services of ancestor worship necessitate . . . the achieve-ment of parenthood."

[22]Morioka (1977:194) shows, however, that slightly later scholars including Fukasaku, Watari, and Hozumi continued to equate ancestors and *kami*, holding that "respect for the *kami* . . . means ancestor venera-tion." Inoue (1911:212–13, in Morioka 1977:192), for example, wrote that

> in one household, the common ancestors of the family are worshipped; in the village, it is the ujigami [tutelary kami], i.e., the common ancestors of the nation. There is a splendid state shrine for the national ancestor.

[23]For the limits of syncretism elsewhere, see Nakamaki 1983.

[24]Here as elsewhere (Nakamaki 1983). On the other hand, Offner (1979:10) found in his 1977 survey of 100 white-collar households in Aichi Prefecture that "for most of the respondents once the spirit of the departed has entered the spirit world there is no need to distinguish *hotoke* from *kami*."

[25]For placement of the *butsudan* elsewhere in Japan, see Nakamaki 1983.

[26]Davis (1980) writes that in the New Religion, Mahikari, the tablets are considered to *be* the ancestors, so literally that one must pick them up for dusting only by the bottom or "feet," to avoid grasping the "head."

[27]Embree 1939:284–87; Hori 1968:56, 138–39, 156–59, 170n.; Smith 1974.

[28]Ooms 1967, 1976; Smith 1974; Bernier 1975; Fujii 1983.

[29]See Fujii 1983 for a discussion of changes in funerals associated with cremation.

[30]This was the young poet's explanation when he and I visited the shallow cave to view the palanquin. It had been left carelessly lying on its side, exposed to wind and rain, the straw and paper accoutrements from the last funeral still attached and in disarray. He said that the

place had a "bad feeling" (*kimochi ga warui*). When I asked him to stand by the palanquin to give scale to a photograph, he demurred, though usually he was willing to be photographed.

[31]Fujii (1983) reports that half of all "seventh-day rites" now are held either on the day of the funeral or on the day after and similarly attributes this to the "needs of busy, widely-scattered people."

[32]Fujii (1983:62) cites a 1981 *Asahi Shinbun* survey asking, "Do you think that people's spirits continue to exist after death?" Sixty percent thought that they do, 30 percent thought that they do not, and 10 percent did not respond. Swyngedouw (1985), citing an NHK Broadcasting Company survey in addition to the *Asahi Shinbun*, gives similar figures.

[33]For example, a woman of fifty-five told me the following story from her youth:

> About the time I came here as a bride—my father was a great sake drinker, you know—well, he came home after drinking. And he said, "Hey, Grandma! Boil some meat, boil some rabbit meat, okay?" So my mother went to get some onions. The road was over on that side; the stone house was on this side. So just then—she was going to boil some meat, right?—she yelled, "*Waa! Kyaa!*" Whatever you'd call it—a "death fire" (*hitodama*)? A flash of light? She said it went out over there, *Raaa!* Yeah. So— this probably sounds funny, but—Mother was yelling, "Quick, come out and look!" So my father went out, but he couldn't see it. According to my mother, something about this big [indicates a sphere about half a meter across] appeared, *Shuuu!*
>
> The next day, while we were still thinking, "It didn't happen," and "A mystery!" we went to cut firewood on the mountain, right? Cut firewood, and bring down branches to burn. Before, around here, there wasn't any gas and things like that. So my mother and I went to do that. But just as we were beginning to work [something happened], you know? My older sister—her child, he was about five years old—he got sick, and it was bad, I tell you! So my mother, without having done any work, came home and headed for the nearest doctor. It was a long way, but she got in a car and got on the train—and just as they left, he died. Yeah. So . . . when that

sort of—light—flies . . . should one say, a "soul" (*tamashii*)? When things like that do that sort of thing, well!

That's what happened, then, thirty-five or thirty-six years ago, when we were still girls.

[34]Kopytoff (1971:129), following Fortes (1965), has noted a similar lack of interest in locations of ancestors in Africa: "The African emphasis is clearly not on how the dead live but in the manner in which they affect the living." Many of his other points about African "ancestor worship," e.g., the importance of seniority, the lack of a sharp division between living and dead, and prayer as communion rather than as worship, fit "ancestor worship" in Yamanaka as well. Ooms (1976) also has noted the absence of clear ideas or strong opinions in Japan about the afterlife.

[35]Bernier refers (1975:143) to "the vague conceptions people have of the other world" in a village in southern Mie Prefecture, and Smith (1974) and Ooms (1976) among others comment similarly. Yanagita (1962:123), in Munakata (1977:36), says that by the end of memorial services thirty-three or fifty years after death, the "individual man melts into a greater body of spirits. . . . The continued existence of the spirit . . . is not considered."

[36]Diviners in Japan are most frequently women in middle age or above, and frequently they are blind (Hori 1968:203–15). This woman was said to have been abandoned in childhood and to have become a diviner in middle age, after a misfortune in love.

[37]The lack of pronounced fear or awe of death and the dead is one feature that most people in the hamlet seem to share with the temple priest, who offered to me as an example of "truth" the unavoidable fact that "everyone dies." Reconciliation to this fact, he said, is the first condition of a happy life. My impression is that most people in Yamanaka have achieved this reconciliation relatively successfully, no doubt aided by the doctrine—and fact—of household continuity.

Offner (1979:12) sees this continuity negatively, describing the Japanese as "lacking a sense of clear-cut separation between the living and the dead." He also notes that rites for the dead are "primarily concerned with the continuation of personal human relationships and memories rather than worship" and cites Nakamura's (1964:361) observation that "one's *tama* (soul/spirit) is supposed to remain in this world . . . after death, and essentially no distinction is drawn between the states of one's *tama* before and after death."

[38]The same strong assumption of continuity between living and dead is noted for Africa by Kopytoff (1971). Both his description of relations between living and dead and his theoretical conclusions apply well to Yamanaka. African ancestors "retain a functional role in . . . the life of their living kinsmen [and] African kin-groups are often described as communities of both the living and the dead" (1971:129). Dead lineage members are appealed to collectively in such crises as serious illness or prolonged misfortune. Relations with them are shaped mainly by seniority: they are "fed" certain foods, and they are addressed, at their graves or at a crossroad, in a conversational monologue. They dispense both favors and misfortune, although they do not actively cause misfortune as much as allow it to happen. In social relations generally, seniority is the guiding principle, and the line between living and dead does not affect it. The English terms "ancestor," "cult," and "worship" are misleading because they suggest a dichotomy between living and dead that does not exist in the African view. We should understand relations with ancestors not as a symbolic projection of the social system, but as part of it.

If we change "lineage" to "household" and "crossroads" to "altar," and add some set formulas to the conversational monologues addressed to the dead, Kopytoff's description fits Yamanaka. People there represent themselves as a single group with their household dead. Relations with everyone in it follow a single model, the household, to which seniority and the parent-child relation are central. Tylor (1924:113, orig. 1871) long ago analyzed "ancestor worship" similarly:

> Its principles are not difficult to understand, for they plainly keep up the social relations of the living world. The dead ancestor, now passed into a deity, simply goes on protecting his family and receiving suit and service from them as of old.

[39]Spiro (1972:14) says that Buddhism does not occur in any culture by itself but is always accompanied by another, complementary religion to which most people simultaneously subscribe. This clearly is true in Japan.

[40]See Dore 1967, Ono 1969, Matsumoto 1972, Bernier 1975.

[41]Ueda's analysis of *kami* parallels Lienhardt's (1961:158) analysis of Dinka "Divinity":

> Divinity, then, images here the lived experience of community and concord, and . . . also represents truth, justice, honesty,

uprightness, and such-like conditions of order and peace in human relations . . . experience of living is here clearly the basis from which comes such purely theoretical or cognitive apprehension of Divinity and the Powers as the Dinka have . . . their notion of Divinity may be seen to arise in the experience of order in relation to disorder, life in relation to death . . . and not merely as a theoretical force from without.

[42]For a recent list of traditional household *kami*, see Nakamaki 1983.

[43]In Japan foxes traditionally (Hori 1968:45; see Davis 1980 for a more extensive account) have the power to bewitch and possess humans. Most people I asked in Yamanaka were skeptical about this power, but at a meeting I attended at the next village to the north, a Kōsei-kai member of about sixty reported his bewitchment by a fox. Another man received exorcism for a fox spirit at a Kōsei-kai "ascetic exercise" (*reikan shugyō*) I attended at the Ueno Church in 1971.

[44]The advice to see a doctor represents a change from the movement's policy of a decade before, when faith-healing was more prominent. The change seems to have been in part a reaction to criticism from newspapers and from the government, in part a response to an increasingly educated membership, and in part a response to increasingly available medical attention. Morioka (1979) reports a similar change in Kōsei-kai policy at the national level and attributes it to a shift in popular concerns from health to family social relations.

[45]Dale (1975) notes that Kōsei-kai links the "circle" (*wa*) to "harmony" (*wa*) by punning. At the same time, the principle of community is balanced against that of seniority. The seat of honor in Japan is the one—occupied here by the *hōza* leader—farthest from the entrance to the room, while the rank of other seats diminishes toward the entrance. The near equality of seating at meetings with the branch chief alone is replaced by a clearer hierarchy when the church chief also is present. Like the branch chief, he sits farthest from the entrance and, in addition, is flanked by the branch chief and any other officers present. Then the circle tends to collapse and be replaced by a somewhat amorphous group facing the chief, especially when there are more than about fifteen people present and when space does not permit an open circle. The church chief's seniority is also expressed by the length of his responses to problems, which tend to become doctrinal lectures. The

least egalitarian meeting is the formal doctrinal lecture, where lay members form a clear single group facing the speaker.

[46]The Great Sacred Hall (*daiseidō*), completed in 1964 as a "sanctuary for the salvation of mankind" (Niwano 1978:204), cost ¥4 billion (about $11 million). It is an eight-story, ferro-concrete structure 33.66 m high, with a total floor area of 23,154 m². The building combines, in eclectic and opulent fashion, elements of traditional Japanese Buddhist art, contemporary technology, and its own idiosyncratic symbolism. Its circular floor plan represents the perfection of the Lotus Sutra, an internal bridge represents the pathway to Nirvana, and a large tower on the roof represents the Eightfold Path. Its technical facilities include central heating, cooling, humidity control, vacuum cleaning, electrical generation, closed-circuit and broadcast television stations, and three deep wells with a daily capacity of 2,200,000 gallons (Risshō Kōsei-kai 1970). Dale (1975, esp. pp. 37–43) gives an excellent description of the interior appearance and atmosphere of this hall and its effect on *hōza* held there.

The "Hall of the Open Gate" (*fumonkan*), completed in 1970 at a cost of ¥10 billion, centers around a lecture hall for 5,000 people and has a floor space of 42,800 m². It is even more opulent and more of a showcase of technology than is the Great Sacred Hall, with a revolving stage and "the latest acoustical and motion-picture equipment" (Niwano 1978:246). Blacker (1971:598) has noted that such opulent, modernistic architecture is widely used by the New Religions as one of the

> outward signs of modern progress . . . too widely accepted as symbols of prestige to be thought dispensable in paradise. The *shinkō shūkyō* . . . are always careful to equip their concrete cathedrals with the latest heating and cooling devices, the latest acoustic equipment, the most up-to-date networks of closed-circuit television . . . the earthly paradise, like these cathedrals which are often conceived to be its miniature forerunners, will boast a modern image.

The design of the Hall of the Open Gate, like that of the Great Sacred Hall, is symbolic (Niwano 1978:246–47):

> The form of the building—two circles joined in one—is derived from the Seal of the Three Laws: "All things are impermanent"; "Nothing has an ego"; and "Nirvana is quiescence." The twenty-eight columns on the exterior of the building symbolize the twenty-eight chapters of the Lotus

Sutra. The statue of Kannon, the Bodhisattva Regarder of the Cries of the World, enshrined in the lobby on the second floor . . . symbolizes the thirty-three forms that Kannon may assume in saving sentient beings from confusion and suffering.

[47]His review for 1963, for example, listed fourteen events, including Kennedy's assassination, the construction of a fire tower in Yamanaka, a train wreck in the Philippines that killed 204 people, a house burning down in a neighboring hamlet, completion of the Ueno City waterworks, and his own appointment as the Ueno Youth Division representative to Kōsei-kai headquarters.

[48]Dore (1978:263) also notes that the contemporary Japanese charismatic healer is "likely, now, to be a modernized one who has assimilated—at least a pop-version of—the science on whose fringes he operates. He is likely to have more in common with macrobiotic foods and Canadian Air Force exercises than with traditional 'prayer ladies' and their trances."

[49]His account also echoes, in alluding to postwar social degeneration and to Niwano's search for a solution among existing religious organizations, traditional accounts of the Buddha's and of Nichiren's wanderings amid suffering and turmoil, looking vainly for an existing religious remedy. Niwano's hope to restore a national spiritual unity to a Japan riven by physical and moral troubles is particularly like that of Nichiren. Nor was he alone: in the mid-1930s there were some 750 "religio-political societies" (Davis 1977:69) directed to the same end.

[50]Offner and van Straelen (1963:274), for example, say that there is an "undeniable pecuniary interest evident" in many of them, and Earhart (personal communication) also has noted this.

[51]Watanabe (1968:221) and Dale (1975:44–45) have noted similar threats by Kōsei-kai to wavering members.

[52]Dale (1975:58) reports the same complaint from a Tokyo member:

One thing that stands between us and the community is that we . . . use too much pressure and propaganda . . . we're always waving the flag in front of us. Wouldn't it be better if we simply led a good life and let people judge for themselves whether or not they want to join our organization?

[53]Hardacre (1984:58) reports that Reiyūkai leaders also sometimes pay the dues of members who quit, evidently for similar reasons.

[54]Kōsei-kai usually counts its members by households and assumes that if the head is a member, everyone is. Kadoya said that his retired parents are members as part of his household, as well as his wife and children. His mother, however, told me with apparent rancor that neither she nor her husband are members and that in fact that only Kadoya had joined. She pointed out that her husband insists on keeping the memorial tablets in the old altar rather than in the new one with Kōsei-kai emblems "because the ancestors don't like to be moved into a new place." Kadoya's wife said that she is a member, but she is unenthusiastic and in 1971 came to the meeting place only once.

[55]This scrutiny and apparent rationality regarding the rewards of membership may be representative not only of other local Kōsei-kai members, as I am maintaining, but of members of other New Religions in other parts of Japan as well. Davis (1977:89) for example, though he does not regard their behavior as particularly rational, notes of the New Religions that "the individual, and his family, often drop out when the sect fails to bring about the kind of health, wealth, and happiness it promised to deliver."

[56]Based on the 1971 village property-tax register. Holdings certainly are undervalued, but probably uniformly so.

[57]The idea of the individual as principally a node in a network of relations, relatively recently developed in Western sociology and anthropology, is characteristically Japanese. As the philosopher Nakamura Hajime (1967:182) put it,

the Japanese in general did not develop a clearcut concept of the human individual *qua* individual as an objective unit like an inanimate thing, but the individual is always found existing in a network of human relationships.

[58]The "empiricism" of subjective experiences such as happiness may seem doubtful to the Western reader, but I think it is self-evident to the Japanese. Kawashima (1967:262) notes that the Japanese world-view has "radical empirical immediacy." Dōgen, founder of Sōtō Zen, wrote (Nakamura 1967:187) that the mind

is infallible. . . . Blue, yellow, red, and white are nothing but
the mind. Long, short, square, and round are nothing but the
mind. Life and death are nothing but the mind.

Kishimoto (1967:113) has argued that "the common concern of all these
[Japanese] religions is the internal problems of man. Their main focus
is on immediate experience." Dōgen also has said (Ueda 1967:170) that
"to study Buddhism is to study oneself. To study oneself is to forget
oneself. To forget oneself is to realize oneself as all things [in the
world]."

[59]Rajana (1975:197) concludes about the New Religions in general
that they "relate atomised individuals to larger society" and "help to
integrate [into the larger society] individuals who have few alternative
means of participating." Whether or not Kōsei-kai "integrates" people
with the larger society, it does provide an alternative route to social
recognition. Hardacre (1986:192–93) similarly states that

the new religions offer cherished avenues to prestige and
recognition seldom open to members in secular society. . . .
The new religions provide ladders of prestige and reward for
achievement. . . . Much as a man rises through the ranks in a
company, members of the new religion can win reward and
recognition that might well be beyond their reach in secular
society.

[60]Kōsei-kai, like many of the New Religions, does not distinguish
between religion and science, or, as Arai (1972:104) puts it, "the new
religions tend to mingle and confuse science and religion." This "confusion" may be seen, for example, in the abundant mechanistic and scien-
tistic metaphor used. A former president of Sōka Gakkai, for instance,
called the mandala a "machine that turns out happiness" (Arai
1972:100), and a Kōsei-kai leader said, "Our answer does not come
simply from our own reason, but it comes from beyond us. We are like a
TV set. Tune it right and the picture comes from beyond onto the
screen" (Dale 1975:62). The use of such images may be in part an
attempt to borrow the prestige of science and modern technology and in
part simply a reflection of popular contemporary figures of speech.
However, I think it is more than this. It seems likely that many
members simply do not distinguish religion and science but see them
rather as contiguous and interpenetrating descriptions of the world.

[61]In the non-Berkeleyan, realist view prevailing in the West, such a
dependent mode of existence must be sharply distinguished from the

independence of "real" existence. But in the "radical empiricism"
(Kishimoto 1967:112) sometimes said to characterize Japanese thought,
this distinction is much less important.

[62]There are, however, anomalous "wandering ghosts" (*muen-botoke*, literally "buddhas without a connection"), who are the spirits of
people without descendants (chapter 3). These are dangerous, in the
view of the few people who now take them seriously, because in their
desperate need to establish relationships, they may draw the living into
the other world.

Bibliography

Arai, Ken. 1972. New religious movements. In *Japanese religion, a survey by the Agency for Cultural Affairs.* Ed. Hori Ichirō, Ikado Fujio, Wakimoto Tsuneya, and Yanagawa Keiichi. Tokyo and Palo Alto: Kōdansha.

Barbour, Ian G. 1974. *Myths, models, and paradigms.* New York: Harper and Row.

Barnes, Barry. 1974. The comparison of belief-systems: Anomaly versus falsehood. In *Modes of thought.* Ed. Robin Horton and Ruth Finnegan. London: Faber and Faber.

Basabe, Fernando M. 1967. *Japanese youth confronts religion, a sociological survey.* Tokyo and Rutland, Vermont: Sophia University and Charles E. Tuttle Company.

____. 1968. *Religious attitudes of Japanese men, a new sociological study.* Tokyo and Rutland, Vermont: Sophia University and Charles E. Tuttle Company.

Beardsley, Richard K., John W. Hall, and Robert C. Ward. 1965. *Village Japan.* Chicago and London: University of Chicago Press.

Beattie, J. H. M. 1970. On understanding ritual. In *Rationality.* Ed. Bryan R. Wilson. Evanston and New York: Harper and Row.

Befu, Harumi. 1971. *Japan, an anthropological introduction.* San Francisco and London: Chandler Publishing Company.

Bellah, Robert N. 1964. Religious evolution. *American Sociological Review* 29:357-58.

Benedict, Ruth. 1946. *The chrysanthemum and the sword.* New York: Houghton Mifflin.

Berkeley, Bishop George. 1939. A treatise concerning the principles of human knowledge. In *The English philosophers from Bacon to Mill.* Ed. Edwin A. Burtt. New York: Random House.

Bernier, Bernard. 1975. *Breaking the cosmic circle: Religion in a Japanese village.* Cornell University East Asia Papers 5. Ithaca, NY: Cornell China-Japan Program.

Black, Max. 1962. *Models and metaphors.* Ithaca, NY: Cornell University Press.

Blacker, Carmen. 1971. Millennarian aspects of the new religions in Japan. In *Tradition and modernization in Japanese culture.* Ed. Donald H. Shively. Princeton: Princeton University Press.

Brown, Keith. 1979. *Shinjō, the chronicle of a Japanese village.* Ethnology Monographs 2. Pittsburgh: University Center for International Studies.

Bunce, William K. 1955. *Religions in Japan.* Tokyo: Charles E. Tuttle Company.

Chinnery, Thora E. 1971. *Religious conflict and compromise in a Japanese village: A first-hand observation of the Tenrikyō church.* The University of British Columbia Publications in Anthropology 5. Vancouver: The University of British Columbia.

Cohn, Norman. 1970. *The pursuit of the millennium.* New York: Oxford University Press.

Crapo, Richley H. 1982. More on a cognitive theory of religion. *Current Anthropology* 23:341-42.

Cross, Whitney R. 1950. *The burned-over district.* Ithaca, NY: Cornell University Press.

Dale, Kenneth. 1975. *Circle of harmony: A case study in popular Japanese Buddhism.* South Pasadena, CA: William Carey Library; Tokyo: Seibunsha.

Davis, Winston. 1977. *Toward modernity: A developmental typology of popular religious affiliations in Japan.* Cornell University East Asia Papers 12. Ithaca, NY: Cornell China-Japan Program.

____. 1980. *Dojo: Magic and exorcism in modern Japan.* Stanford: Stanford University Press.

Dore, Ronald P. 1967. *City life in Japan.* Berkeley and Los Angeles: University of California Press.

____. 1978. *Shinohata: A portrait of a Japanese village.* New York: Pantheon Books.

Douglas, Mary. 1968. Pollution. In *International encyclopedia of the social sciences*, vol. 12. Ed. David R. Sills. New York: Macmillan.

Durkheim, Emile. 1976. *The elementary forms of the religious life.* London: George Allen and Unwin, Ltd.

Earhart, H. Byron. 1969. The interpretation of the "new religions" of Japan as historical phenomena. *Journal of the American Academy of Religion* 37.3 (September):237–48.

____. 1970. *The new religions of Japan: A bibliography of Western-language materials.* Tokyo: Sophia University.

____. 1974a. *Japanese religion: Unity and diversity.* 2nd ed. Encino and Belmont, CA: Dickenson Publishing Company.

____. 1974b. *Religion in the Japanese experience: Sources and interpretations.* Belmont, CA: Dickenson Publishing Company.

____. 1980a. Toward a theory of the formation of the Japanese new religions: A case study of Gedatsu-kai. *History of Religions* 20.1–2 (August-November):175–97.

____. 1980b. Translator's introduction. In *Japanese religion in the modern century*, by Shigeyoshi Murakami. Tokyo: University of Tokyo Press.

____. 1983. *The new religions of Japan: A bibliography of Western-language materials.* 2d ed. Ann Arbor: University of Michigan Center for Japanese Studies.

Embree, John F. 1939. *Suye Mura, a Japanese village.* Chicago: University of Chicago Press.

Evans-Pritchard, Edward Evan. 1956. *Nuer religion.* Oxford: Clarendon Press.

Fernandez, James W. 1982. *Bwiti: An ethnography of the religious consciousness in Africa.* Princeton: Princeton University Press.

Festinger, Leon, Henry W. Riecken, and Stanley Schachter. 1956. *When prophecy fails.* Minneapolis: University of Minnesota Press.

Fortes, Meyer. 1965. Some reflections on ancestor worship. In *African systems of thought.* Ed. Meyer Fortes and G. Dieterlen. London: Oxford University Press.

____. 1976. An introductory commentary. In *Ancestors.* Ed. William H. Newell. The Hague: Mouton.

Frazer, Sir James. 1935. *The golden bough.* New York: Macmillan.

Freud, Sigmund. 1961. The future of an illusion. In *The standard edition of the complete psychological works of Sigmund Freud,* vol. 21. Ed. J. Strachey. London: Hogarth Press.

Fujii, Masao. 1983. Maintenance and change in Japanese traditional funeral and death-related behavior. *Japanese Journal of Religious Studies* 10.1:39-64.

Fukasaku, Yasufumi. 1911. Kazoku seido hiken [The family system: A personal view]. In *Kokumin kyōiku to kazoku seido* [National education and the family system]. Ed. Tōa Kyōkai. Tokyo: Meguro Shoten.

Fukutake, Tadashi. 1967. *Japanese rural society.* London: Oxford University Press.

____. 1974. *Japanese society today.* Tokyo: University of Tokyo Press.

Geertz, Clifford. 1966. Religion as a cultural system. In *Anthropological approaches to the study of religion.* Association of Social Anthropologists Monographs 3. Ed. Michael Banton. London: Tavistock Publications.

_____. 1975. Comon sense as a cultural system. *Antioch Review* 33:5-26.

Gellner, Ernest. 1970. Concepts and society. In *Rationality.* Ed. Bryan R. Wilson. Evanston and New York: Harper and Row.

Gōrai, Shigeru. 1984. Folk religion and the cult of the ancestors. *Japanese Religions* 13.2:26-32.

Griaule, Marcel. 1980. *Conversations with Ogotemmeli.* London: Oxford University Press.

Guthrie, Stewart Elliott. 1980a. A cognitive theory of religion. *Current Anthropology* 21:181-203.

_____. 1980b. Reply (to Bourdillon, de Mahieu, Sahay, and Teran-Dutari on "A cognitive theory of religion"). *Current Anthropology* 21:537-38.

_____. 1982. Reply (to Adams and Crapo on "A cognitive theory of religion"). *Current Anthropology* 23:342-44.

Hardacre, Helen. 1984. *Lay Buddhism in contemporary Japan: Reiyūkai Kyōdan.* Princeton: Princeton University Press.

_____. 1986. *Kurozumikyō and the new religions of Japan.* Princeton: Princeton University Press.

Hesse, Mary. 1966. *Models and analogies in science.* Notre Dame: University of Notre Dame Press.

Hockett, Charles. 1973. *Man's place in nature.* New York: McGraw-Hill Book Company.

Hori, Ichirō. 1968. *Folk religion in Japan.* Ed. Joseph M. Kitagawa and Alan L. Miller. Tokyo: University of Tokyo Press.

Horton, Robin. 1960. A definition of religion and its uses. *Journal of the Royal Anthropological Institute* 90:211.

____. 1962. The Kalabari world-view: An outline and interpretation. *Africa* 32.3:197–219.

____. 1970. African traditional thought and Western science. In *Rationality*. Ed. Bryan R. Wilson. Evanston and New York: Harper and Row.

Horton, Robin, and Ruth Finnegan. 1973. *Modes of thought*. London: Faber and Faber.

Hozumi, Yatsuka. 1913. Yasokyō izen no Ōshū kasei [The family system in Europe before Christianity]. In *Hozumi Yatsuka hakase ronbunshū* [Collection of essays by Hozumi Yatsuka]. Ed. Uesugi Shinkichi.

Hsu, Francis L. K. 1975. *Iemoto: The heart of Japan*. New York: John Wiley and Sons, Inc.

Inoue, Tetsujirō. 1911. Waga kokutai to kazoku seido [Our national polity and the family system]. In *Kokumin kyōiku to kazoku seido* [National education and the family system]. Ed. Tōa Kyōkai. Tokyo: Meguro Shoten.

Kawa Mura Yakuba [Kawa Village Office]. 1971. *Kawa Mura son-sei yōran* [Kawa Village affairs survey].

Kawashima, Takeyoshi. 1967. The status of the individual in the notion of law, right, and social order. In *The Japanese mind*. Ed. Charles A. Moore. Honolulu: East-West Center Press, University of Hawaii Press.

Kishimoto, Hideo. 1967. Some Japanese cultural traits and religions. In *The Japanese mind*. Ed. Charles A. Moore. Honolulu: East-West Center Press, University of Hawaii Press.

Kitagawa, Joseph. 1971. New religions in Japan: A historical perspective. In *Religion and change in contemporary Asia*. Ed. Robert Spencer. Minneapolis: University of Minnesota Press.

Kluckhohn, Clyde. 1979. A general theory of myth and ritual. In *Reader in comparative religion*, 4th ed. Ed. William A. Lessa and Evon Z. Vogt. New York and London: Harper and Row.

Kopytoff, Igor. 1971. Ancestors and elders in Africa. *Africa* 41: 129, 141.

Kōsaka, Masaaki. 1967. The status and role of the individual in Japanese society. In *The Japanese mind*. Ed. Charles A. Moore. Honolulu: East-West Center Press, University of Hawaii Press.

Kuhn, Thomas S. 1970. *The structure of scientific revolutions*, 2d ed. Chicago: University of Chicago Press.

Leach, Edmund. 1954. *The political systems of highland Burma*. London: Bell.

Levi-Strauss, Claude. 1966. *The savage mind*. Chicago: University of Chicago Press.

Lienhardt, Godfrey. 1961. *Divinity and experience*. Oxford: Clarendon Press.

Maeda, Takashi. 1976. Ancestor worship in Japan. In *Ancestors*. Ed. William H. Newell. The Hague: Mouton.

Malinowski, Bronislaw. 1925. Magic, science, and religion. In *Science, religion, and reality*. Ed. James Needham. New York: Macmillan.

____. 1979. The role of magic and religion. In *Reader in comparative religion*, 4th ed. Ed. William A. Lessa and Evon Z. Vogt. New York and London: Harper and Row.

Maranda, Elli Koengaes. 1971. The logic of riddles. In *Structural analysis of oral tradition*. Ed. Pierre Maranda and Elli Koengaes Maranda. Philadelphia: University of Pennsylvania Press.

Marwick, M. G. 1973. How real is the charmed circle in African and Western thought? *Africa* 43:59-71.

Matsumoto, Shigeru. 1972. Introduction. In *Japanese religion, a survey by the Agency for Cultural Affairs*. Ed. Hori Ichirō, Ikado Fujio, Wakimoto Tsuneya, and Yanagawa Keiichi. Tokyo and Palo Alto: Kōdansha.

Matsunaga, Alice. 1969. *The Buddhist philosophy of assimilation*. Tokyo: Monumenta Nipponica, Sophia University.

McFarland, H. Neil. 1967. *The rush hour of the gods: A study of new religious movements in Japan.* New York: Macmillan.

Mishima, Yukio. 1963. *After the banquet.* New York: Alfred Knopf.

Morioka, Kiyomi. 1970-71. The impact of suburbanization on Shinto belief and behavior. *Social Compass* 42:37-65.

_____. 1977. The appearance of "ancestor religion" in modern Japan: The years of transition from the Meiji to the Taishō periods. *Japanese Journal of Religious Studies* 4:183-212.

_____. 1979. The institutionalization of a new religious movement. *Japanese Journal of Religious Studies* 6:1-2:239-80.

Morioka, Kiyomi, and William H. Newell. 1968. *The sociology of Japanese religion.* Leiden: E. J. Brill.

Munakata, Iwao. 1977. Symbolic structure of the traditional folk-religion in Japan and its transformation through the proliferation of the techno-industrial civilization. Unpublished manuscript.

Murakami, Shigeyoshi. 1980. *Japanese religion in the modern century.* Trans. H. Byron Earhart. Tokyo: University of Tokyo Press.

Nakamaki, Hirochika. 1983. The "separate" existence of *kami* and *hotoke*—a look at *Yorishiro. Japanese Journal of Religious Studies* 10.1:65-86.

Nakamura, Hajime. 1964. *Ways of thinking of Eastern peoples.* Honolulu: East-West Center Press.

_____. 1967. Consciousness of the individual and the universal among the Japanese. In *The Japanese mind.* Ed. Charles A. Moore. Honolulu: East-West Center Press, University of Hawaii Press.

Nakane, Chie. 1970. *Japanese society.* Berkeley and Los Angeles: University of California Press.

Needham, Rodney. 1972. *Belief, language, and experience.* Oxford: Basil Blackwell.

Niwano, Nikkyō. 1968. *Travel to infinity.* Tokyo: Kōsei Publishing Company.

____. 1978. *Lifetime beginner*. Tokyo: Kōsei Publishing Company.

Norbeck, Edward. 1970. *Religion and society in modern Japan: Continuity and change*. Houston: Tourmaline Press.

Offner, Clark B. 1979. Continuing concern for the departed. *Japanese Religions* 11.1:1–16.

Offner, Clark B., and Henry van Straelen. 1963. *Modern Japanese religions, with special emphasis on their doctrines of healing*. Tokyo: Rupert Enderle.

Ono, Sokyō. 1969. *Shinto, the kami way*. Tokyo and Rutland, Vermont: Charles E. Tuttle Company.

Ooms, Herman. 1967. The religion of the household: A case study of ancestor worship in Japan. *Contemporary Religions in Japan* 8.3–4:201–334.

____. 1976. A structural analysis of Japanese ancestral rites and beliefs. In *Ancestors*. Ed. William H. Newell. The Hague: Mouton.

Plath, David. 1964. Where the family of god is the family. *American Anthropologist* 66.2:300–17.

Popper, Sir Karl. 1985a. Against the sociology of knowledge. In *Popper selections*. Ed. David Miller. Princeton: Princeton University Press. Reprint from 1945.

____. 1985b. Realism. In *Popper selections*. Ed. David Miller. Princeton: Princeton University Press. Reprint from 1970.

____. 1985c. The self. In *Popper selections*. Ed. David Miller. Princeton: Princeton University Press. Reprint from 1977.

Putnam, Gareth. 1977. New intellectual and ecumenical emphases in Risshō Kōsei-kai: A seminar report. *Japanese Religions* 10.1:57–62.

Radcliffe-Brown, A. R. 1922. *The Andaman Islanders*. Cambridge: Cambridge University Press.

Rajana, Eimi Watanabe. 1975. New religions in Japan: An appraisal of two theories. In *Modern Japan: Aspects of history, literature, and society*. Ed. W. G. Beasley. Berkeley: University of California Press. See also Eimi Watanabe.

Risshō Kōsei-kai. 1966. *Risshō Kōsei-kai*. Tokyo: Kōsei Publishing Company.

_____. 1970. *Risshō Kōsei-kai, a new Buddhist laymen's movement in Japan*. Tokyo: Kōsei Publishing Company.

_____. 1980. *Risshō Kōsei-kai, an organization of Buddhist laymen*. Tokyo: Kōsei Publishing Company.

Roberts, John M., Saburo Morita, and L. Keith Brown. 1986. Personal categories for Japanese sacred places and gods: Views elicited from a conjugal pair. *American Anthropologist* 88.4:807–24.

Rodd, Laurel Rasplica. 1980. *Nichiren: Selected writings*. Hawaii: University of Hawaii Press.

Simpson, George Gaylord. 1961. *Principles of animal taxonomy*. New York: Columbia University Press.

Shibata, Chizuo. 1983. Some problematic aspects of Japanese ancestor worship. *Japanese Religions* 13.1:35–48.

Smith, Robert J. 1974. *Ancestor worship in contemporary Japan*. Stanford: Stanford University Press.

_____. 1978. *Kurusu: The price of progress in a Japanese village, 1951– 1975*. Stanford: Stanford University Press.

Sōrifu Tokei Kyoku (Bureau of Statistics, Office of the Prime Minister). 1970. *Shōwa yonju-go nen kokusei chōsa hōkoku, dai 3 kan, sono 10, Gunma-ken* [1970 population census of Japan], vol. 3, part 10, Gunma Prefecture.

Spae, Joseph J. 1966. Popular Buddhist ethics. *Japan Missionary Bulletin* 20:101–9, 232–41.

Spiro, Melford E. 1972. *Buddhism and society*. New York: Harper and Row.

Suenari, Michio. 1972. Yearly rituals within the household: A case study from a hamlet in northeastern Japan. *East Asian Cultural Studies* 11.14:77–82.

Sugihara, Yoshie, and David Plath. 1969. *Sensei and his people: The building of a Japanese commune.* Berkeley and Los Angeles: University of California Press.

Swanson, Guy E. 1960. *The birth of the gods: The origin of primitive beliefs.* Ann Arbor: University of Michigan Press.

Swyngedouw, Jan. 1985. The quiet reversal: A few notes on the NHK survey of Japanese religiosity. *Japan Missionary Bulletin* 39:4-13.

Takeda, Choshu. 1976. "Family religion" in Japan: *Ie* and its religious faith. In *Ancestors.* Ed. William H. Newell. The Hague: Mouton.

Tamaru, Noriyoshi. 1972. Buddhism. In *Japanese religion, a survey by the Agency for Cultural Affairs.* Ed. Hori Ichirō, Ikado Fujio, Wakimoto Tsuneya, and Yanagawa Keiichi. Tokyo and Palo Alto: Kōdansha.

Thomsen, Harry. 1963. *The new religions of Japan.* Tokyo and Rutland, Vermont: Charles E. Tuttle Company.

Tomikura, Nariyoshi. 1972. Confucianism. In *Japanese religion, a survey by the Agency for Cultural Affairs.* Ed. Hori Ichirō, Ikado Fujio, Wakimoto Tsuneya, and Yanagawa Keiichi. Tokyo and Palo Alto: Kōdansha.

Toulmin, Stephen. 1972. *Human understanding.* Princeton: Princeton University Press.

____. 1982. The construal of reality: Criticism in modern and postmodern science. *Critical Inquiry* (September):93-111.

Tsukamoto, Zenryu. 1974. Formalism in Buddhism. In *Religion in the Japanese experience: Sources and interpretations.* Ed. H. Byron Earhart. Belmont, CA: Dickenson Publishing Company.

Turner, Victor. 1967. *The forest of symbols: Aspects of Ndembu ritual.* Ithaca and London: Cornell University Press.

Tylor, Sir Edward B. 1924. *Primitive culture,* 7th ed. New York: Brentano's Publishers.

Ueda, Kenji. 1972. Shinto. In *Japanese religion, a survey by the Agency for Cultural Affairs.* Ed. Hori Ichirō, Ikado Fujio, Wakimoto Tsuneya, and Yanagawa Keiichi. Tokyo and Palo Alto: Kōdansha.

Ueda, Yoshifumi. 1967. The status of the individual in Buddhist Mahayana philosophy. In *The Japanese mind.* Ed. Charles A. Moore. Honolulu: East-West Center Press, University of Hawaii Press.

Wallace, Anthony F. C. 1966. *Religion, an anthropological view.* New York: Random House.

Watanabe, Eimi. 1968. Risshō Kōsei-kai: A sociological observation of its members. *Contemporary Religions in Japan* 9.1-2 (March-June):75-151. See also Eimi Watanabe Rajana.

Watari, Shōzaburō. 1915. *Kokumin dōtoku joron* [An introduction to national morality]. Tokyo: Chūbunkan.

Weber, Max. 1963. *The sociology of religion.* Trans. Ephraim Fischoff. Boston: Beacon Press.

Webster's new collegiate dictionary. 1977. Springfield, MA: G. and C. Merriam Co.

Weeks, J. Stafford. 1974. Risshō Kōsei-kai: A cooperative Buddhist sect. In *Religious ferment in Asia.* Ed. Robert J. Miller. Lawrence, KS: University of Kansas Press.

White, Leslie. 1969. *The science of culture.* New York: Farrar, Straus and Giroux.

Wilson, Bryan R. 1970. *Rationality.* New York: Harper and Row.

Wittgenstein, Ludwig. 1958. *Philosophical investigation.* 2d edition. Oxford: Basil Blackwell.

Worsley, Peter. 1957. *The trumpet shall sound.* London: McGibbon and Kee.

Yanagawa, Keiichi, and Abe Yoshiya. 1978. Some observations on the sociology of religion in Japan. *Japanese Journal of Religious Studies* 5.1:5-36.

Yanagita, Kunio. 1937. Oyakata kokata [Roles of *oya* and *ko*]. Pp. 89-124 in *Kazoku seidoshi zenshū, part I: Shiron-hen; vol. 3: Oyako.* Tokyo: Kawada Shobo.

____. 1962. Senzo no hanashi [Concerning the ancestors]. In *Teihon Yanagida Kunio shu*, vol. 10. Tokyo: Chikuma Shobo.

INDEX

A

Abe, Yoshiya, 43
Adoption, 41
Adoptive husband, 41
African ancestor worship, 213(*n*.34), 214(*n*.38)
Afterlife
Buddhist view of, 78, 82–83, 200, 211(*n*.24), 213(*n*.34, 37)
individual concepts of, 149–50, 176–77, 212(*n*.33)
see also Ancestor worship; *Hotoke*; *Kami*
After the Banquet (Mishima), 89
Aged. *See* Older people; Old people's association
Agricultural cooperative, 49–50
Agriculture. *See* Holidays; Yamanaka, agriculture; crop names
Allegory, 4
All Souls' Festival, 48, 60, 68, 82, 85, 91, 195
observance activities, 69–70
Altars
All Souls', 69–70
funeral, 73, 74
household, 64, 68, 134, 136
meeting place, 119–21
see also God-shelf
Amaterasu-ō-mikami. *See* Sun Goddess
Analogy, 6–7
see also Isomorphism
Ancestor
defined, 41, 43, 210(*n*.21)
and household status, 85
relationship of, 66, 68

Ancestor worship
in Africa, 213(*n*.34), 214(*n*.38)
All Souls' Festival, 69–70
and death/extinction fears, 83, 87–94, 200–1
and gratitude, 25, 132, 133
and household continuity, 83–93, 190, 195–96, 199–200, 205–6, 213(*n*.37), 214(*n*.38)
personal views of, 12, 155, 161, 164, 165, 166, 176, 197
in Reiyūkai, 19
religious/social context, 5, 24, 210(*n*.19)
in Risshō Kōsei-kai, 24–25
senzo and *hotoke*, 65–68
state-fostered, 86–87
see also Parent-child relationship
Anomie, 201, 207(*n*.3)
Anthropology, on religion, 3–4, 10, 15, 17, 103, 193, 197, 206
Anthropomorphism, 5, 14, 194
Arai, Ken, 207(*n*.3), 219(*n*.60)
Architectural style, 216(*n*.46)
Aristotle, 6
Ascetic exercises, 21, 123, 134, 136
Atheists, 84
Autumn equinox. *See* Equinox
Azande witchcraft, 13, 14, 206

B

Barbour, Ian G., 4
Barnes, Barry, 4, 14–15
Beattie, J.H.M., 4, 10, 14, 103
Behavior, instrumental, 181
Behavioral traits, 148, 209(*n*.12)
Bellah, Robert N., 16, 17

Z